THE DIVE SITES OF PAPUA NEW GUINEA

Series Consultant: Nick Hanna

Bob Halstead, internationally known in diving circles, runs the dive boats Telita and Tiata and has over twenty year's experience of diving in Papua New Guinea.

First published in the UK in 1996 by
New Holland (Publishers) Ltd
London • Cape Town • Sydney • Singapore

24 Nutford Place
London W1H 6DQ
UK

P. O. Box 1144
Cape Town 8000
South Africa

3/2 Aquatic Drive
Frenchs Forest, NSW 2086
Australia

ISBN 1 85368 677 8

Project development: Charlotte Parry-Crooke
Series editors: Catherine Randall/Charlotte Fox/Paul Barnett
Design concept: Philip Mann, ACE Ltd
Design/cartography: ML Design
Cover design: Peter Bosman
Index: Alex Corrin

Typeset by ML Design, London
Reproduction by Hirt and Carter, South Africa
Printed and bound in Singapore by Tien Wah Press (Pte) Ltd

All the photographs in this book were taken by Bob Halstead.

Title page: *A yellow crinoid dominates this colourful reef scene.*
Contents page: *Lush growths of delicate purple Lace Coral, Stylaster sp. on the vertical wall of Balaban's Bommie.*

Author's Acknowledgements

Sincere thanks to the following, who helped me collect information for this book:

Dr Chris Acott, Kevin Baldwin, Franco Banfi, David Barker, Peter Barter, Greg Bates, Telita Bates, Max Benjamin, Frank Butler, Owen Coney, Craig De Wit, Barry Fitzpatrick, Dave Flinn, Peter Jennings, Tony Karacsonyi, Linda Kavanagh, Dik Knight, Peter Leggett, John Lippman, David Miller, John Miller, Geoff Murphy, Rob Padfield, Rodney Pearce, Alan Raabe, Tim Rowlands, Nikhil Sekhran, Peter Stone, Ken Weaving

and my wife Dinah, who has shared the adventure of exploring PNG's underwater paradise with me. Without her magic eyes I would have missed so much, and without her laughter it would not have been such joy. For those who always wondered, there is no one finer.

Publisher's Acknowledgements

The publishers gratefully acknowledge the generous assistance during the compilation of this book of the following:

Nick Hanna for his involvement in developing the series and consulting throughout and Dr Elizabeth M. Wood for acting as Marine Biological Consultant and contributing to The Marine Environment.

CONTENTS

How to use this Book

THE REGIONS

The dive sites included in the book are arranged within nine main geographical regions: Milne Bay Province, Port Moresby area, Tufi, Lae, Madang Province, Walindi and Kimbe Bay, Rabaul, New Ireland, and Manus Island, the Western Isles and Wuvulu. Regional introductions describe the key characteristics and features of these areas and provide background information on climate, the environment, points of interest, and advantages and disadvantages of diving in the locality.

THE MAPS

A map is included near the front of each regional or subregional section. The prime purpose of the maps is to identify the location of the dive sites described and to provide other useful information for divers and snorkellers. Though certain reefs are indicated, the maps do not set out to provide detailed nautical information such as exact reef contours or water depths. In general the maps show: the locations of the dive sites, indicated by white numbers in red boxes corresponding to those placed at the start of the individual dive site descriptions; the locations of key access points to the sites (ports, marinas, beach resorts and so on); reefs and wrecks. In some instances, a dive site is not indicated on the map in order to protect the site from shark-finners (see page 39). The site description gives details of how to access the dive site. (Note: the border around the maps is not a scale bar.)

MAP LEGEND

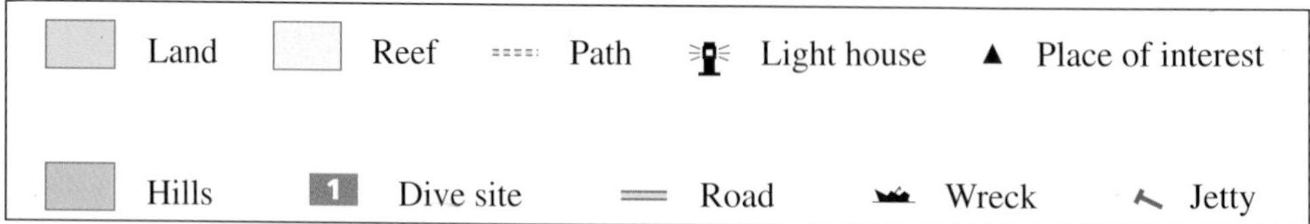

THE DIVE SITE DESCRIPTIONS

Placed within the geographical sections are the descriptions of each region's premier dive sites. Each site description starts with a number (to enable the site to be located on the relevant map), a star rating (see below), and a selection of key symbols (see below). Crucial practical details (on location, access, conditions, typical visibility and minimum and maximum depths) precede the description of the site, its marine life and special points of interest. In these entries, 'typical visibility' assumes good conditions.

The Star Rating System

Each site has been awarded a star rating, with a maximum of five red stars for diving and five blue stars for snorkelling.

Diving
★★★★★ **first class**
★★★★ **highly recommended**
★★★ **good**
★★ **average**
★ **poor**

Snorkelling
★★★★★ **first class**
★★★★ **highly recommended**
★★★ **good**
★★ **average**
★ **poor**

The Symbols

The symbols placed at the start of each site description provide a quick reference to crucial information pertinent to individual sites.

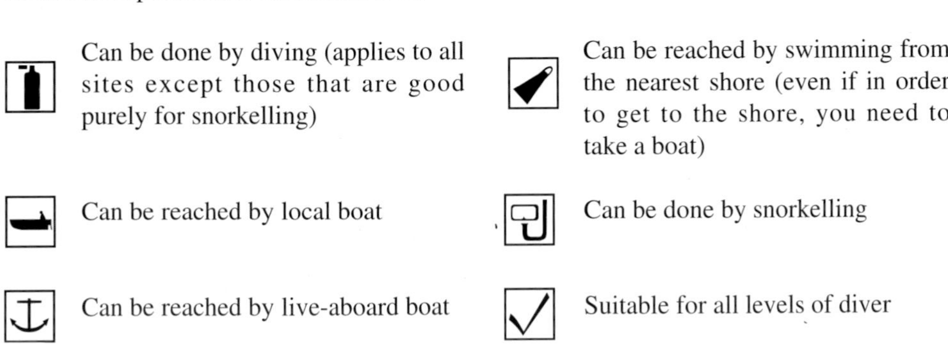

Can be done by diving (applies to all sites except those that are good purely for snorkelling)

Can be reached by swimming from the nearest shore (even if in order to get to the shore, you need to take a boat)

Can be reached by local boat

Can be done by snorkelling

Can be reached by live-aboard boat

Suitable for all levels of diver

The Regional Directories

A 'regional directory', which will help you plan and make the most of your trip, is included at the end of each regional section. Here you will find, where relevant, practical information on how to get to an area, where to stay and eat and available dive facilities. Local 'non-diving' highlights are also described, with suggestions for sightseeing and excursions.

Other features

At the start of the book you will find practical details and tips about travelling to and in Papua New Guinea, as well as a general introduction to the country itself. Also provided is a wealth of information about the general principles and conditions of diving in the area. Throughout the book, features and small fact panels on topics of interest to divers and snorkellers are included. At the end of the book are sections on the marine environment (including coverage of marine life, conservation and codes of practice) and underwater photography and video. Also to be found here is information on health, safety and first aid as well as a guide to marine creatures to look out for when diving in Papua New Guinea.

INTRODUCTION TO PAPUA NEW GUINEA

In the era when the Pacific and Asia were being explored, invaded and colonized by Europeans, Papua New Guinea was largely ignored. Its formidable ranges might have held the promise of fabled golden treasures, but the mountains soared above shores tangled with impenetrable jungle and were protected by fierce inhabitants and treacherous reefs, both capable of giving intruders some lethal surprises.

What made this astonishing country so difficult for early foreign explorers is the very thing that draws modern adventurers. PNG (as the locals now call it) is one of the world's last remaining wildernesses, but the quality that has kept it pristine is not climatic severity but the opulence and abundance of its wildlife. Nature went crazy in PNG and produced such a lush display of mountains, volcanoes, rivers, swampy plains, rainforests and coral reefs that Europeans had a hard time taming them and surviving. Even Papua New Guineans, whose ancestors are believed to have settled from Asia some 50,000 years ago, have mostly stayed isolated from each other; this has resulted in the evolution of over 750 languages and a kaleidoscope of colourful and distinct traditional cultures.

Eventually, in the late 19th century, coastal regions were visited by pioneering missionaries and traders, but, incredibly, it was not until the 1930s that the first outside explorers ventured into the Highland valleys in the centre of PNG. Here over a million people lived who had never seen, nor even contemplated, an outside world. The first white Europeans who ventured into the Highlands were thought to be spirit ancestors returning from the dead.

From 1906 there was an Australian Administration in Papua, the southeastern section of the island of New Guinea. After World War I the Australians gained control also of the northeastern mainland and islands, previously German New Guinea, eventually combining them to form the Territory of Papua and New Guinea. (The western half of mainland New Guinea was originally colonized by the Dutch but in the 1960s was handed over to Indonesia and is now known as Irian Jaya.) Colonial exploitation of the `Territory' by

Opposite: *The coral island of Deka Deka near Samarai offers superb snorkelling.*
Above: *Young men paddle their brightly decorated canoe to a celebration.*

Australians was controlled, and a paternalistic approach protected native rights, with much of the Administration's resources allocated to provide quality education with the aim of eventual independence. This came on 16 September 1975, and PNG has since demonstrated to the world a lively and unique, but nevertheless strong, adherence to the principles of democracy.

One thing the Australians did that has been tremendously beneficial to the development of PNG was to insist that English was the only language used in schools. English is thus spoken throughout the country and is the language of commerce. Two other languages were used by the Administration to communicate with village people: Police Motu and Tok Pisin. Motu was used primarily in Papua and these days is seldom heard outside Central Province, whereas Tok Pisin has thrived and is the most usual form of conversation in much of the country.

TOK PISIN

Of the 750 or so languages spoken in PNG, Tok Pisin is the most widely understood after English. This colourful language has derived from English – or, perhaps more correctly, Australian, if you consider such words as *bagarup*, meaning 'broken' – with input from German, Indonesian and Melanesian. Primers in the language are readily available, and recommended.

Tok Pisin has a lot of humour and a refreshing sense of logic. *Numbawan pikinini bilong misis kwin* is of course Prince Charles (say it out loud if you're bemused), but you are advised not to request help to *pus(h)im car bilong me*, and you should be cautious when calling the cat . . . since *pus pus* means 'sex'.

Opposite: *Some villages remain as picturesque today as they have always been.*

THE COUNTRY

Modern PNG consists of the eastern half of the island of New Guinea and several chains of islands ranging from the equator through the Bismarck Sea, the Solomon Sea and south into the Coral Sea, where the Louisiade Archipelago's eastern tip almost touches latitude 12°S.

The northern islands start with the tiny but exquisite island of Wuvulu in the west, made famous by Jean-Michel Cousteau when he used it as a base for his educational Project Ocean Search. Further east are the Admiralty Islands – including Manus Island, where anthropologist Margaret Mead did much of her pioneering work and where there was a large US base during World War II. New Hanover's people were known for their cargo-cult beliefs – that, if they made the right magic, ships and planes would arrive with their share of the goods they saw foreigners accumulate so quickly. Immediately eastward New Ireland, a long skinny island, arcs southeast towards Bougainville Island. Bougainville, part of North Solomon's Province, has been the site of a long dispute between the islanders and the Government over a huge copper mine; as I write, it is unlikely any quick resolution will allow visitors or diving there for some time.

Along the mainland's north coast a 'ring of fire' of active volcanoes – including Manum and Karkar Islands – link Long Island and Umboi and eventually New Britain, ending in Rabaul Town, not far from the coast of New Ireland. This ring of volcanic cones produces some of the world's most dramatic landscapes. South of New Britain are the Trobriand 'Islands of Love' – subject of the researches of another famous anthropologist, Bronislaw Malinowski. Here some of the finest canoe-builders in the Pacific produce the biggest yams from their gardens, but what everyone remembers is that they encourage their teenagers to have as many sexual partners as possible. Life on the Trobriands is in fact very highly structured, with all sorts of restrictions and obligations. One of the Trobriand Islanders' most admirable traits is their belief that their culture is superior to all others; theirs is consequently still among the strongest traditional societies in the Pacific.

Still further south are the imposing D'Entrecasteaux Islands, with the peak of Goodenough Island – over 2500m (8200ft) – being higher than any mountain in Australia and especially impressive for an island just 37km (23 miles) long. Finally, sweeping away to the southeast is the Louisiade Archipelago, consisting of literally hundreds of islands and reefs, the largest being Misima, Tagula and Rossel islands.

The mainland is dominated by two major rivers, the Fly to the south and the Sepik to the north. Both are navigable for several hundreds of kilometres inland. The Fly supports transport to a major mine at OK Tedi, and the Sepik a thriving tourist industry. Sepik villagers are famed for their traditional carvings, and you can purchase these from villagers along the riverbanks.

A major road, the Highlands Highway, connects the coastal town of Lae to Highlands towns including Goroka, Kundiawa, Mount Hagen, Mendi, Tari and Wabag. Branching from it is the Ramu Highway, connecting the Highlands to Madang on the north coast (as yet no road connects the Highlands to the south coast). These roads are rugged and subject to landslides and flooding, so a four-wheel drive is considered essential for travelling in many areas.

Madang has a superb and scenic natural deep-water harbour, and is thus a centre for much of PNG's tourist activity. Further down the north coast, at Tufi, there is a totally different landscape. This is PNG's fiord country: deep, long channels cut into steep coastal hills that rise eventually to Mount Victoria, towering nearly 2000m (6500ft) tall.

Milne Bay lies at the mainland's southeastern tip. The bay itself is some 10km (6 miles) wide and 30km (19 miles) long, with the town of Alotau nestled in the hills on the northern shore. Milne Bay was in 1942 the site of a famous battle when, after the stalemate of the Battle of the Coral Sea, the Japanese suffered their first land defeat attempting to seize the bay. At the entrance to the bay's southern side is the China Strait, so named by Captain John Moresby in 1873 during the first European exploration of the area; he believed he had found a shortcut to China. In the strait sits the beautiful island of Samarai; once a staging post for miners, missionaries, pearlers and Government patrols, Samarai was among the most colourful and loved towns in the South Pacific, and the largest town in the 'Territory'. It is today a friendly but rather seedy reminder of its glorious past.

The national capital, Port Moresby, is situated around a magnificent protected harbour on the south coast. It could be among the most beautiful cities in the world – with the Owen Stanley mountain range as backdrop, with its barrier reef producing a fringe of blue, green and breaking surf just offshore, and with the hills and bays that make up the city. However, an explosion of development and a rapid population-growth (villagers come from all over the country to find their fortune but mostly end up living in squalid squatter settlements) have produced chaos, with power, road, cleaning, police and water services unable to cope.

CLIMATE

The coastal climate is tropical, with much of the year being hot, still and humid – perfect diving weather! The rainy seasons take place during different months in different parts of the country; the most prominent windy season results from the Southeast Trade Winds, which blow from about May through to November and affect the southern part of the country more than the north. Tropical thunderclouds often build during a calm day and bring a refreshing shower in the evening. PNG is too close to the equator to suffer much from cyclones – only the Louisiade Archipelago's eastern tip regularly experiences them. The Highlands climate is much cooler, with certain areas – particularly those over 2000m (6500ft) – experiencing overnight frosts in August and September. The highest mountain, Mount Wilhelm (4509m; 14,800ft), is snow-capped for several months each year.

THE PEOPLE

PNG's population remains small compared to those of other, similar-sized countries: about four million, giving a population density of about eight people per square kilometre (20 per square mile). No significant areas are uninhabited so, outside the towns, the population is

fairly evenly distributed. With population pressures low and industrialization limited, the country is like a giant nature park. Harvesting PNG's rich forests and mineral wealth has accelerated during the past decade and causes great concern; however, many Papua New Guineans make their living from the land and sea and are acutely aware of environmental problems and protective of their resources.

Their vast and scattered land is divided into 19 Provinces and the National Capital District of Port Moresby. Only the five Highlands Provinces are landlocked, so the sea is a vital part of PNG's culture. Many islands are famous for their inhabitants' seafaring history and skills. Village children learn to paddle small outrigger canoes from a very early age, and most learn to swim as they learn to walk. The dugout canoe, which has many different styles throughout PNG, is still the most important means of transport for coastal villagers, especially as it is often easier to paddle along the shore than trek along a rainforest path.

Although considered Melanesian, Papua New Guineans have a wide variety of racial backgrounds. It is still easy to learn to distinguish a Highlander from someone from the Gulf or the islands by their appearance, but Polynesians, Micronesians, Asians and Europeans have mingled with the Melanesians to produce a diverse people.

The Highland Shows and Sing-Sings

The Highland Shows are gatherings of Highlands clans at either Mount Hagen or Goroka to display their traditional dress and dances. Held annually in August and/or September, the shows are colourful and exciting events. There are competitions to encourage clans to do their best to preserve their culture, and plenty of opportunities for tourists to photograph Highlanders in all their finery.

Village Sing-Sings are local gatherings to celebrate a wedding – or just about anything else – and can involve dressing up, dancing, singing and feasting. They can be very good fun. Visitors are often welcome to join in – and may have to: it is very bad form just to sit back and watch.

Opposite: *Kula canoes at Egum Atoll sail the islands in Milne Bay Province.*

Papua New Guineans are fiercely proud and protective of their clan and area origins. This is the source of many problems in terms of political representation, and is also the source of the infamous Payback, where even an innocent member of a clan accused of injuring a member of a different clan, accidentally or otherwise, can be the target of fatal retaliation. There are certainly cultural resentments between some groups, particularly the Coastals and Highlanders, but these tend to be short-lived and fluid; in general, PNG must be among the most successful multicultural societies as far as race relations go – at least in the Bush. Town life distorts the culture to such an extent that it is hard to consider it typical of PNG. Visitors should be aware of the tendency of Papua New Guineans to take the law into their own hands, particularly in connection with road and other accidents.

One characteristic typical of all PNG people is a love and talent for visual art. The expression of this in body painting and decoration is unrivalled. Each clan has its own distinctive style of decoration, though there is plenty of scope for individual variation. The originality and imagination of the designs, and their brilliant colours and skilful application, are quite astounding.

In certain areas skilled carvers turn tropical hardwoods into traditional sculptures – from walking-sticks and bowls to fearsome masks or mural 'storyboards'. Canoes and buildings can also be works of art. Traditional designs are often used for inspiration for modern buildings – PNG's Parliament House is a particularly fine example of a modern and practical interpretation of a traditional building. The preservation of these customs is encouraged by the Government, and throughout the year several Shows and other celebrations occur when villagers dress up in their traditional finery and meet other groups, performing dances or enacting past events – often in competition.

Inevitably, the modern commercial world is invading even the most remote villages, though most still rely on farming and fishing for their daily sustenance. Fortunately the soils are fertile and food abundant. Occasionally a drought or flood causes temporary hardship, but the Government is quick to respond with food shipments. There are no starving masses in PNG: any malnutrition is due to dietary ignorance rather than long-term food shortages. Cash crops are encouraged, and markets have been established enabling villagers to earn money to buy popular items like radios. Many Papua New Guineans now own successful businesses, and the Government has reserved certain activities for PNG citizens only. Foreigners wishing to work in PNG are welcome, but restricted to businesses where skilled citizens are not available or are in short supply, and they are expected to train citizens as a part of their licence to operate.

DIET

Villagers in PNG are blessed with naturally fertile soil that produces rich harvests. Although historically accused of cannibalism, they usually enjoy not 'baked beings' but a mainly vegetarian diet. Village pots are always on the boil with sweet potato, yams, taro, tapioca and greens, generally cooked with creamed coconut. Villagers eat when they feel like it throughout the day, rather than at set mealtimes (although the main meal is eaten around noon). Only very occasionally are pork, chicken or fish added to the mixture. Fruit and nuts are a regular part of the diet. Surprisingly, since the PNG climate is perfect for growing many exotic spices, the meals are very bland, with no attempt being made to jazz up the flavours.

The shock of moving from a traditional society to a Western commercial one has proved too traumatic for many citizens, and this is probably the biggest challenge facing PNG today. In the towns, youths desiring glamorous Western goods but lacking the ability to earn the money necessary to buy them, and alienated from their traditional cultures, form criminal street gangs known – not affectionately – as 'rascals'.

Visitors to villages away from the towns will mostly find themselves in a spotlessly clean environment, with village leaders, pastors, health orderlies and schoolteachers working to organize their communities. The traditional hospitality is generous and warm – it would be a matter of shame if a visitor were shabbily treated. But in the towns rubbish remains unswept and homes are guarded by razor wire and barking dogs.

FLORA AND FAUNA

So the real PNG is out of the towns, in the Bush. The most typical coastal scene is of dense rainforest smothering saw-toothed mountains that often rise straight from the sea, but there are also swampy plains near river-mouths and, inland, grasslands, lakes and pine forests. The tropical hardwoods of the coastal rainforests are very high-quality and of the most valuable species; this unfortunately makes them a target for logging companies. The strips of coastal plain have been developed into plantations, but much of the nation's commercial agriculture occurs in the fertile valleys of the Highlands.

Wherever you go in PNG you can find a unique flora and fauna. The most famous exotic plants are members of the Orchid Family, and PNG has more species than any other country. They are not at all hard to find – a short walk into the forest will immediately reveal the commoner varieties. Other species are known only from certain areas, and there is little doubt that as-yet-unknown species decorate trees in remote valleys.

Insects abound and, although the malarial mosquito is widespread, otherwise most are fascinating and harmless; the world's largest butterfly, the Queen Alexandra's Birdwing, is among them. There are no monkeys or dangerous members of the Cat Family; the most dangerous mammal is probably the Wild Pig. Tree Kangaroos and many attractive species of native marsupials flourish. Crocodiles live in certain areas and form an important part of the culture, particularly in the Sepik region, where initiation ceremonies for young men include cutting their backs with small slashes to leave scars resembling crocodile-skin. Lizards and snakes are common, too, but live snakes are difficult to observe in the wild – particularly if you're travelling with villagers, who habitually kill them on sight.

PNG is famous for its birdlife. With over 700 species, including 38 of the world's 43 Bird of Paradise species, this is a true paradise for birdwatchers. Birds of Paradise live at the higher elevations, but birds of one sort or another thrive in all areas of PNG. Anchoring a boat at a typical coastal bay surrounded by rainforest can be a noisy experience, with Sulphur-crested Cockatoos screeching, Blackbirds crowing and dozens of others squawking and chirping! The insects add to the din and, when nightfall eventually comes and Flying Foxes flap overhead, it is a relief that quiet is settling at last over the forest.

The onshore flora and fauna are a miracle of nature, but even this pales beside what you can find beneath the waters around Papua New Guinea.

BIRDS OF PARADISE

The majority of the 43 species of Bird of Paradise (*Paradisaea* spp) are found in PNG. Although the females are rather drab, the males have magnificent plumage and perform elaborate mating dances. The plumage has been used traditionally by Highland clans as part of their ceremonial body decoration; headdresses made from the plumes are prized and considered heirlooms. The commercial trade and export of Birds of Paradise are strictly forbidden, and birds may be killed only for traditional purposes.

The specimens sent to Europe by early explorers for some reason had had their feet removed. This led people to believe that the birds spent their whole life in the air! PNG's national crest is based on the Bird of Paradise.

This perfectly sheltered lagoon near Madang offers easy snorkelling.

TRAVELLING TO AND IN PAPUA NEW GUINEA

VISAS

A tourist visa is available on arrival for a fee of K10; it is valid for 30 days and cannot be extended. Restrictions apply for travellers from some Asian, Eastern European and African countries. For longer stays, a visa should be obtained before departure for PNG. All tourists are required to have a valid passport, sufficient funds and onward or return tickets.

The rules have been known to change at short notice, so it is always better (if possible) to obtain a visa before leaving for PNG. Visas are issued at various PNG Embassies, High Commissions or Consulates in Australia (Canberra, Sydney, Brisbane, Cairns), Belgium, Fiji, France, Germany, Indonesia, Japan, Malaysia, New Zealand, Philippines, Solomon Islands, UK and USA (Washington, New York). The usual visa granted is for 60 days and in theory you can extend this for a further 30 days once in PNG. If this becomes necessary, use an agent (see Visa Services in the Yellow Pages) rather than try to do it yourself. On no account overstay your visa or engage in any employment while in the country: the penalties are severe.

If planning to travel via Australia, remember you must also have an Australian visa. Do not rely on any 'in transit' exemptions unless you have absolute faith in airline schedules.

HEALTH

You must have adequate health insurance in case of serious illness while in PNG. Although some centres have adequate hospitals or private doctors, in many others there are none, or the services are poor or overloaded. If you get sick, get out!

Divers can obtain Evacuation Insurance from a variety of diving organizations, which provide cover not only for diving accidents but for other illnesses or accidents that require evacuation. A popular one is: Divers' Alert Network (DAN), Box 3823, Duke University Medical Center, Durham, NC 27710, USA, tel 800 446 2671/fax 919 490 6630. Vaccinations are not required unless you have visited, or come from, a country with yellow fever or cholera. An International Health Card is likewise not required.

Opposite: *Villagers paddle out to dive boats to trade vegetables and artefacts.*
Above: *The Longnose hawkfish, Oxycirrhites, grows to around 10cm.*

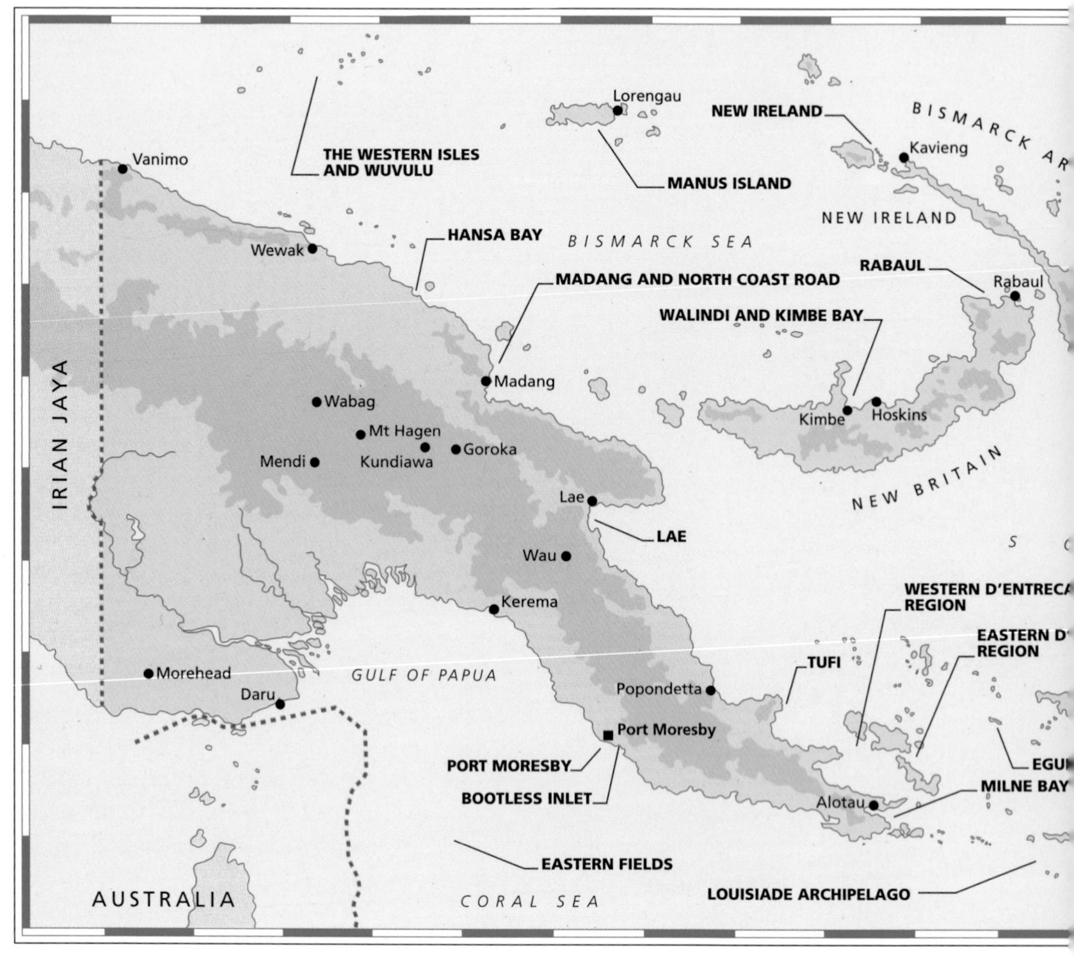

MALARIA

Malaria is a big problem, and you must take precautions. Follow a course of prophylaxis recommended by your doctor; however, these are far from foolproof, and the best action is to avoid being bitten by mosquitoes. This is not so difficult as it might seem, but a fanatical approach is the best! The danger is at night, so make sure you wear appropriate long-sleeved and long-legged clothing in the evenings and sleep in a protected area using a good insect repellent. Never sleep ashore in the open without a mosquito net and repellent.

Chloroquine prophylaxis, although helpful, is not considered adequate by itself. Several new drugs are available, but some have side-effects which make them unsuitable for divers; Larium, for example, can produce symptoms similar to those of decompression sickness. Since individual susceptibilities are very varied, try the drug well before your journey to test for side-effects. Whatever you do in the way of prevention, after returning home it is vital you inform your doctor of the possibility of malaria should you get fevers or flu-like symptoms – even if this happens months later.

The good news is that live-aboard boats provide very good protection, since the malaria mosquito does not travel any distance over water.

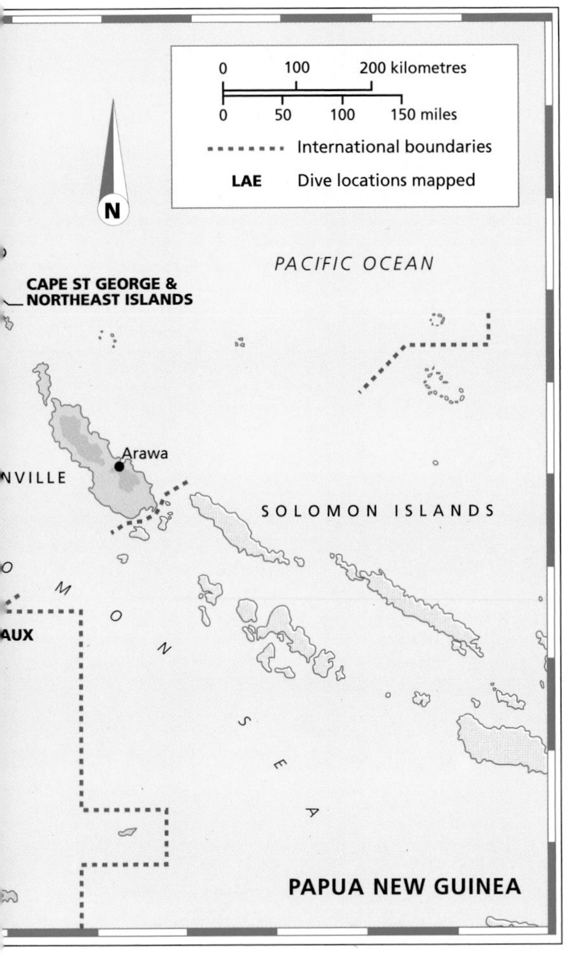

OTHER MEDICAL CONSIDERATIONS

Apart from malaria, PNG is a healthy place to be. With no pollution to speak of, wonderful weather and fresh air the dangers are more from carelessness than from disease. The following are the cause of 90% of health problems on diving cruises:

Ears. You must dry your ears after every day of diving to avoid external-ear infections. I strongly recommend alcohol-based eardrops used after your evening shower. These are easily available without prescription.

Coral Cuts. Any cuts or scratches, whether from above or below the water, must be attended to immediately. The scratch needs to be thoroughly scrubbed out and an antibiotic or at least antiseptic ointment applied. Failure to do this will result in infection, possibly serious.

EMERGENCY PROCEDURES

All divers who feel unwell after diving and are unsure of what to do should contact Divers' Emergency Service (DES) Australia, on 61 8 373 5312, for advice. If this number is engaged call 61 8 223 0230 and ask for Doctor on Call, Hyperbaric Medicine, or 61 8 224 5116 for the Hyperbaric Medicine Office. When calling, have as much of the following information ready as possible:

- symptoms
- dive profiles
- patient's age, sex, and relevant personal and medical details
- nearest town/airstrip
- hours of oxygen supply available on site
- access to intravenous fluids and person to administer them
- insurance status of patient (important for evacuation: note that DES does not organize evacuation and is independent of DAN and Dive Master – see below)

If evacuation to a recompression facility is advised:

- Members of the Divers' Alert Network (DAN) can call the Australian DAN Alarm Center (on 61 7 371 3255), who will arrange evacuation; the costs of this are covered by DAN membership. Actual treatment costs in Australia may be covered by additional DAN or other insurance, or by Medicare if you're an Australian citizen. The next nearest DAN Alarm Center is in Singapore (on 65 226 3813).
- Members of Dive Master/Medex can call the International Medex Centre (at either

[UK] 44 1273 202141 or [USA] 1 410 321 4426), who will arrange evacuation. Dive Master membership will cover all your evacuation and treatment costs.

The nearest recompression facility in Australia is at Townsville:

Townsville General Hospital
Eyre Street
Townsville, Queensland 4810
tel 61 (0)77 819 455
fax 61 (0)77 726 711

Divers who are not members of DAN or Dive Master, or do not have other insurance, must make private arrangements, which may involve considerable expense. DAN or Dive Master membership is, for this and other reasons, strongly recommended. Membership and other details can be obtained from:

DAN
Box 3823, Duke University Medical Center
Durham, NC 27710, USA
tel 800 446 2671
fax 919 490 6630

DAN Australia
PO Box 134, Carnegie
Victoria, Australia 3163
tel 61 (0)3 563 1151
fax 61 (0)3 569 4803

Dive Master
PO Box 146, Leigh-on-Sea
Essex SS9 1SZ, UK
tel 44 1702 76902
fax 44 1702 471892

Dive Master
AIBA Group Insurance
Brokers
PO Box 1809,
North Sydney
Australia 2059
tel 61 2 923 1066
fax 61 2 929 4584

DRESS

Wear a hat and lightweight clothing that covers most of the body. This offers protection against the sun and insects; just as significantly, the wearing in public places of scant clothing, particularly very short shorts or bikini bottoms, invites ridicule or worse.

CUSTOMS FORMALITIES

PNG Customs handle many tourist divers every year, and welcome them. You may bring in personal diving and photographic gear on the understanding that you'll take it out again on departure. Having a tourist visa and a booking with a known diving operator in PNG is usually enough to ensure trouble-free passage through Customs. If you have a particularly large amount of gear, it is a good idea to have a list should the Customs officer request it.

PNG has strict importation bans against guns and ammunition, pornography (including Playboy) and narcotics. You're allowed 200 cigarettes and a litre of alcohol duty-free – the latter is advisable, since alcoholic beverages are incredibly expensive in PNG.

On departure there are no problems for the genuine tourist, although be aware that exporting certain wildlife and artefacts is illegal. Note that many countries forbid the import of certain items from PNG, particularly if animal products are involved. Australia is one such country, so do some research if you plan a stopover in Australia en route home.

TRANSPORTATION

People travel to and around PNG by air. A road system connects some Highland areas to the coast, but most roads are poor and limited. There are no trains, and only the north coast has a regular service shipping passengers from port to port. The occasional cruise ship makes a visit and private yachts call in now and again, but PNG is a nation for aviators.

The national airline, Air Niugini, has for over 20 years provided a reliable and accident-free service to the main centres, and several private airlines and air-charter companies fly aircraft and helicopters to the remotest islands and valleys.

Air Niugini's international flights operate between Port Moresby and Sydney, Brisbane and Cairns in Australia (a joint service with Qantas), Singapore (a joint service with Singapore Airlines) and Hong Kong, Manila, Jayapura and Honiara. Port Moresby is still the main port of entry, but it is planned to open other centres, like Milne Bay, to direct international flights in order to help the tourism industry.

Air Niugini's domestic flights connect all the main centres, mostly using Fokker F28 jets – affectionately called 'pocket rockets' by regular users. Bookings on Air Niugini flights can be made worldwide through reputable travel agents.

Air Niugini
PO Box 7186, Boroko
tel 675 325 9000
tel 675 327 3444 (bookings)
fax 675 327 3482/327 3550

Milne Bay Air, the largest private airline, makes daily flights to Alotau in Milne Bay (alongside Air Niugini) and services over 40 other airports. It has a large and varied fleet of aircraft and can provide pressurized aircraft for medical evacuation on charter:

Milne Bay Air
PO Box 170, Boroko
tel 675 325 0555
fax 675 325 2219

Other domestic airlines include:

AirLink – New Guinea Islands
Mission Aviation Fellowship (MAF) – Highlands and North Coast
Nationair – charter, based in Port Moresby
Sandaun Air Services – North Coast
South West Air – Western PNG
Island Airways – Madang area
Islands Aviation – New Guinea Islands
Pacific Helicopters – charter throughout Papua New Guinea

Children provide a warm welcome to a village guest house.

Land Transport

Taxis are available in most centres, as are Public Motor Vehicles (PMVs); most look unroadworthy and probably are. Adventurers who try them out should not be disappointed – pick one that at least looks as though it will reach your destination – but in general they are to be avoided. Hotels and dive operators all run pick-up services from the airports, and hire cars are available, so the need for other transport is very limited.

If you hire a car, remember to drive on the left-hand side of the road, a rule not easily apparent merely from observing the other traffic or trying to spot the occasional traffic signs, most of which lie flattened by the roadside or are covered in graffiti. Drive carefully and defensively – avoid accidents at all costs: if someone is injured you could, however blameless, be blamed. Do not stop but go directly to the nearest police station.

TOURISM DEVELOPMENT AUTHORITY

The Papua New Guinea Tourism Development Authority actively promotes PNG tourism overseas and has produced some useful guides to the various tourist activities available. They are happy to provide information on request:

PNG Tourism Development Authority
PO Box 1291, Port Moresby
tel 675 20 0211
fax 675 20 0223

MONEY

The PNG currency is named after traditional shell money. The kina is divided into 100 toea. There are K50, K20, K10, K5 and K2 notes, and a distinctive K1 coin with a hole in the middle. The value of the kina, which suffered a large devaluation in 1994, is presently 25% less than the US dollar and is likely to fluctuate for a while.

Credit cards are used, but only American Express has widespread acceptance. Diners' Club and, more recently, MasterCard have been introduced, but are not as common. So, if planning to use credit cards, make sure you have American Express. Banks are open Mon–Thu 09:00–14:00, extended until 17:00 on Fri. Travellers' cheques are easily cashed with a passport for identification. A bank at the airport opens to coincide with arrival and departure times of international aircraft.

Carry some small change with you – particularly if going on a live-aboard where there are opportunities to make minor purchases of shells or artefacts from villagers. It is unwise to carry and show large quantities of cash. In many areas it is common to bargain with villagers for artefacts, but if this is taken to extremes it can cause insult. Pay what you think is a reasonable price; do not keep pushing for an obviously unfair bargain. Haggling is not expected with every purchase, and not at all for food.

Tipping is not universal, but is becoming more widespread. It should never be done as a matter of course, and is generally discouraged.

ELECTRICITY

Most towns have fairly reliable power supplies; 240V 50Hz power is the standard. Sockets use Australian-type plugs with three flat pins angled to one another. Many hotels and diveboats have 120V power (but usually still 50Hz) with US-style sockets to enable low-power appliances like battery chargers to be used.

Underwater photographers should bring with them a small transformer and adaptor

Specialist Travel Agents

The following travel agents sell Diving Tours to PNG:

PNG
South Pacific Tours
PO Box 195, Boroko
tel 675 21 3500/fax 675 21 3136

Melanesian Tourist Services
PO Box 707, Madang
tel 675 82 2766/fax 675 82 3543

Trans Niugini Tours
PO Box 371, Mount Hagen
tel 675 52 1438/fax 675 52 2470

Australia
Dive Adventures
9th Level, 32 York St
Sydney, Australia 2000
tel 61 2 299 4633/fax 61 2 299 4644

Allways Dive Expeditions
168 High Street
Ashburton, Australia 3147
tel 61 3 885 8863/fax 61 3 885 1164

Pro Dive Travel
Shop 620, Royal Arcade
255 Pitt Street
Sydney, Australia 2000
tel 61 2 264 9499/fax 61 2 264 9494

Sea New Guinea
100 Clarence Street
Sydney, Australia 2000
tel 61 2 267 5563/fax 61 2 267 6118

Peregrine Adventures
382 Little Bourke Street
Melbourne, Australia 3000
tel 61 3 670 0888/fax 61 3 670 1268

Singapore
Friendly Tour
5 Coleman Street, #03-06
Excelsior Shopping Centre
Singapore 0617
tel 65 336 7072/fax 65 336 7073

UK
Scuba Safaris
Nastfield Cottage
The Green, Frampton-on-Severn
Gloucestershire GL2 7DY
tel 44 1452 740919/fax 44 1452 740943

USA
See and Sea Travel
50 Francisco Street, Suite 205
San Francisco, CA 94133
tel 1 415 434 3400/fax 1 415 434 3409

Tropical Adventures
111 Second North
Seattle, WA 98109
tel 1 206 441 3483/fax 1 206 441 5431

Adventure Express
650 Fifth Street, Suite 505
San Francisco, CA 94107
tel 1 415 442 0799/fax 1 415 442 0289

Poseidon Venture Tours
359 San Miguel Drive
Newport Beach, CA 92660
tel 1 714 644 5344/fax 1 714 644 5392

Rainbowed Sea Tours
75-5751 Kuakini Highway, Suite 103
Kailua-Kona, Hawaii 96740
tel 1 808 326 7752/fax 1 808 329 8000

Aqua Trek
110 Sutter Street #810
San Francisco, CA 994104
tel 1 415 398 8990/fax 1 415 398 0479

International Diving Expeditions
11360 Matinicus Court
Cypress, CA 90630
tel 1 714 897 3770/fax 1 714 891 2154

Niugini Odyssea
26961 Hilltop Road
Evergreen, CO 80439
tel/fax 1 303 674 0252

necessary to convert 240V Australian to 120V US supply if they need it. Note these should be proper transformers, which are unfortunately rather heavy, and not electronic converters, which can damage battery chargers.

Departure Tax

A K15 departure tax is levied on leaving PNG, and must be paid in PNG currency. This tax may change without notice.

Telecommunications and Mail

PNG has a modern and extensive telephone system. In all main centres it is generally very easy to make domestic and international telephone or fax calls by direct dialling, although sometimes lines are congested. Mail services are efficiently run and reliable, even to distant villages (eventually!), and courier services are available in most main centres.

Time

PNG is 10hr ahead of GMT.

Photographers

Photographers should bring with them all their equipment and film. Although print film is widely available, slide film is less so and expensive.

Among diveboats, only the *FeBrina* has E6 processing. However, E6 processing is available in Port Moresby at Images (tel 25 5106/fax 25 3835) and PNG Colour Laboratories (tel 25 4665/fax 25 0358).

DIVING AND SNORKELLING IN PAPUA NEW GUINEA

The most significant feature of PNG's reefs is that very deep water comes very close to shore at most places around the coast. If the continental shelf is defined as the region from the shore to 100 fathoms (183m), then much of PNG has no continental shelf: just a few metres from the shore, depths plunge in vertical cliffs from 1m (40in) to 1km (3300ft) or more.

This type of underwater wall or dropoff exists along much of the mainland's north coast and around much of New Britain, the southwest coasts of New Ireland and New Hanover and many other islands in the Bismarck and Louisiade archipelagoes. These deep walls often exist where the prevailing winds are offshore, producing calm seas and upwellings as the surface waters are blown away to be replaced by deep ocean water. Where currents also move along the walls, the deep cliffs support a multitude of marine creatures. Delicate coral formations which could never grow on barrier reefs subjected to storm waves thrive in these sheltered waters. Sea fans and soft corals often reach enormous size, and large pelagic fish patrol the reef-edge.

Although the sites are sheltered, anchoring a diveboat is not always easy, since the reeftop may be less than 1m (40in) deep and indeed, at low tide, exposed. Even when there is enough water to anchor, the shore is sometimes so close you have to fend off from cliffs and overhanging trees. However, it is not always necessary to anchor, as divers may prefer to swim or drift along the reef and be picked up when they surface. Snorkellers can enjoy the sheltered coral gardens along the shore and peer down the walls, where they'll often see some of the larger pelagic species.

So close to shore the local weather plays an important part in the underwater conditions. Even in perfect weather, the many streams dribbling fresh water into the sea may cause a hazy layer in the top few centimetres as the fresh water mingles with the brine. Torrential rains can make streams flood, so that a thick brown plume of fresh water, nutrients and debris is washed into the ocean; at such times the water can, from the surface, look too dirty to dive – although in fact, because fresh water floats on top of brine, there is still clear water

Opposite: *A cloud of Anthias feed around a Green Tree Coral, the dive boat above.*
Above: *Diving celebrity Valerie Taylor explores a reef in Milne Bay.*

on the reef. When the rain stops it takes only minutes for the offshore winds to blow the dirty water out to sea.

It is this regular flushing of chemical-free nutrients into the sea that gives such unbelievably rich life on the reefs. If the runoff is incessant and into shallow water, as at the mouth of the Fly River, then siltation is too heavy for coral reefs to survive, while excessive nutrients produce algal blooms; but in areas where there is a balance between (a) discharge of runoff, (b) flushing with deep ocean water and (c) currents to stir everything up, the coral reef's productivity reaches a climax. Such places include the reef systems at the mouth of Milne Bay, the deep-water entrances to the passes between New Ireland and New Hanover, the lagoon entrances at Madang and many others. Finding the best time to dive here is not always easy, since incoming currents (and best visibility) do not always accord with the published tide tables or the lunar phases, but when the conditions are right the fish congregate to feed on the current-borne plankton and the abundance of marine life is staggering.

Further away from the mainland are countless small islands and reefs, mostly uninhabited and uncharted. Although more exposed to the weather, they are usually blessed with year-round visibility in excess of 40m (130ft). Some are close enough to the mainland or big islands to support soft corals and giant sea fans and sea whips; these occur deeper than their inshore relatives, usually at 20–50m (65–165ft). Reefs far offshore, especially those in very clear water, are not necessarily the best, although dramatic exceptions do exist – and, if the reef is small and acts as an oasis in the middle of a watery desert, sometimes the big-fish action is formidable.

UNEXPLORED REEFS

Reefs closer to the mainland and big islands are, when conditions are good, the most interesting. There are so many that it can be hard to decide which one to dive. Much exploration has still to be done to find not only the best reefs but the best parts of them.

Away from the principal shipping routes around the coasts of PNG the charts are marked 'Caution, Unsurveyed'; and it is these areas – a large proportion of PNG's waters – that contain some of the best dive sites. Dotted lines on the charts show approximately where reefs are known to exist, but are highly inaccurate. Reefs may be found outside the areas marked, and some charted reefs simply do not exist, or do so a kilometre away from the position marked. One regularly dived reef is charted in no fewer than four different positions – none of them correct!

That word 'Caution' has to be heeded: only in good light, when reefs can be seen clearly from the boat, should entry to these areas be attempted. Nevertheless, divers have over the years systematically explored and charted several previously unsurveyed reef systems. (These include the Dart Reefs between Cape Vogel and Goodenough Island; unnamed reefs north of Sanaroa and Fergusson Islands; and reefs in Kimbe Bay and around New Hanover Island.) Many more still remain to be discovered.

The fact that much of underwater PNG is still unexplored is a key reason why it has gained a reputation as a top destination for experienced divers. Weary of diving where many have dived before, adventurous divers can charter diveboats to explore remote reefs. Even on regular dive cruises it is often possible to spend some time diving new sites. The reports of these sites have led other types of experienced divers to head for PNG: naturalists, wreck fanatics and underwater photographers.

PANDA CLOWNFISH

Many divers think the Panda Clownfish (*Amphiprion polymnus*) is rare – and on coral reefs it is. But, as with many supposedly rare creatures, the secret is knowing where to look. These beautiful anemonefish make their home on sand and muck! Sea-grass beds in shallow water are particularly rewarding. The fish usually live in the sand anemone *Stichodactyla haddoni*, which will retract into the sand if disturbed, but I have also seen them in *Heteractis crispa* and *H. aurora*.

The juveniles are black and yellow, with a single white stripe near the head and a broader white saddle across the back. As they grow older they lose the yellow, becoming eventually black and white – hence the common name Panda. Eggs are laid on a rock or coconut-husk next to the anemone. When startled, the Panda Clownfish sometimes dives into the stomach of the anemone, a strange behaviour which apparently does the fish no harm.

Opposite: *The Telita was the first live aboard dive-boat in PNG and it is still one of the most popular in PNG.*

BARRIER REEFS

The Papuan coast, Bougainville Island and a few other areas have barrier reefs running parallel to the coast, with relatively shallow water in the lagoon between shore and reef and very deep water outside the barrier, which marks the edge of the continental shelf. The Papuan Barrier Reef is as rich a coral wonderland as the Great Barrier Reef of Australia, with the advantage of being just a few kilometres offshore. The passes through the barrier, where tidal waters enter and leave the lagoon, are bursting with marine life and therefore make the most exciting dive sites. In calm conditions the outside of the barrier can be dived, but in many places the reeftop is relatively barren because of regular pounding by the ocean swells.

Some parts of the barrier are 'sunken' (i.e, the reeftop is deeper than normal – 6–10m; 20–33ft). Large waves can pass over without breaking, so these areas do not act as very effective barriers; however, for the same reason, the reeftop coral formations are generally much better than on the true barrier reefs. Down the dropoff the corals are better formed and, depending on the currents, very clear water can be found.

If water is being flushed from the lagoons (which are cauldrons of living marine soup) the outside slopes can remain dirty well past diving depths – not so good for divers though excellent nutritionally for the reefs. The inside slopes of the barrier reefs, by contrast, offer sheltered water that may be dived in most conditions, and it is here you can see the more delicate coral gardens. The patch reefs and islands inside the lagoons likewise have an abundance of marine life.

The closer to shore, the poorer the visibility and the more stressed the coral growth. Where mangroves line the shore, the bottom becomes muddy rather than sandy, with only the occasional coral outcrop. This mangrove and mud environment is, however, fascinating to dive. It acts as a secure nursery area for fish that will eventually live on the outer reefs, and supports many interesting animals, particularly molluscs, that can be found nowhere else. Shallow sandy areas off beaches, some sloping quickly to deep water, make an ideal environment for sea-grass beds, and the different fauna found here makes for fascinating 'muck diving' – seahorses, ghost pipefish, cowfish, Panda Clownfish and dugong live among other exotic marine life in these sand-and-sea-grass areas.

THE PORT MORESBY SUB-AQUA CLUB INC

Established in 1975, the Port Moresby Sub-Aqua Club runs regular dive trips and social meetings. It has its own 6m (20ft) outboard-powered diveboat, fitted with safety gear and a sun-shade, which can make fast trips out to the dive sites with up to six divers. Regular departure times are 07:00 on Saturdays and 08:00 Sundays from the DPI boat ramp at downtown Port Moresby, but there are sometimes special weekday trips and night-dives. You usually book space on the boat by calling the current divemasters; second trips are organized if numbers are sufficient. Current membership numbers about 90 qualified divers. Details of club membership, trips and the photo competition can be obtained from the club (address on page 86).

WRECKS

In addition to the magnificent reefs there are hundreds of wrecks scattered throughout the waters. These include ships, boats, submarines and aircraft, many in excellent condition and now transformed into coral wonderlands. Many have yet to be dived, and rarely does a year go by without some significant discovery being made. All of PNG's war wrecks are now protected, so the more recently discovered wrecks offer you the same thrill they did the discoverers.

MARINE LIFE

PNG has – along with its neighbour Indonesia – more marine species than any other region in the world. The totals are unknown, since new species are constantly being discovered (for example, my wife Dinah and I recently discovered seven new fishes), but it is estimated that PNG has twice the number of fish species as the Red Sea and over five times the number found in the Caribbean. As for the invertebrates, there are undoubtedly hundreds of undescribed species within diving depths. Since divers visiting PNG for the first time are likely to be bewildered by the quantity of marine life new to them, underwater naturalists commonly travel with a specialist marine biologist who can point out which creatures are known and which are very unusual. Diving 'ecotours' of this kind are becoming more and more popular in PNG, with the result that discoveries are increasing rather than decreasing.

Conditions are excellent for underwater photography, sites are rich and varied, and photographers searching for the unusual are quickly rewarded. In recognition of this the PNG Government has sponsored the Port Moresby Sub-Aqua Club to organize the world's richest underwater photography competition.

WEATHER

Weather patterns vary considerably from one part to another: while Port Moresby is having its dry season Milne Bay is having its wet season, and so on. PNG is blessed with year-round diving, but tropical weather is notoriously unpredictable, so that 'dry' seasons can turn out to be very wet and 'wet' seasons clear and sunny.

Fortunately the seasons do not affect the underwater conditions as much as might be expected – indeed, some areas have clearest water during their wet season. The most important factor in determining underwater visibility is the ocean current, and when blue water flows into an area, as it regularly does throughout most of PNG, the rain does not matter very much. For any particular location, however unpredictable the weather, diving is guaranteed; even if a particular dive site cannot be reached, it is unheard-of to lose a day's diving because of the weather.

The Southeast Trade Winds blow about May/Nov. The south is most affected, the wind-strength becoming less the further north you go. Since most diving is close to shore, the high mountains produce local land breezes and early mornings are often calm; it is not until later in the day that the Trade Winds start to take over. When these are mild the weather is perfect for diving; but unfortunately during this season the wind will occasionally and unpredictably pick up strength and start blowing at 20–25 knots, so that exposed reefs become impossible to dive. However, all diving areas have excellent sites that are sheltered from the Southeast Trades, and one big advantage of this season is that a blue current usually pushes through the country from the Coral Sea, producing excellent visibility.

This season is the coolest time of the year, and water temperatures that drop as low as 25°C (77°F) around Port Moresby and Milne Bay require the use of a thin wetsuit (the better-quality lined lycra suits may be used, but only if a hood is included). North of New Britain the water temperature rarely drops below 28°C (82°F), so that wetsuits are never required (although lycra suits with hoods are still strongly recommended). The Southeast season is considered the dry season through much of the country, but some areas – like Milne Bay and the southern coast of New Britain – can experience rain.

The Northwest season, running about Jan/Mar, brings hot, calm but squally weather to much of the country. As

Red sea whips are a feature of many of the reefs in PNG, and colourful subjects to photograph.

might be expected, the north is most affected and, although this is the rainy or monsoon season there, the water temperature can rise to a delicious 30°C (86°F). This is among the best times to dive in Milne Bay: the water is at about 28°C (82°F) and the days are often calm and hot. Cyclones in the Coral Sea seldom have any effect in northwestern Milne Bay, though the eastern Louisiade Archipelago should be avoided.

Between the two seasons the winds are usually light, but rainfall and visibility can be very unpredictable.

SKILL LEVELS

Diving in PNG has been pioneered by very experienced divers, and consequently this is one of the few diving destinations where experienced divers get an opportunity to dive without the restrictions seen elsewhere. Deep, decompression and solo dives are routinely made and in conditions that could be suicidal for novices. Because of the dangers of divers attempting dives beyond their level of competence, some operators require evidence of experience before allowing certain dives.

That said, the great majority of dives require little more than basic skills. There are several dive schools in the country where internationally qualified instructors continually train novices, and visiting divers with little experience will find many extraordinary dives well within their capability, while professional divemasters and dive guides will be there to ensure the dives are as safe and enjoyable as possible.

It is important, though, to realize that dive operators in PNG treat their guests as adults. Because undue restrictions are not imposed, it is essential you behave responsibly and do not attempt dives that are beyond your skill and experience level. Although the dive operators are very happy to teach their guests new techniques, it is obviously not possible to turn a novice diver into an experienced deep-wreck diver in the course of just one week's vacation!

For recently certified divers, or those whose diving has been limited to establishments geared to large numbers of poorly skilled divers, many of the techniques seem at first glance to fly in the face of conventional wisdom concerning the 'rules' for safe diving. However, you would be mistaken to think that PNG divers are ignorant or gung-ho. The reality is that they have learned that the conventional way is not always the best for the challenges they face. The joy of diving here is that the unexpected can and often does happen: diving is still an adventure ... and there is no such thing as a perfectly safe adventure: there must always be an unknown factor, and the challenge is to be able to respond effectively to the changing circumstances and yet avoid injury.

Responsible diving means that, before any dive, each individual must make the decision that, for him or her, the dive will be 'safe' – i.e., that it is unlikely (although not impossible) that injury will occur. You must thus know both the risks of diving this particular dive and your ability to cope with them. Dive operators will provide briefings outlining the less obvious risks, but only you yourself can know if you have the ability. Divemasters may stop you making a particular dive if you visibly lack the necessary skills, but they vastly prefer that you make this decision for yourself.

Let's define terms. The risks increase with increasing depth, increasing current, reduced visibility, poor surface conditions, a difficult underwater topography to navigate, longer underwater swims, the presence of sharks or crocodiles or overhead obstructions, etc. So much is a matter of fact. By contrast, the dangers are not so absolute: they depend on your ability to cope with those risks. For example, a dive in clear, calm shallow water is a low-risk dive – but would be very dangerous if you didn't know not to hold your breath during ascent. A dive in deep, murky, shark-infested water, with a current running, although high-risk, may be safe if you have the training and experience to cope with these conditions.

Very few PNG operators require the buddy system. If you wish to dive with a buddy you're of course welcome to do so, although each diver needs to be self-sufficient: one buddy should not be dependent on another. Most PNG operators believe that the really important buddy is the one above the water, looking out for the divers, who can assist them immediately if they surface away from the main boat or shore.

Many of the best wreck-dives and a few reef dives require an ability to dive deeper than generally recommended for recreational scuba divers. Operators routinely supervise dives to 50m (165ft), more rarely to 60m (200ft). These extreme depths should be attempted only by very experienced divers properly equipped for deep diving.

EQUIPMENT

Because exploration often implies significant underwater mobility, streamlining of dive gear is considered important, and PNG divers generally use dive-skins rather than wetsuits (although tropical wetsuits are necessary in the south during the 'winter' months). Buoyancy compensators are of the low-drag, low-volume variety. Regulators are typically equipped with a pressure gauge but not a full bulky console, and masks are worn without snorkels. As yet no operators provide facilities for nitrox or trimix diving, but I would not be surprised to see this in the near future.

Divers are expected to bring their own diving computers and keep track of their own dive profiles. Advice is always available, and operators prefer all divers to make conservative decompression stops after every dive even when they are not dictated by the computer. This is usually no hardship, since dives are mostly from shallow-water anchorages, so you can enjoy the shallow reef while effectively making a safety stop.

There are no recompression facilities in PNG and, although every operator has standby oxygen available, you face evacuation to Australia if chamber treatment is required. Transport can be arranged by means of a specially equipped aircraft with a portable two-person chamber on board. But be warned: evacuation and treatment are incredibly expensive, and you should carry insurance to cover this. Avoidance of the problem, by doing only carefully planned and skilfully executed dives well within your personal capability, is far preferable.

Many shallow reef tops have exquisite coral gardens, perfect for snorkelling.

MILNE BAY PROVINCE

Between the Coral Sea and the Solomon Sea lies a beautiful and intricate chain of pristine volcanic peaks, coral islands and reefs. The two seas surge back and forth, flushing plankton-rich lagoon waters with liquid blue from their abyssal depths and causing a frantic profusion of marine growth. Humans are few, and live in harmony with a bountiful nature. Incredible creatures have evolved to creep and swim in this underwater Eden, and marine giants from near and far gather to feast on the almost obscene abundance.

The volcanically active and massive D'Entrecasteaux Islands, the Louisiade Archipelago, the Trobriand 'Islands of Love' and the hundreds of other islands that radiate from the deep natural harbour of Milne Bay itself are surrounded and laced by a maze of reefs that would take several lifetimes to explore. The most commonly dived areas are:

- near the mouth of Milne Bay
- the Eastern D'Entrecasteaux region
- the Western D'Entrecasteaux region (including Cape Vogel)

Many other regions, although they are further from Alotau and harder to get to, offer amazing diving.

Not only is Milne Bay Province the largest and most undisturbed of all PNG's coastal areas, it is, as far as exotic marine life goes, the most exciting. Kavieng may have its unbeatable giant schools of barracuda and indomitable Silvertip Sharks (*Carcharhinus albimarginatus*), and Walindi its exquisite reefs and heart-stopping whale encounters, but Milne Bay is special for the extraordinary richness not only of its classic tropical reefs – packed with the usual creatures that divers would expect to find, large and small – but of marine animals so unusual that many are new to science. In addition, one of the most fantastic scorpionfish in the world, *Rhinopia aphanes*, can be regularly found; this incredible fish mimics crinoids and, although hard to spot, can usually be seen once you know what to look for.

Opposite: *View of China Strait from historic Samarai Island.*

Above: *Soft Corals, Dendronephthya sp. occur in every colour of the rainbow.*

There seems no end to the discoveries that divers can make here. An important reason, apart from the unpolluted and minimally exploited surroundings, is the great variety of the dive sites. There are classic coral walls, some sheltered almost all year round from heavy seas; reef passes that capture the surging tides and thus huge numbers of feeding fish; long barrier reefs and miniature atolls; sandy beaches with delicate coral gardens; and quiet bays where sea-grasses hide seahorses, Panda Clownfish, frogfish, rare species of garden eel and the occasional dugong. Mangroves and rivers provide vital nurseries and nutrients but, because of the deep water so close to shore, have no negative effect on the diving. There are also some spectacular wreck-dives – including probably the world's best aircraft wreck-dive, the amazing B17 bomber Blackjack.

Visiting divers fly into Gurney Airport, the gateway to the provincial capital, Alotau; work is underway to upgrade the airstrip to international standards for direct jet flights from Cairns. Four live-aboard diveboats and one expedition ship operate out of Alotau: *Telita, Tiata*, *Barbarian II* and *Chertan*, plus the 42-passenger expedition vessel *Melanesian Discoverer*. Of these only *Telita* and *Chertan* are based there. Since conditions are sometimes unpredictable the flexibility of live-aboard diving and the time on the water it affords are useful to ensure you reach the very best diving area for the prevailing conditions. The usual problem is too much choice, not too little!

It is important to realize that the weather patterns in Milne Bay are not the same as in the rest of the country. Good diving is available all year round, including Jan/Mar, considered the wet season elsewhere but definitely not in Milne Bay – during these months the water is at its warmest and mostly calm. Cyclones very rarely affect the diving areas, except among the islands to the far southeast of the Louisiade Archipelago, where little diving is done at present. The water temperatures range from a wonderful 30°C (86°F) around Dec/Jan to 25°C (77°F) in Jul/Aug. Tropical wetsuits are recommended in all but the warmest months, though many divers are happy with lycra suits – particularly if they have a hood. Visibility is usually at least 25m (80ft) and often much better, especially when the Southeast Trades cause a blue-water current to flow through the islands.

Milne Bay does not have as many wrecks as other provinces, but what it lacks in number it makes up for in quality, especially if the diver is interested in aircraft. The best are a beautiful P38 Lightning in 27m (90ft) and the incredible B17 Blackjack, which is in 45m (150ft) (see pages 64 and 58). Both aircraft were ditched, and the wrecks are upright and in excellent condition, with the original guns still in place. Souveniring from wrecks is not allowed in PNG, so visiting divers will see these just as they were found. A great way to end a cruise in Milne Bay is to visit the wreck of the Muscoota (see page 36). The bay is also home to the China Straits drift-dive – a 4km (2$^1/_2$-mile) drift at 4 knots in 30–40m (100–130ft) of water!

Although many dive sites are known and visited regularly, even the busiest rarely see more than 20–30 divers a month. Since commercial pressure is negligible and village populations very small, the reefs are effectively part of a great marine park, and you see reefs unspoiled by human hand. Milne Bay is so vast that many reefs remain undived, and it is not unusual for diveboats to make a couple of exploratory dives during a cruise: it is always a special thrill to be the first to dive a new site.

In short, Milne Bay is a very special place where divers can experience coral reefs the way that nature made them – a privilege and joy indeed.

Milne Bay

There is one very interesting wreck-dive (Site 2) right in Milne Bay, but otherwise you must cruise from Alotau east to the mouth of the bay to reach the best dive sites. Here – from East Cape and the northeast side of the mainland in a wide arc through Nuakata Island and south to Basilaki Island and Samarai – are hundreds of reefs and dozens of islands with superb diving. Currents are common on the exposed reefs and passes, and are variable: the strongest usually, but unfortunately not always, coincide with the spring tides, and may be avoided by studying the Port Moresby tide tables. The tide tables for Alotau are of little use for predicting diving conditions.

1 CHINA STRAIT

★★★★★

Location: Samarai Island.
Access: By boat drifting through strait. Strait is shipping channel, so good lookout must be taken before starting dive to make sure strait free from large vessels. Large divers' flag must be shown.
Conditions: Light winds required (any direction). Currents up to 6 knots flow through strait. For experienced divers only.
Typical visibility: 15m (50ft)
Minimum depth: 30m (100ft)
Maximum depth: 40m (130ft)

If you wish to attempt this dive you need a copy of the navigation chart for the China Strait plus tide tables for Port Moresby; a table on the chart enables you to predict the direction and strength of the current. The usual dive starts 2 n. miles (3.7km) northeast of Samarai Island with the current (4 knots ideal) flowing northeasterly. You descend a heavily weighted line lowered behind the boat; each diver has an individual line, with a fixed loop on the end, attached to this at the bottom – you must be able to let go of the line at any stage, and must be confident in your ability to surface in a strong current, after ascending through murky water with no reference, should you have to ditch the line.

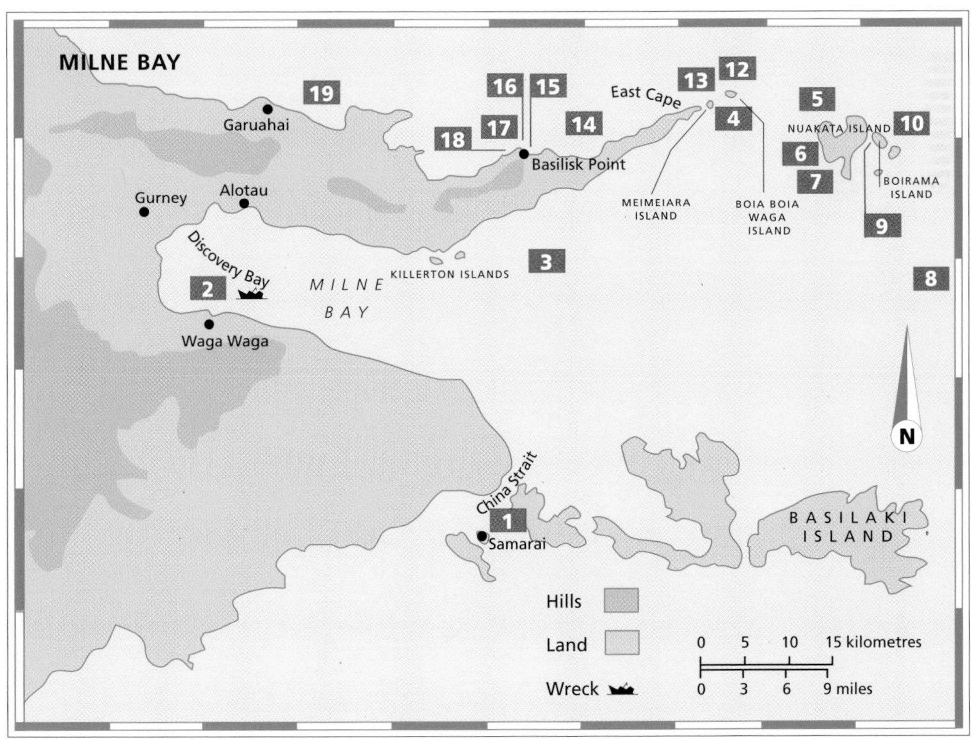

The effect is like water-skiing underwater, with a constant pull on the line and buffeting caused by turbulence. The sensation of speed is extraordinary as the bottom, covered in soft corals and other marine growth, rushes by. You need constant vigilance, as deep ledges and occasional rocks appear suddenly out of the gloom. Divers try to get as close to the bottom as possible without hitting anything, then fly up and around each other; in their exhilaration divers often 'maypole' their lines. Cameras are not advised.

After a maximum bottom-time of 15min the boat starts to haul the line up to avoid it catching the bottom as you start your ascent. It may be the most memorable 15min you'll ever spend underwater! If you do the drift at a slower speed you may, if you've sharp eyes, spot Goldlip Pearl (*Pinctada maxima*) shells.

2 MUSCOOTA

★★★★★★★★

Location: Discovery Bay, 6 n. miles (11km) across Milne Bay from Alotau.

Access: By boat (preferably) or road from Alotau. Wreck partly above water and easily found, with secure anchorage surrounding it.

Conditions: Sheltered in all weather conditions.

Typical visibility: 20m (65ft) – can be greatly reduced after heavy rain

Minimum depth: as shallow as you like

Maximum depth: 24m (78ft)

The wreck is of the *Muscoota*, an iron-hulled clipper ship launched by Queen Victoria and originally named the *Buckingham*. It was converted to a coal-refuelling barge for World War II, and scuttled at the end of the war

when it sprang a leak. The large sliding gantry over the hull is home to many schools of fish; its top can be seen above the surface, as can the bow-tip, but the rest is underwater, the stern in mud at 24m (70ft). The Muscoota is covered with marine life, including many colourful clams, soft corals and sponges. The surrounding sea-grass-and-silt bottom is home to seahorses (*Hippocampus* spp), ghost pipefish (*Solenostomus paradoxus* and *S. cyanopterus*), Flying Gurnard (*Dactyloptena orientalis*), ribbon gobies (*Oxymetopon* spp) and a host of other interesting creatures. The ship had no engine, but there is a boiler-room forward that was used to power the winches of the refuelling gantry. Tomato (Spine-cheeked) Clownfish (*Premnus biaculeatus*) abound on the ship's foredeck. A resident Wobbegong Shark (*Eucrossorhinus dasypogon*) is often seen. The wreck is very colourful, and makes an excellent night-dive. Take care not to collide with the gantry – the clams are sharp – and always wear a knife, as old fishing-lines tangle on the wreck. Dramatic wide-angle photographs are possible in clear conditions, and the macro opportunities make this a great dive for photographers even when visibility is reduced.

The bow can be easily snorkelled, and harbours a host of interesting creatures.

3 SULLIVAN'S PATCHES

★★★★★★★★

Location: 4 n. miles (7.4km) east of Killerton Islands.
Access: By boat from Alotau. Anchor on northerly tip of western reef or easterly tip of eastern reef in sand patches only, to avoid damage to exquisite coral reefs.
Conditions: Although protected from ocean swells, may be dived only in calm conditions. Currents slight.
Typical visibility: 30m (100ft)
Minimum depth: 6m (20ft)
Maximum depth: 50m (165ft) plus

Two main reefs, the more easterly running approximately east–west and the westerly running north–south. At least two dives are needed to explore these. In the early 1980s these reefs were rendered barren by Crown-of-Thorns Starfish (*Acanthaster plancii*) but an amazing rejuvenation has since taken place, and the reefs are now packed with vibrant corals and schools of fish. Deep water surrounds the reefs, but the best diving is in the first 20m (65ft). Large animals are frequently seen, especially Manta Rays (*Manta birostris*) but also the occasional Hammerhead Shark (*Sphyrna lewini*) and, less commonly, Tiger Shark (*Galeocerdo cuvier*). A large navy anchor east of the westerly reef was left during World War II, when it secured a navigational buoy.

Opposite: *Banana Bommie displays an extraordinary abundance of marine life.*

BOMMIES

Anyone who dives in Australia or with Australians will be mystified by continued reference to 'bommies'. Don't be alarmed – this isn't Australian baby-talk for unexploded ordnance. The word is derived from an Aboriginal term, *bombora*, meaning a coral growth that sticks out from its surroundings. Bommies can be small – a coral bommie on a sandflat may be just 1m (40in) across – or large – an isolated coral reef that could take 30min to swim around – and anything in between. Coral towers are certainly bommies, but the word 'tower' is generally reserved for bommies that are particularly tall and slim. Bommies tend to be places that attract particularly rich marine growth and healthy fish populations.

There is good snorkelling on top of both reefs, but people nervous of sharks should not wander too far from the diveboat.

4 BANANA BOMMIE

★★★★★

Location: 1.75 n. miles (3.2km) south-southeast of Boia Boia Waga Island.
Access: Anchor on barren scar caused by grounded ship (since salvaged) in 5m (16ft) near northern end of reef.
Conditions: Best diving conditions are in the prevailing slight current from the west; this can reach 2 knots. Some shelter, but can be uncomfortable in windy conditions.
Typical visibility: 20–40m (60–130ft), but can get murky
Minimum depth: 5m (16ft)
Maximum depth: 30m (100ft)

This patch reef is just small enough to swim around on a single tank, but it is best to dive only whichever side is receiving the current – usually the west. Reasonable shelter from the current is possible once you're over the front face. The reef is incredibly rich, and the sheer numbers of fish and other marine life are staggering. The reef-side slopes down to a sandy bottom at about 27m (90ft) with rich coral outcrops. Garden eels (*Heteroconger* spp) live in the sand. A huge school of very friendly Batfish (*Platax tiera*) is often seen, as are Grey Reef Sharks (*Carcharhinus amblyrhynchos*), colourful Red-lined Sea Cucumbers, nudibranchs and myriads of reef fish. This is a wonderful site for wide-angle photography in clear conditions.

There are other sites with similar features nearby. Snorkelling is possible only in the rare circumstances of calm water and slack currents.

5 HIBWA REEF

★★★★★★★★

Location: Hibwa sand cay, near Nuakata Island.
Access: Best to anchor off reef in 10–20m (33–65ft).
Conditions: Currents can be fierce on south side: pick times of slight current. Little current in shallows.
Typical visibility: 30m (100ft), sometimes reduced
Minimum depth: 1m (40in)
Maximum depth: 50m (165ft)

Different dives are possible around the island; the best scuba diving is at the southern end. It is easy to get disoriented on this dive, and care should be taken with navigation. Once on a coral mound, choose the side receiving any current to get the best fish action. Move from mound to mound towards the shallow reef, where the dive can be ended in very shallow water. A pick-up from here back to the main boat is a good idea.

The shallow reef around Hibwa sand cay can be snorkelled, and you can land on the cay.

6 TUNNEL REEF

★★★★★★★

Location: 1½ n. miles (2.8km) west of Nuakata Island.
Access: Anchor on rubble patch on top of middle of reef.
Conditions: Partly sheltered; can be dived in light wind conditions. Sometimes strong currents over reef.
Typical visibility: 30–40m (100–130ft), sometimes reduced
Minimum depth: 6m (20ft)
Maximum depth: 50m (165ft)

An isolated, sausage-shaped reef running north–south. Near the southern end a tunnel runs through the reef, starting at 27m (90ft) and rising to exit at 15m (50ft); it is approximately 2m (6½ft) wide, and the morning sun shines directly down it much of the year. Inside the tunnel there is good marine growth, and the surrounding reef is well covered with soft and hard corals and many fish. At the northwestern end three coral towers rise from the bottom, close to the reef; the hanging lace sponge covering them looks like icing on a fancy cake! Manta Rays have been seen around the reef.

The rather small area for snorkelling is pleasant when current is slack.

7 TRISH'S BOMMIE

★★★★★

Location: 2 n. miles (3.7km) southwest of Nuakata Island's southern tip.
Access: Take great care to anchor on the several rubble patches on reef, not on live coral areas.
Conditions: Calm seas and light currents necessary.
Typical visibility: 30–40m (100–130ft)

Crystal clear waters enable divers to enjoy spectacular reef scenes.

Minimum depth: 9m (30ft)
Maximum depth: 40m (130ft)
Quite a large patch reef, best dived when the current is from the east. The front face, a sloping dropoff, is covered with soft corals; the reef also has areas of lettuce and other hard corals, Giant Clams and many anemones, some with very colourful mantles. A deep trench runs close by, so sharks are seen more often than on some local reefs. An unbelievable number of fish gathers on the front face of the reef when the current is running – it's sometimes difficult to see the reef! Schools of surgeonfish, fusiliers, mackerel, unicornfish and great clouds of anthias all compete for the current-borne plankton. This is a difficult reef to dive unless the conditions are perfect, but it should then be a first choice.

8 HEINECKE HEAVEN

★★★★★

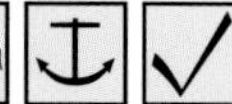

Location: $6^1/_2$ n. miles (12km) southeast of Nuakata Island.
Access: Because of the depth over it, reef difficult to see until you're very close. Anchor on sand patch in middle of reef.
Conditions: Calm or light winds required, as reef has little shelter. Often slight current.
Typical visibility: 30–40m (100-130ft)
Minimum depth: 13m (43ft)
Maximum depth: 50m (165ft) plus
The best plan is to circumnavigate this small reef in a single dive, pausing at whichever side is receiving any current, where there will be the most fish-life. There is something different to see all around the reef, some areas having exceptionally colourful and lush soft corals. Sharks, pelagics and turtles are frequent, and a great many different species of reef fishes thrive here. An excellent wide-angle site for photographers.

This uncharted reef was discovered accidentally and first dived in 1994. There are no other reefs nearby, so Heinecke's Heaven acts as a particularly rich oasis.

9 BOIRAMA REEF

★★★★★★★★

Location: Western side of Boirama Island.
Access: Anchor in gutter to northwest of sand beach.
Conditions: Sheltered from southeast winds. Sometimes strong currents.
Typical visibility: 30m (100ft)
Minimum depth: as shallow as you like
Maximum depth: 40m (130ft)
If a current is running, this can be done as a drift-dive, with divers being dropped in the water 100m (110yd) or so to the south, off the island's sand beach. The drift starts slowly, along a wall richly decorated with fans and sponges. Near the beach the reef dies out and you encounter a sand slope populated with shrimp gobies, garden eels and sand darters. Deep down the slope, soft corals grow from the sand bottom and there is a giant school of Bannerfish (*Heniochus diphreutes*). A rare school of Moorish Idols (*Zanclus cornutus*) is often on the reef just before the sand slope. After about 50m (165ft) a second reef starts, incredibly rich in marine growth, abounding with soft corals, sponges and crinoids. The current is usually strongest here, and careful navigation is needed to ensure the boat is not overshot. Many large fish feed in front of the reef-wall, including Dogtooth Tuna, Spanish Mackerel (*Scomberomorus commerson*), barracuda (*Sphyraena putnamiae*) and Grey Reef Sharks. After diving the front reef-wall, rise to the reeftop to find a garden of coral heads separated by sand gutters. Giant Clams are on the reef, as is a resident Wobbegong Shark.

In the Northwest season the reef on the other side of the passage near Nuakata Island can be dived, but is not as rich as Boirama Reef.

There is excellent safe snorkelling close to the shore on the reef's southern part, but avoid the northern part except in light current conditions.

SHARK-FINNING

Demand for shark-fin soup has never been higher. In PNG, wholesalers are offering up to US$50 per kilogram for shark-fins, which are then exported to Asia at even higher prices. Such sums represent an enormous amount of money for village people, and the temptation to catch sharks is hard to resist. But the fin is the only part of the shark that has any commercial value. Although fisheries officials claim that the flesh, skin and teeth can also be used, the wholesalers purchase only the fins. So shark fishermen catch the fish, remove its fins, and throw the usually still-living creature back into the sea, where it suffers a miserable, slow death.

VILLAGE CHOIRS

Many villages have choirs, usually formed in connection with the local church. The best I have heard are at Nuakata Island in Milne Bay. Up to 20 people of both sexes, ranging from 8 to 25 years old, paddle out to the visiting diveboats and, for a small contribution to the church fund, perform a lively concert. A couple of the older boys have well worn guitars and accompany the choristers, who sing both counterpoint and harmony with surprising skill and great enthusiasm. Most of the songs are in the local language, and have obvious religious significance.

10 WHALE REEF

★★★★★★★

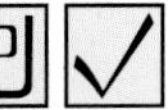

Location: On the eastern side of Boirama Island.
Access: Anchor on top of detached part of reef.
Conditions: Calm during westerly winds but exposed during Southeast Trades. Detached part of reef experiences a current, usually from south.
Typical visibility: 30m (100ft), sometimes reduced
Minimum depth: as shallow as you like
Maximum depth: 40m (130ft)

Start by descending along and down the detached bommie in a southerly direction. There are beautiful coral growths with excellent fish-life. For a second dive, swim across a saddle to the fringing reef, which has several indentations and spurs. In the Northwest season Manta Rays are frequent, including large schools of the small Manta species called Mobula (*Mobula tarapacana*). The reef was discovered one year when Minke Whales (*Balaenoptera acutorostrata*) were seen feeding around the detached part.

Snorkellers should immediately cross to the fringing reef, where safe, current-free snorkelling may be found right up to the shore.

11 PEER'S REEF

★★★★★

Location: Nuakata Island; exact location withheld because of shark-finners.
Access: Refer to Telita Cruises.
Conditions: Best diving is during Southeast season, when a constant current sweeps over the reef from east at 1/2–1 knot; it can reach 2 knots, in which conditions diving is difficult. Can be uncomfortable in windy weather.
Typical visibility: 20–40m (65–130ft)
Minimum depth: 5m (16ft)
Maximum depth: 50m (165ft) plus

A steep dropoff runs along the front of the reef. The reeftop is very lush, but the best diving is at the edge of the drop in 18–25m (60–80ft). Soft corals adorn the front face, and the fish action is impressive. Schooling Hammerhead Sharks are frequent in the Southeast season. It is often possible to photograph large animals, but handling big cameras is difficult in the current. Photographers should keep it simple.

The site can be dived either by using a current-line to get to the front face and then staying still and watching the world go by, or by using a dinghy to drop divers up the reef to drift back to the anchored boat. Great care and careful navigation is needed since divers who get lost can easily be swept by the current into deep, rough and sharky waters.

A memorial to a much-loved, tragically killed diving mate, Peer Kirkemo, is at 30m (100ft) down the slope. It is now covered with soft corals, and should not be disturbed.

There is excellent snorkelling on the reeftop, but only at rare times of calm, still water and only if you're happy about snorkelling with sharks. Dugong have been seen by snorkellers here.

THE HARBOURMASTER

Visitors to East Cape are greeted by John, whose family owns land near the anchorage. John paddles out to all the boats visiting the anchorage to welcome them and to see if anyone needs to buy food or betelnut or other supplies. He uses his canoes to help ferry passengers ashore, and has earned the nickname 'Harbourmaster' – which he accepts with good humour.

John has built a traditional guesthouse on his land right by the beach, and you can stay here for a very modest cost. You need to provide your own camp-bed but the house, built of bush materials and on stilts, is completely weatherproof and cool. Whether you arrive by road (from Alotau) or by sea, John's warm hospitality includes cooking meals if required and offering canoe rides, fishing expeditions and visits to the two islands. He has a vast knowledge of local traditions and provides an opportunity for you to experience village life.

12 BOIA BOIA WAGA ISLAND

★★★★★★

Location: The second of the two islands near East Cape.
Access: Anchor in sand patches in 7m (23ft).
Typical visibility: 30m (100ft), sometimes reduced
Minimum depth: 7m (23ft)
Maximum depth: 50m (165ft) plus

Of several possible dives, the best is on the spur of reef on the northwest side and when a slight current is coming from the northwest; you dive the west dropoff and swim south along the wall. There are soft corals and small sea fans deeper down the wall, at about 30m (100ft), and good coral growths in the shallows. Turtles are frequent. The spur of reef on the northeastern side offers similar features to those of the western spur. Look out for Manta Rays and Hammerheads.

In the Southeast season the island provides a good anchorage close to the beach. Extensive areas of shallow coral gardens all around the island offer excellent snorkelling.

Opposite: *A common, but vibrant, variety of nudibranch, Notodoris minor.*

13 COBB'S CLIFF

★★★★★★★★★★

Location: Between Boia Boia Waga and Mei Mei'ara islands.
Access: Anchor in 18m (60ft) on sand in middle of small lagoon.
Conditions: Sheltered in most conditions. A strong current often moves through nearby reef passage, but dive itself experiences only eddies; these can be confusing and change direction during course of dive, but are seldom strong enough to trouble a diver.
Typical visibility: 40m (130ft) plus, depending on direction of current in channel; best when current is moving into Milne Bay from north. However, visibility can be excellent with either current – and anyway the currents are largely unpredictable.
Minimum depth: 5m (16ft)
Maximum depth: 50m (165ft) plus

Start by swimming south along the outer dropoff. A deep dive is possible, but most action takes place in the first 20m (65ft). A leisurely 10min swim takes you to the end bommie, where most fish congregate. It is worth spending most of your time hanging around the bommie looking out for large animals or searching for Leaf Scorpionfish (*Taenianotus triacanthus*) and Lacy Scorpionfish (*Rhinopias aphanes*). Return to the boat along the ridge-top in 5-8m (15–26ft). You can do alternative dives along the ridge's lagoon side or along the dropoff to the north. At this site Dinah and I have photographed rare deep-water anthias (*Pseudantias* spp) and sand tilefish (*Hoplolatilus* spp) in 60m (200ft) down the outer dropoff.

A broad expanse of superb coral reef on the lagoon's other side, largely unaffected by current, provides snorkelling opportunities. Manta Rays sometimes visit the area and Whale Sharks (*Rhiniodon typus*) have been seen.

14 WAHOO REEF

★★★★★★★★

Location: On the north coast 6 n. miles (11km) west of East Cape.
Access: Anchor immediately east of bommie off shallow fringing reef.
Conditions: Sheltered in Southeast Trades; unreliable in Northwest season. Can be slight current over site.
Typical visibility: 40m (130ft)
Minimum depth: as shallow as you like
Maximum depth: 50m (165ft) plus

A steep dropoff plunging from 12m (40ft) to more than

60m (200ft) is vertical on its northern side and slightly sloping on its western side. The reef has a definite right-angled corner, and gradually slopes up here to about 8m (26ft), where an interesting wall with crevices and swimthroughs rises to the surface. You may not always be lucky at this reef, but over the years it has produced some memorable encounters for me. Big creatures habitually swim along the edge of the dropoff and over the sloping corner, among them Hammerhead Sharks (the commonest), Whale Sharks, Manta Rays and Mobula, Queensland Groupers, dugong and Tiger Sharks. A small school of barracuda resides on the reef; plenty of other reef fish are very approachable. In 1989–92 the reef was infested by Crown-of-Thorns Starfish, but coral regrowth is now obvious and the reef will soon recover its former splendour. Anchoring boats should be careful to avoid some significant stands of cabbage coral (*Turbinaria reniformis*).

The excellent snorkelling along the edge of the shallow dropoff includes a chance to see some bigger creatures.

15 KATHY'S CORNER

★★★★★★★★★

Location: Point immediately east of Basilisk Point (Sites 17-18).
Access: Anchor in sand at 20m and tie stern to tree ashore.
Conditions: Sheltered in all but northwesterly winds.
Typical visibility: 40m (130ft)
Minimum depth: as shallow as you like
Maximum depth: 60m (200ft) plus

The cliff face to the east descends into the water as a wall covered with sponges and black corals above a black sand bottom; this wall is home to many nudibranchs, including Spanish Dancers (*Hexabranchus sanguineus*), and is an excellent night-dive. The wall continues round the point; in the shallows on its top is an exquisite coral labyrinth with sea fans. Flashlight fish (*Photoblepharon palpebratus*) can be found in the labyrinth at night, as can juvenile Pinnate Batfish (*Platax pinnatus*) and turtles.

On the west are two small coral reefs stacked with an incredible number of Cardinalfish. Lionfish hunt among them and Leaf Scorpionfish are sometimes seen. Beware the dangerous stinging corallimorpharians on the rocks near these reefs. A scattered, scruffy coral garden in shallow water is home to many unusual marine animals, including frogfish, various lionfish, ghost pipefish, Mantis Shrimp and Moray Eels (*Gymnothorax javanicus*). Deep down the sand slope at 60m (200ft), two large rocks are home to three species of rare anthias (one not yet scientifically described) and one (*Pseudanthias hutomoi*) known previously only from trawl specimens. This extraordinary site has many different features, all outstanding, and is good for both wide-angle and close-up photography.

Snorkelling along the wall and on top of the labyrinth is first class, easy and safe.

16 BASILISK POINT

★★★★★★★★

Location: Basilisk Point, on north coast 10 n. miles (18.5km) west of East Cape.
Access: Although site close to shore, access to water is difficult except from a boat. Do not anchor on site: the holding is poor and damage to reef would be unavoidable.
Conditions: May be dived in all but northwesterly winds. Any current usually runs from east; this is preferable.
Typical visibility: 40m (130ft) plus
Minimum depth: 1m (40in)
Maximum depth: 50m (165ft) plus

This dive is usually made as a drift/swim: you start by dropping into the water at a vertical wall on the point's eastern side. At the point the wall changes into a steep slope, and here a school of barracuda may be found hanging in about 10m (33ft). Further round, the slope becomes a vertical wall once more, now with large cracks and crevices that deserve exploration. The usual pick-up point is at the end of this. Hammerhead Sharks, Manta Rays and schools of Mobula are sometimes seen.

The shallows around the point offer fine current-free snorkelling with plenty of live reef and fish. You might see the barracuda.

17 DEACON'S REEF

★★★★★★★★★★

Location: At the west end of Basilisk Point.
Access: Although site very close to shore, there are no roads, so access only by boat. Anchoring possible only in calmest conditions (any wind tends to push boat against cliff) and only on one particular coral head. Great damage to reef could result from careless or ignorant anchoring. Often one anchors at beach nearby and drops divers off in a dinghy, which later picks the divers up again, or they can complete the dive by swimming back to anchored boat.
Conditions: Usually calm; may be dived in anything but northwesterly winds. Slight current runs over reef.
Typical visibility: 40m (130ft) plus
Minimum depth: 5m (16ft)
Maximum depth: 50m (165ft) plus

A steep dropoff rises from beyond 300m (1000ft) to

form a series of coral towers very close to a cliff with overhanging trees. Between towers and cliff is an area of sea fans and whips and exquisite coral growth. To start with, work along the outer drop, keeping an eye open for Hammerhead and other Sharks and rays; but don't neglect to dive the shallows right up against the cliff in 5m (16ft). Dramatic photographs are possible as the sun rises later in the morning to shine through the canopy of trees onto the reef. In the cliff face are deep crevices and even a cave (hazardous to penetrate except with cave-diving techniques).

Snorkellers who follow the cliff face will see reef scenes usually reserved for scuba divers.

18 DINAH'S BEACH

★★★★★★★★

Location: On north coast west of East Cape, in bay past Basilisk Point (Sites 17-18).
Access: No roads to beach. Anchor in front of large tree to east of village and tie stern to tree.
Conditions: Exposed in northwesterly weather; however, wind usually from southeast, and bay then provides shelter in all but extreme conditions.
Typical visibility: 15–40m (50–130ft)
Minimum depth: as shallow as you like
Maximum depth: 50m (165ft) plus

To the east of a stream running into the sea lies a shallow coral and rubble garden, beyond which the bottom slopes away to very deep water. Some rare creatures (including shells) have been found down the deep slope, but the most interesting area is the shallows, where several families of octopus live along with five species of lionfish, Blue Ribbon Eels (*Rhinomuraena quaesita*), Mantis Shrimp, Cleaner Shrimp at cleaning stations, juvenile angelfish (*Pomacanthus imperator*), cuttlefish and many others. Since the water is shallow, many hours of diving time can be spent in the area. The dive is particularly rewarding just before sunset when the lionfish become active, but be careful: lionfish are fearless and will approach divers. Octopus are active throughout the day. This is a superb site for macro photography.

Ashore, a vigorous walk up the stream leads through tropical rainforest to two splendid waterfalls, and the birdlife is rich and varied.

Much can be seen by snorkelling through the shallows. Big creatures sometimes come by – one morning I snorkelled with a marlin (*Makaira* spp)!

19 BETHA'S BOMMIE

★★★★★★★★★

Location: 1 n. mile (1.85km) north of Awaiama Bay, off rocks on beach on north coast.
Access: You must anchor in gutter between two halves of reef – not on reeftops.
Conditions: Sheltered from southeast winds; not possible when northwesterlies blowing. Often currents over deeper reef.
Typical visibility: 25–35m (80–115ft)
Minimum depth: 5m (16ft)
Maximum depth: 50m (165ft) plus

It is usual to make at least two dives on this site. The first is to the deeper table and dropoff, where large schools of trevally and other fish are found on the side receiving any (usually slight) current. There are some large sea fans, barrel sponges and tree coral stands. Secondly, the shallow reef is delicate and exquisite, with wonderful coral growths, bommies, soft corals and sponges. The reef is full of life and often visited by larger fish like Hammerhead and Grey Reef Sharks, Manta Rays and turtles. Surprisingly, the best place to see Hammerheads is on the edge of the shallow reef closer to shore.

A third dive can be made where, 100m (110yd) or so along the beach towards the bay, a coral bommie rises to 12m (40ft) before plunging to the dropoff. The bommie is split and has swimthroughs, but be careful to avoid damaging the many growths of black coral and sponges. This bommie makes an excellent and colourful night-dive, having many tube corals (Tubastraea spp) with brilliant yellow polyps. Awaiama Bay offers a good anchorage on its southern side. The sheltered shallows near the shore offer snorkellers many healthy corals with sand passages between.

The Blue ribbon eel, Rhinomuraena quaesita, is usually seen singly.

The Eastern D'Entrecasteaux Region

The reefs in this region are beyond the mouth of Milne Bay but still accessible within a day's sailing from Alotau. Normanby Island (Sites 1 and 2) has interesting diving on its southeast corner, off its western shore and at its northern extremity. Dobu Island (Site 9), on Normanby Island's northern side, is a perfectly formed extinct volcano with gas vents bubbling in the waters around its northeast corner. Further north, Sanaroa Island (Sites 10–13) shelters the excellent diving in the passage (Site 10) between it and Fergusson Island, and when the weather is calm there are many unsurveyed reefs north and east of Sanaroa blessed with very clear water and plenty of big-fish action. North of Fergusson Island , near the Amphlett Islands, are further exceptional dives (Sites 19 and 20).

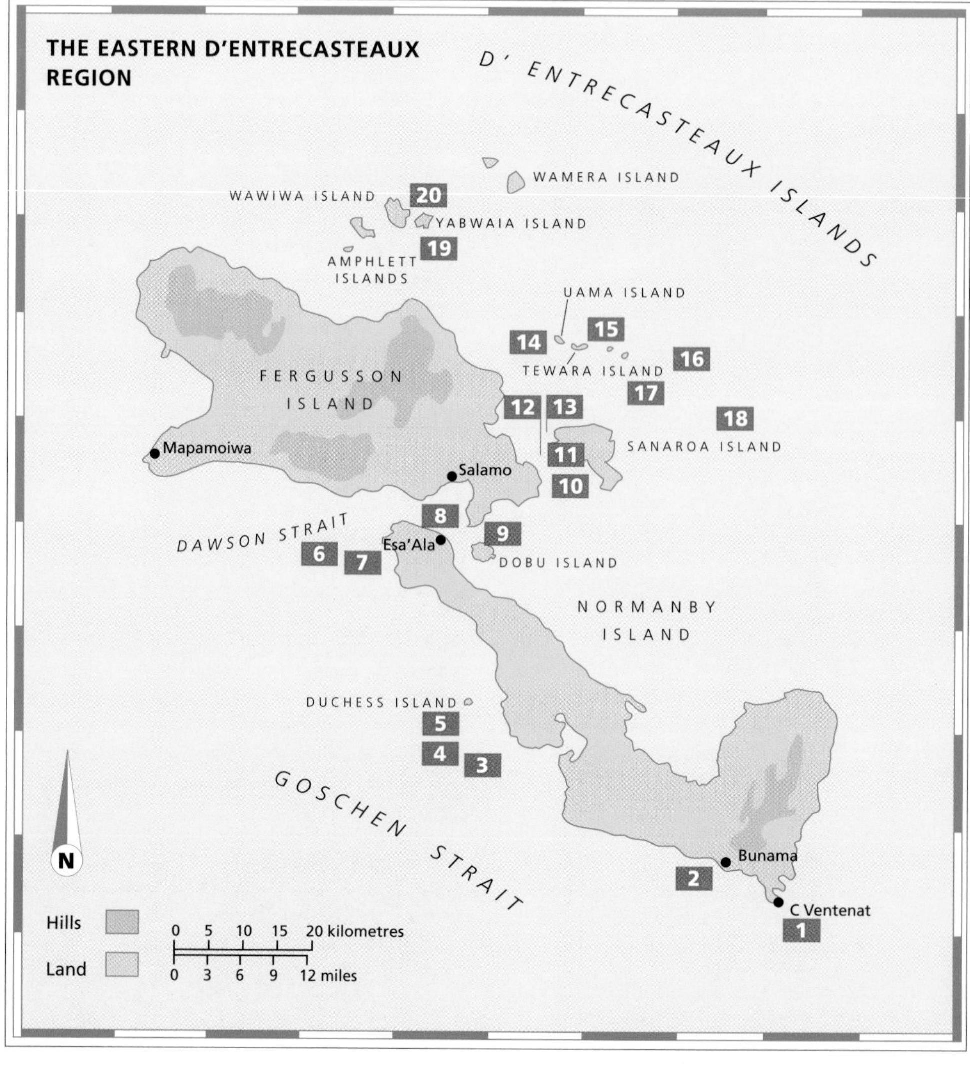

1 LIPSON SHOAL

★★★★

Location: 1 n. mile (1.85km) east of Cape Ventenat, Normanby Island.
Access: Anchor on eastern edge of reef.
Conditions: Sheltered from northwest; generally not accessible in Southeast season.
Typical visibility: 45m (150ft)
Minimum depth: 8m (26ft)
Maximum depth: 40m (130ft)

Situated in a break in the barrier reef outside the Ventenat Islands, the reef collects an exceptional number of pelagic fish and sometimes Grey Reef Sharks. It is predominantly hard corals, of many different kinds. You should start the dive into any current from the east, then go down the dropoff, where the effect of the current is minimal. The fish will usually approach you, so excessive swimming is not necessary. Eagle Rays (*Aetobatus narinari*) are seen in the area.

Other sites with similar features are nearby. This is too deep for comfortable snorkelling, but there is excellent snorkelling nearby when the current permits.

2 BUNAMA

★★★★★★★★

Location: Bays either side of Bunama Mission on Normanby Island's south coast.
Access: The only access to Bunama is by boat. Western bay: Anchor in 15m (50ft) west of wharf ruins; tie stern to tree ashore. Eastern bay: Anchor in 15m (50ft) in front of first large trees after reef ends.
Conditions: Use western bay in Southeast season, eastern bay otherwise. Swells sometimes affect eastern bay.
Typical visibility: 10–40m (33–130ft), very variable
Minimum depth: as shallow as you like
Maximum depth: 40m (130ft) plus

Sea-grass beds in the shallows change to other algal species and a silty 'muck' bottom deeper. In the shallows are myriad sand anemones of various species along with Panda Clownfish (*Amphiprion polymnus*), often with eggs, and Porcelain Crabs (*Neopetrolisthes ohshimai*). Seahorses are often found along with ghost pipefish, Double-ended Pipefish (*Syngnathoides biaculeatus*), garden eels, cuttlefish, frogfish, cowfish (*Lactoria cornuta*), Dwarf and other lionfish and octopus. Both sites are excellent night-dives, especially for those interested in shells. Small Manta Rays and dugong are sometimes seen in the western bay. This site is a macro photographer's paradise, but take care not to stir up the bottom. You can spend a long time in the shallow sea-grass beds.

IN THE MUCK

Over the past 10 years there has developed an awareness that coral reefs are not the only tropical habitats that make great dive sites. A group of sophisticated and very experienced divers started to look at alternatives, the main objective being to search for creatures they had not seen before. Some of the areas they found most rewarding were not glamorous – perhaps a sand slope or a rubble patch, or the mouth of a stream or a sea-grass bed, with visibility perhaps less good than on the offshore reefs – but the results have been quite stunning. Many of these places are packed with fascinating marine creatures, some new not only to the divers but to science.

We have found that the best 'muck' dives, as they have come to be called, are usually in sheltered water subject to slight currents, which bring food. The diving is usually easy, but great observational skills are required. We consider these dives to be treasure hunts, and the rewards are fabulous animals never seen on coral reefs.

Many creatures can be seen just by snorkelling. Both bays have a coral reef along the beach at the seaward sides, offering good, easy snorkelling close to shore.

3 CALYPSO REEF

★★★★★★★★

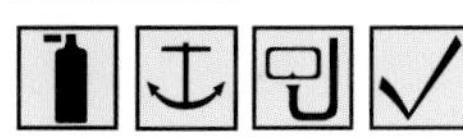

Location: 3.4 n. miles (6.3km) south of Duchess Island, near Normanby Island.
Access: Anchor only in the sand patches to avoid damage to luxuriant coral growths.
Conditions: Cannot usually be dived in strong southerly winds, but get there early in morning and you can sometimes do 1–2 dives before wind makes site uncomfortable.
Typical visibility: 40m (130ft) plus
Minimum depth: 6m (20ft)
Maximum depth: 50m (165ft) plus

A beautiful scenic reef packed with marine life. The occasional mild currents determine which side of the ridge has the greatest concentration of fish.

After diving the dropoff you can browse on the ridge-top, which has very rich corals and coral 'bommies' with large barrel sponges and an enormous concentration of crinoids. This is an excellent site to find the rare Lacy Scorpionfish.

The ridge starts at the end of a very shallow reef; when approaching in the boat take care not to run aground. Once the ridge is located it can be dived anywhere along its 1km (1100yd) length.

Other sites with similar features are nearby. For best snorkelling, anchor near the shallow portion of the reef. Snorkellers can see the beautiful coral gardens on the reeftop and the many schools of fish on the edge of the dropoff.

4 JENNIFER'S REEF

★★★★

Location: 3 n. miles (5.6km) south-southwest of Duchess Island, near Normanby Island.
Access: Anchor in sand patches at 18m (60ft).
Conditions: Difficult to dive in strong southerly winds, though early-morning dives may be possible before wind has effect. Currents usually slight. Set a decompression-line beneath boat.
Typical visibility: 40m (130ft) plus
Minimum depth: 15m (50ft)
Maximum depth: 50m (165ft) plus

A coral mound rises to 15m (50ft) from a wide ridge at 20m (65ft) and deeper. Directly north of the mound a dropoff plunges to 60m (200ft); a deeper dropoff, further south, is not usually dived. After descending the anchor-line you should see the mound; find its up-current side. A large school of Pacific Barracuda (*Sphyraena putnamiae*) is usually there and will often form a circle around you as you swim into it. Coral rocks covered with crinoids are plentiful, as are other schools of fish and pelagics.

5 BARBARIAN REEF

★★★★★★★★

Location: 1 n. mile (1.85km) south-southwest of Duchess Island, near Normanby Island.
Access: Take care when anchoring to avoid coral damage: usual procedure is to anchor northeast of reef, next to adjacent shallow reef attached by a ridge.
Conditions: Not usually dived in strong southerly winds, except in early morning before wind takes effect.
Typical visibility: 40m (130ft)
Minimum depth: 10m (33ft)
Maximum depth: 60m (200ft)

Two shallow reefs are connected by a ridge approximately 500m (550yd) long, with a coral tower near one end. You enter the water near the northerly reef, then proceed along the ridge to the tower. The whole area has many stands of Green Tree Coral (*Tubastraea micrantha*), and the top of the tower has a big garden of cabbage coral and a huge three-mouthed barrel sponge. There is also an unusual sand anemone (*Heteractis aurora*) on a small sand patch on top of the tower. A current runs through the pass over the ridge, and many fish congregate to feed. Coming back from the tower you can explore the reef, which has a splendid coral garden, before surfacing.

Although the tower cannot be snorkelled, the adjacent shallow coral reef is excellent.

BULLETS

Often, excellent dive sites are situated in the lee (sheltered side) of islands. Wind blowing over a flat island flows evenly, so that a boat anchoring on the lee is held away from the island. This effect changes when the island is tall. The anchored boat, even in calm water, may be subjected to back-eddies of wind that blow it towards the island. Even more alarmingly, sudden gusts of wind (bullets) can blow with very great strength, causing dragged anchors and loss overboard of loose items. To give an idea of the wind-speeds involved, when the average wind-strength is 20 knots, bullets of 40 knots are not uncommon.

Dive sites that suffer from bullets are to be avoided in windy weather. They can often be detected before anchoring by noticing the periodic violently ruffled appearance of the otherwise calm surface.

6 BALABAN'S BOMMIE

★★★★★★★★★

Location: 1½n. miles (2.8km) off the northwesterly tip of Normanby Island.
Access: Only dinghies can anchor over most of reef, which is very shallow on top; in calm conditions you may be able to anchor a boat on its southwestern tip. Do not anchor on reef's northeasterly side, which has one of PNG's finest shallow coral gardens.
Conditions: Can be dived in all conditions except strong southeasterly winds.
Typical visibility: 40m (130ft) plus
Minimum depth: 1m (40in)
Maximum depth: 50m (165ft) plus

The reef is too large to circumnavigate on a single dive. Divers usually start by exploring the deep dropoff and caverns at the southwestern tip, then move along the north side to the coral gardens on the reeftop. Here there is also a large population of anemones and their resident fish, including the White-bonnet Anemonefish (*Amphiprion leucokranos*). The caverns are along the reef's south side, near the western end. Along the northeast side a sand slope replaces the dropoff and is populated with shrimp gobies and sand tilefish.

The coral gardens are best seen by snorkelling. In calm conditions, with sun overhead, they offer unique opportunities for wide-angle reef photography. Superb.

7 OBSERVATION POINT

★★★★★★★★★

   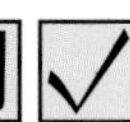

Location: Westerly point of Normanby Island.

Opposite: *Black corals and barrel sponges.*

Access: Anchor boat on sand slope in passage between point and small island, with stern tied to tree on sandy beach. The friendly villagers have rest-houses to welcome visiting divers, and provide a night-time security service guarding boats (fee K10).
Conditions: Sheltered in all weathers; particularly good in Southeast season. Sometimes current over the site.
Typical visibility: 8–30m (25–100ft)
Minimum depth: as shallow as you like
Maximum depth: 40m (130ft)
Not a glamorous site, but the opportunities for finding unusual marine life are outstanding. A coral reef, with sea-grass and mangroves in the shallows, borders a steep sand slope littered with crinoids and debris. Deep down the slope, in the middle of the passage, live sea pens and small soft corals. The area supports an incredible array of creatures not found on coral reefs: ghost pipefish, sand darters and razorfish (*Xyrichtys* spp), shrimpfish (*Aeoliscus strigatus*), Dwarf Lionfish (*Dendrochirus brachypterus*), octopus, cuttlefish, Inimicus and other scorpionfish, Helmet Shells, frogfish, fire urchins and juvenile batfish. A new species of sand darter named after Dinah and myself, *Trichonotus halstead*, was discovered here. This rather sophisticated dive may be a disappointment for devotees of glorious reefs, but is amazingly rewarding for macro photographers seeking rare creatures: the range of species present varies, but is always superb – take care not to stir up the bottom. A Saltwater Crocodile (*Crocodilus porosus*) was once photographed here.

For snorkellers, the shallows in the sea-grass, reef and mangrove areas have many resident fish, including seahorses. Village people regularly swim here, though the area has crocodiles.

8 AYER'S ROCK

★★★★★★

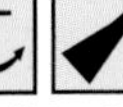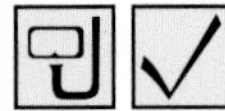

Location: Off the first village on Normanby Island after you enter Dawson Strait from the west.
Access: Anchor in sand east and well clear of reef.
Conditions: Calm sea in all winds. However, anchorage subject to 'bullets' of wind in strong southerly winds and then prone to dragging.
Typical visibility: 15–30m (50–100ft)
Minimum depth: 8m (26ft)
Maximum depth: 40m (130ft) plus
A black sand beach has sea-grass beds close to shore, then slopes steeply down. A single large coral reef rises from the sand at right-angles to the beach, the shallowest part rising from the sand at 15m (50ft) to about 8m (26ft). The reeftop gradually slopes down while the bottom plunges to about 40m (130ft). The reef is packed with life, including big black coral trees, hard and soft corals and many fish. In clear water there are good wide-angle opportunities for photographers, but more usually the visibility is moderate and you would be better to concentrate on the area's great variety of marine life. Panda Clownfish are common in the shallows near the reef. This is an excellent night-dive (you can anchor here overnight). Use a repellent to counter the copious mosquitoes that can mar the evenings.

The sea-grass beds offer interesting snorkelling, with anemones, cowfish and other inhabitants.

FINDING NEW FISH SPECIES

Many divers imagine that discovering a new species of fish is a question of stumbling upon a creature obviously different from all the other fish they have seen before. No doubt in the early days that is how it was, but today new species are more often discovered by very careful observation of the commoner fishes. The reason is that fish often mimic each other: a fish may gain a biological advantage by looking very like another sort of fish, particularly if it has no natural protection, such as venomous spines, and the other fish has. So it pays to know the common fishes in great detail, and then observe them carefully underwater, looking for any slight variation that could signify a distinct new species rather than just a variety.

9 DOBU BUBBLEBATH

★★★

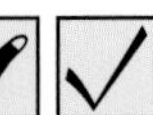

Location: Northeast corner of Dobu Island.
Access: Anchor in sand close to the northeast point.
Conditions: Sheltered in all winds; sometimes a slight but easily manageable current.
Typical visibility: 10–20m (33–65ft), sometimes (unpredictably) poor
Minimum depth: 1m (40in)
Maximum depth: 10m (33ft)
Dobu Island, site of one of the area's very first Christian missions, is a classic small extinct volcano. In the surrounding area are several places where gas (principally carbon dioxide but with some hydrogen sulphide) continues to vent through the sea bed. Some vents are large and continually gush hot gas but many emit just a single fine stream of bubbles, and these often appear through the reef and sea-grass.

This is a shallow dive, ideal for a long afternoon swim. The reef is surprisingly healthy, with abundant marine life. The Bubblebath is wonderful for unusual wide-angle photographs which are best taken in natural light with a faster-than-normal shutter speed of 1/125th or even 1/250th sec. There are also numerous macro subjects, including anemonefish, anglerfish and scorpionfish, nudibranchs and Mantis Shrimp.

Snorkelling is not recommended: the gas from the vents is foul-smelling and possibly harmful.

I have always been wary of the terms 'dormant' and 'extinct' as applied to volcanoes so I was not too surprised when I found out that the 'extinct' volcano called Dobu Island, between Normanby and Fergusson islands in Milne Bay Province, had an underwater vent that was still actively bubbling gas.

In June 1989 we dived the vent for the first time. It is a very strange sight. On one hand you are aware of the turmoil that must be going on beneath the seabed to cause the venting of the gas; on the other, what you actually see is an idyllic reef scene with all the usual residents of our underwater world, but diffused through a curtain of bubbles emerging from the bottom.

The gas, presumably because of the hydrogen sulphide it contains, has a foul smell. Because of this, even though the vents are in shallow water, we preferred, instead of snorkelling, to use scuba gear and breathe the fresh air from our tanks.

We expected to see a barren reef, but this was not so. In fact, the sea-grasses seemed to thrive. Although the biggest vents bleached the rock around their bases and were surrounded by bits of dead reef, we could see the gas from smaller vents emerging right through living coral. Fish and other marine creatures seemed unaffected.

We returned to the vents in October the same year and, with clear water about, I took some photos. We came back in November and again in December, but this time the water was dirty. I was at a loss to explain why, since there had not been any particularly heavy rain recently. Our divers did enter the water to examine the vents, but they returned with uneasy feelings, describing patches of very warm water and strange vibrations.

Two days later the area was put on alert. Clouds of smoke were seen emerging from the sea nearby, and the region experienced a 'seismic swarm' of earthquakes. That explained the dirty water ... nothing like a good shake to stir up the sediment.

Now all is quiet again, and our visiting divers can once more enjoy making this unusual dive.

Diver enjoying the Bubblebath.

10 DOUBLE TOWER, SANAROA

★★★★

Location: Passage between Sanaroa and Fergusson islands, 0.67 n. mile (1.24km) from west cape of Sanaroa.

Access: Anchor on east tower's relatively barren top in 8m (26ft).

Conditions: The sometimes strong currents in the area from either north or south do not debar experienced divers; easier if current is from north (when nearby sites very difficult). Partly sheltered from all winds. Has blue-water current.

Typical visibility: 20–40m (65–130ft) – good in Southeast season; sometimes murky in Northwest season

Minimum depth: 8m (26ft)

Maximum depth: 40m (130ft)

Two towers with a narrow passage between them. The westerly tower is connected to a large shallow reef by a saddle dipping to 22m (70ft) and is the more dramatic – being covered with different-coloured sea fans and Red Sea Whips (*Ellisella* spp) – but the whole area has excellent diving. Between the towers is a garden of Olive Sea Whips (*Junceella fragilis*) at the edge of a dropoff from 30m to 40m (100–130ft). Beside the towers is a sandy plateau at 30m (100ft), with garden eels. The shallow reef reached via the saddle has excellent corals and plentiful fish-life; you can sometimes see Lacy Scorpionfish.

HOT SPRINGS

As well as active volcanoes, several areas in PNG have hot springs. The best-known are at Fergusson Island in Milne Bay Province and Talesea in West New Britain. Villagers use the springs' boiling hot, clear-water pools for cooking, placing food in woven baskets which they lower into the pools. There are also geysers, which obligingly shoot their jets of water high into the air when village elders call on them to do so. Bubbling mud-ponds are separated by creeks, down which hot water runs to the shore. Around the geysers, encrusted salt gives the illusion of firm rock. Take care – a guide is recommended – because some of the salt-crusts are thin and weak. Several people have been badly scalded when their legs dropped unexpectedly through the salt.

11 SONIA SHOAL

★★★★

Location: 1 n. mile (1.85km) southwest of Sanaroa Island's western tip.

Access: Anchor in sand patches on westerly side of reef – and nowhere else: not only is the water shallow, a magnificent stand of cabbage coral covers most of the reef's eastern side.

Conditions: Sheltered from most winds. Can be a very

Giant Clams, Tridacna gigas, are sadly under threat (see box on page 57).

unusual current-dive when current is from the north, but still interesting when current not flowing.
Typical visibility: 20–40m (65–130ft)
Minimum depth: 2m (6½ft)
Maximum depth: 40m (130ft)
This reef makes up a part of a complex arrangement of adjoining reefs. The dive starts on a cliff-face, and the current then pushes you along (left shoulder to cliff). Soon a valley appears and you turn left, though with the current still behind you, through a sand gutter with gorgeous growths of sea fans and whips. Resisting the temptation to turn left again immediately, you pass over a saddle at about 9m (30ft) to enter another sand gutter, which turns left again. A glance at the garden eels on the sand bottom shows you the current is now pushing you northward! This sand gutter rapidly narrows and rises to a shallow (8m; 26ft) pass, and here you finally meet the force of the current. However, the pass is only a few metres wide, and once you pull through you reach the reef's front face where, by descending slightly, you exit the current and can complete the circumnavigation to the boat. Make sure there is someone to pick you up in case you get lost and finish down-current of the boat.

A great snorkel when the tide is slack (otherwise impossible).

12 RHINO REEF

★★★★★★★★

Location: 0.45 n. mile (830m) southwest of Sanaroa's western tip.
Access: Anchor in sand patches between coral ridges close to dropoff.
Conditions: Sheltered in most winds, but watch out for currents; best with slight current from the north.
Typical visibility: 20–40m (65–130ft)
Minimum depth: 4m (13ft)
Maximum depth: 40m (130ft)
A shallow reef drops away steeply to a sand bottom littered with coral heads. The slope, particularly its top, has a bewildering array of corals, sponges and sea whips and many fish. Rays and sharks are sometimes seen in the deeper water, where many large sea fans grow; a Tiger Shark has been seen on this dive. In the shallows, exquisite coral bommies with sand gutters abound. The reef's name derives from the fact that the rare Lacy Scorpionfish (*Rhinopias aphanes*) is often found in the area. On the sand patches are occasional black crocodilefish (*Thysanophrys* spp). A wonderful site for wide-angle photography. In slack current there is great snorkelling on the reeftop.

RHINOPIAS

Soon after we started diving in Port Moresby, Dinah discovered a fish that neither of us recognized. We sent a photograph to the Smithsonian Institution for identification, who came back with the dramatic news that Dinah had found the second-ever specimen of a type of scorpionfish known as Merlet's Scorpionfish (*Rhinopias aphanes*), named from a single specimen found in New Caledonia only a few years before. Since then many specimens have been found in PNG, on reefs out of Port Moresby, Milne Bay and also Madang.

Now more commonly called the Lacy Scorpionfish, the species is spectacular and mimics featherstars. It is found on the edge of dropoffs, usually those that experience some current or surge, and can be in various colours from lime-yellow and pink to, more typically, dark green and black. A related species, *Rhinopias frondosa*, is much rarer in PNG but has been recorded from Milne Bay.

13 VALLEY REEF

★★★★★★★★★

Location: 0.4 n. mile (740m) off Sanaroa Island's northwest side.
Access: Anchor on top of northernmost coral bommie.
Conditions: Sheltered in all conditions except strong northwesterlies. Ideal if strong currents running over Sanaroa Passage reefs (Sites 10–12) make them difficult to dive.
Typical visibility: 30–40m (100–130ft)
Minimum depth: 5m (16ft)
Maximum depth: 50m (165ft)
From the small coral bommie at the north the reef stretches south with various branches and passes; you need several dives to explore it all. The 'valley' is east of the main reef. The reef has many attractive features and is easier to dive than some nearby, but does not have their massive fish-life. Nonetheless, turtles are frequent, as are all the common reef creatures. Anemonefish are frequent on the reeftop, including the much-sought White-bonnet Anemonefish (*Amphiprion leucokranos*).

This is an excellent night-dive. Sea hares are common, and a rare and beautiful nocturnal Pink Lacy Scorpionfish (*Rhinopias* sp.) can sometimes be found.

The very attractive reeftop is shallow and easily snorkelled, with a great variety of different corals, all in excellent condition.

14 WONG'S REEF

★★★★★

Location: 1/2 n. mile (930m) west of Uama Island.
Access: Anchor on bald spot on southern part of reef.
Conditions: Impossible in strong winds, although partly sheltered from ocean swells. Currents (mainly oceanic) can run to 2 knots; best with slight current (1/2 knot).
Typical visibility: 50m (165ft), rarely poor
Minimum depth: 8m (26ft)
Maximum depth: 50m (165ft) plus

The reef-front is a vertical dropoff with black corals and schools of fish, including a resident barracuda school. The sides have sea fans and whips, sloping down to a coral sand bottom at 30–50m (100–165ft), where there are garden eels and many small fish. I found a new species of wrasse (*Novaculichthys* sp) here in the sand at 40m (130ft). Many Giant Clams can be found on the reeftop, some with scarlet soft corals growing on them; a large school of Bumphead Parrotfish (*Bolbometopon muricatum*) is often seen and rather easier to approach than most schools of this species. Sharks can be seen down the dropoff. Once you're over the front drop there is shelter from the current. A good lookout is required on this reef in case divers drift away.

There are other reefs with similar features nearby.

15 MARY JANE (MJ) REEF

★★★★★★★★

Location: North of Sanaroa Island, 3 n. miles (5.6km) east of Tewara Island.
Access: Anchor on rubble patches near westerly end of reef; avoid damaging plate corals.
Conditions: Requires calm seas. A current often runs over reef from south.
Typical visibility: 40m (130ft) plus
Minimum depth: 6m (20ft)
Maximum depth: 50m (165ft)

Typically the boat hangs in deep water at the reef's back (north side), but there is far more life on the south side; swim over the reeftop to the south side (a current-line may be required) and descend there. The best sea-fan growth is close to the end of the reef, but pelagics patrol all along the front. After making a deep dive to see the fans, explore the extensive coral gardens on the reeftop, where turtles are frequent. This is an excellent site for wide-angle photographs: the morning sun shines down the dropoff and can be included in the background, with fans and soft corals in the foreground.

Other sites with similar features are nearby.

The extensive reef to the east has brilliant snorkelling in shallow water. Baby Whitetip Reef Sharks (*Triaenodon obesus*) are common and some sea fans grow on the reeftop. The current is less in the shallow water, but do not attempt to snorkel if it is too strong easily to swim against.

16 HICKSON'S REEF

★★★★★★★★

Location: Northeast of Sanaroa Island, 5 n. miles (9.3km) from Tewara Island.
Access: Anchor according to current and interests.
Conditions: Requires calm weather. A current from southeast often runs over reef.
Typical visibility: 40m (130ft) plus
Minimum depth: 6m (20ft)
Maximum depth: 50m (165ft) plus

For the best pelagic life anchor on the southeast corner, where a steep wall drops to a slope at 40m (130ft). Large schools of fish patrol the reef-edge; deeper down, Grey Reef and sometimes Silvertip Sharks are found. Whitetip Reef Sharks are common on the reeftop, where there is an extensive staghorn-coral garden.

Alternatively, you can dive the pass between the two parts of the reef; this is filled with large pink sea fans and Red Sea Whips. The water here is almost invariably clear, and the reef is bursting with life.

Other sites with similar features are nearby. You can snorkel the reeftop when the current is low.

17 FARRINGTON SHOAL

★★★★

Location: An isolated bommie near Ribbon Reef, 5 n. miles (9.3km) east-northeast of Sanaroa Island.
Access: Anchor on reeftop on southeast side.
Conditions: Requires calm seas. Often strong current on reef.
Typical visibility: 40m (130ft) plus
Minimum depth: 6m (20ft)
Maximum depth: 50m (165ft) plus

This steep-sided coral tower, rising from deep water, is barely 60m (200ft) across, but is well placed to be a shark-feeding station, especially as the usual current helps spread the bait slick. The top of the reef has – set in a garden of staghorn and other hard corals with a few rubble patches – some coral bommies, behind which divers can perch while watching the sharks. However, a while ago a new electronic shark repellent was tested here with Valerie Taylor, and the sharks have declined to accept bait ever since.

Opposite: *Fergusson Island.*

18 END PASS

★★★★★

Location: Southeast of Tewara Island; exact location withheld because of shark-finners.
Access: Refer to Telita Cruises.
Conditions: Requires calm weather. Often currents over site from southeast or southwest.
Typical visibility: 40m (130ft) plus
Minimum depth: 8m (26ft)
Maximum depth: 50m (165ft) plus

You enter the water on the reeftop where the reef narrows to a ridge. This ridge starts to drop away to the east, but rises again to a coral bommie shallowing to about 12m (40ft). Your route should depend on the strength and direction of the currents that typically flow over the area, but for maximum fish-life try to reach the place where the current meets the reef. Both dropoffs are interesting, but the end bommie, the pass and the ridge-top are the most active places. This site has been a regular shark-feeding station.

19 HUMANN'S COLOUR BOOK

★★★★★

Location: 2½ n. miles (4.6km) south of Yabwaia Island, Amphlett Islands.
Access: Anchor in middle of reef on rubble patch; ensure anchor is secure.
Conditions: Can sometimes be dived in early morning even in Trade Wind conditions, as Fergusson Island's land breeze provides some shelter; as the day goes on land breeze disappears and Southeast Trades can start blowing surprisingly quickly (hence the caution about anchoring). Often strong current from southeast.
Typical visibility: 40m (130ft) plus
Minimum depth: 8m (26ft)
Maximum depth: 50m (165ft)

A ridge reef aligned at right-angles to the prevailing southeast current; the current side is far richer in marine life than the lee. You need to get to the front of the reef where, beyond 15m (50ft) or so, the current's effects can be easily handled. The front face could be fully swum by an energetic diver on one dive, but is big enough for a couple of dives. This beautiful colourful reef, with many soft corals, is sometimes current-free – but then the soft corals do not reveal their splendour. Commonly conditions are calm when you enter the water and choppy when you exit.

20 AMPHLETT FANS

★★★★★★★

   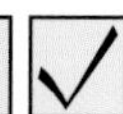

Location: In the pass between Wawiwa and Yabwaia islands in the Amphlett group north of Fergusson Island.
Access: Do not anchor too close to the reef for fear of damaging the many sea fans.
Conditions: This pass looks a tempting and sheltered anchorage but is impossible in strong Southeast Trades, when the wind funnels between the two high islands causing 'bullets' of wind of amazing intensity. In light winds, from any direction, shelter can be found.
Typical visibility: 30–40m (100–130ft)
Minimum depth: 2m (6½ft)
Maximum depth: 25m (80ft)

Off a white sand beach you can see this small shallow reef patch. At the bottom (15–25m; 50–80ft), along the patch's south side, are a series of giant sea fans, Fan Sponges and other interesting coral growths. Eagle Rays, turtles and other fish-life have been seen. Shallower parts have formations of cabbage and 'knob' coral (*Pavona spp*). In calm weather the reef makes a convenient night-dive.

Only slight currents pass between the islands, and the water is always calm, so snorkelling is quite convenient. Unusual corals can be seen on top of the shallow reef.

The Western D'Entrecasteaux Region

The reefs in the Western D'Entrecasteaux region are the furthest to which regular cruises from Alotau go. Dart Reefs (Sites 6–11), between Goodenough Island and Cape Vogel, are particularly good in the Northwest season, when Goodenough Island provides partial shelter. Further reefs to the north of Fergusson Island are excellent in the Southeast season, while Cape Vogel's main claim to fame is the wreck of the B17 Bomber Blackjack (Site 13).

1 MAPAMOIWA ANCHORAGE

★★★★★★★

Location: Just north of Fergusson Island's southwest corner.
Access: The jetty in the anchorage is in constant use by village and mission boats, so anchor just to the north of it and secure the boat's stern to a tree ashore.
Conditions: Completely protected and calm in Southeast Trades; partly protected in other seasons by a reef projecting either side of anchorage. No current.
Typical visibility: 10–30m (33–100ft)
Minimum depth: as shallow as you like
Maximum depth: 50m (165ft) plus

At first glance a rather unappealing site, but since it is the logical place to anchor for the night it is definitely worth a look, and even a night-dive. You can explore the reef, but the most fascinating animals are in shallow water near or in the sea-grass beds. In the extreme shallows are found seahorses, frogfish (*Antennarius pictus*), cowfish and shrimpfish. Panda Clownfish are abundant in sand anemones, often living with Porcelain Crabs, and Dwarf Lionfish are easy to find. The reef and sea-grass beds offer interesting snorkelling. There is a tap with fresh water on the beach, but supply is limited.

2 MAPAMOIWA REEF

★★★

Location: 3 n. miles (5.6km) north of Mapamoiwa, the mission station on Fergusson Island.
Access: Exercise extreme caution when approaching

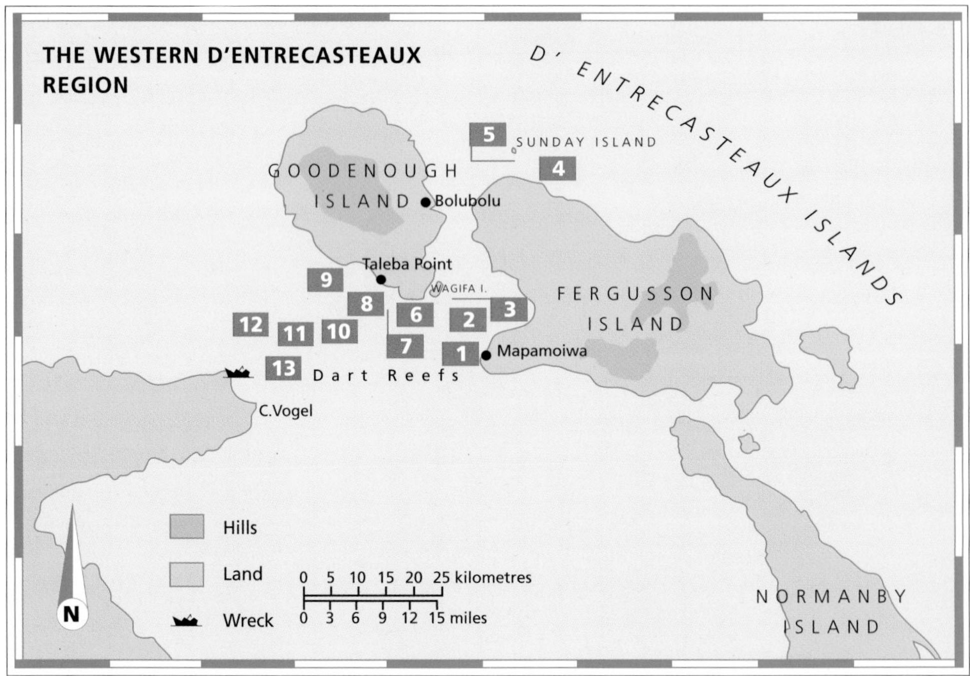

this reef as nearby is a large, poorly charted reef just beneath the surface. (Many other local reefs are too shallow to allow boats to pass over them.)
Conditions: Good even in strong Southeast Trades. Generally a slight current from the east.
Typical visibility: 15–40m (50–130ft), very variable
Minimum depth: 2m (6½ft)
Maximum depth: 50m (165ft) plus
This is one of a series of local reefs with similar characteristics. A very deep, steep dropoff gives little warning of the reef. However, apart from the occasional shark, this dropoff is not the most interesting part, mainly because the prevailing current runs from the other side. Swim round the reef to the eastern side, where bommies and valleys make a fascinating landscape. On this side is a second, shallower dropoff where many fish congregate. There is good hard and soft coral on the reef.

Other sites with similar features are nearby. One reef to the north has an attractive tunnel running through it.

3 CHARLIE'S TOWER

★★★

Location: In Moresby Strait, 1½ n. miles (2.8km) northeast of Wagifa Island.
Access: Can be hard to locate, as top of tower is 15m (50ft) deep.
Conditions: Partly sheltered. Can be dived in light winds from any direction.
Typical visibility: 30–40m (100–130ft)
Minimum depth: 5m (50ft)
Maximum depth: 50m (165ft) plus
The tower rises from very deep water. Its quite small top can easily be circumnavigated on a single dive. There is a deep ridge with sea fans on the western side. This attractive site looks very promising for big animals, but has yet to prove itself.

4 TROTMAN SHOALS

★★★★★★★

Location: 1½ n. miles (2.8km) north of Cape Labillardiere, Fergusson Island.
Access: Choice of patch reefs to anchor on. Take care on approach: one reef is shallower than the others.
Conditions: Excellent shelter in strong southeast winds. Exposed to the north. Slight currents common.

Juvenile Baramundi Cod, Cromileptes altivelis.

Typical visibility: 30–50m (100–165ft)
Minimum depth: 5m (16ft)
Maximum depth: 50m (165ft)
The reefs are circular near the surface, but deeper down often have ridges extending from them. They may be easily circumnavigated during a single dive, but it is usual to dive just that side of the reef receiving any current, where most fish gather. All the reefs have excellent coral growths and fish-life, though few pelagics.

The reefs are rather small for snorkellers, though the shallow tops are rich in marine life.

5 KNIGHT PATCHES

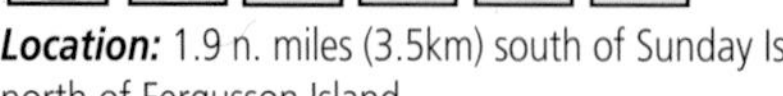

Location: 1.9 n. miles (3.5km) south of Sunday Island, north of Fergusson Island.
Access: Take care navigating in this area as several reefs are awash. Best anchorage is west of the large, very shallow reef.
Conditions: Sheltered in southeast winds. Little current action.
Typical visibility: 30–50m (100–165ft)
Minimum depth: 1m (40in)
Maximum depth: 50m (165ft)
There are several alternative sites here. Choose a sand patch on top of one of the reef areas and explore. The reef formations are quite complex and interesting, with areas of hard-coral growth on top and sea fans and whips down the slopes. The fish-life is nothing special (sharks and turtles are occasionally seen) but the scenery is beautiful. Some particularly large coral formations are excellent for wide-angle photography.

Other sites with similar features are nearby.

The reefs here are quite extensive, rich and of variable depth, so the snorkelling is excellent, particularly as the surface is usually calm.

6 CAMEL REEF

★★★★

Location: 1 n. mile (1.85km) south of Goodenough Island's southern tip.
Access: Anchor on middle of reef's western end, which is relatively barren.
Conditions: Partly sheltered. Occasional mild currents.
Typical visibility: 30–40m (100–130ft)
Minimum depth: 10m (33ft)
Maximum depth: 50m (165ft) plus
From the anchorage it is a short swim to the first hump, a beautiful clump of pillar coral. Beyond is a saddle, descending to 25m (80ft), and then a second, larger hump, bursting with fish-life. A slight current from the east is best; if it is from the west, swim west down to the end of the gradually descending ridge; here the fish-life congregates. Crocodilefish, Lacy Scorpionfish and cuttlefish are common on this interesting reef.

The B17 Bomber Aircraft Blackjack (Site 13, page 58).

7 TRIPLE TOWER BOMMIE

★★★★★★★

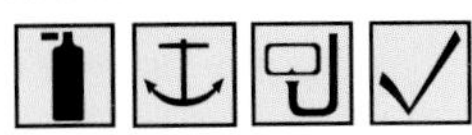

Location: Dart Reefs, 3 n. miles (5.6km) south of Goodenough Island.
Access: Anchor on easternmost bommie.
Conditions: Partly sheltered; not suitable in strong southeasterlies. Sometimes currents in area.
Typical visibility: 30–40m (100–130ft)
Minimum depth: 6m (20ft)
Maximum depth: 50m (165ft) plus

A pass between the two smaller towers has loads of fish plus the coral-covered remains of an old fishing net. You can circumnavigate both these towers in a single dive. Deep diving around the towers reveals some shark action, and small Manta Rays are sometimes on view. The coral growth is good, with some sea fans and soft corals.

Other sites with similar features are nearby. The larger reef has extensive areas of shallow coral for snorkelling.

8 CECILIA'S REEF

★★★★★★★★★

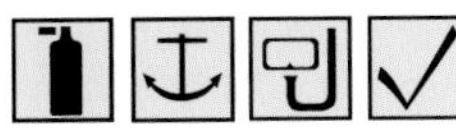

Location: 2 n. miles (3.7km) southwest of Galaiwa Bay, Goodenough Island.
Access: Anchor with care on the reeftop in 5m (16ft).
Conditions: Partly sheltered. Sometimes slight current.
Typical visibility: 30–40m (100–130ft)
Minimum depth: 5m (16ft)
Maximum depth: 50m (165ft)

A small reef bursting with life. Find the reef's active side, where the fish are feeding in the current. The best action is shallow, at the edge of the reef and just over it, so this is an ideal dive for later in the day; since the anchorage at Galaiwa Bay is a short and easily navigated distance away, this is a perfect spot for a night-dive before anchoring for the night. The reef-ledges are full of colourful corals at night.

Many other sites with similar features are nearby, but are uncharted and sometimes very shallow, so take great care navigating. The reefs here are good for snorkelling, though there are sometimes significant currents.

9 PEER'S PATCHES

★★★★★★★★★

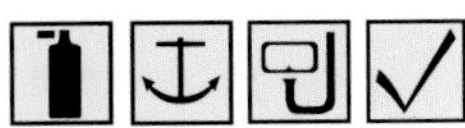

Location: Reefs off Taleba Point, on southern side of Goodenough Island.
Access: Anchor in barren patch on top of western bommie.

POACHING CLAMS

Clam poachers from Taiwan and other Asian nations have for many years raided PNG waters. The poachers usually stay well clear of the mainland and towns – there are plenty of distant reefs and islands seldom visited by Government patrols. The poachers use masks and primitive diving gear. They slice the main adductor muscle of the Giant Clam, then scrape the flesh from the shell. All but the adductor muscle is discarded – an horrific waste, since virtually the whole clam is wonderful eating – and the dead shell is left on the reef. Traditionally village fishermen harvested juvenile clams but left the large clams as breeding stock – they might transport young clams back to the reef beside their village and form clam gardens. Poaching Giant Clams is, therefore, destructive to the traditional lifestyle.

There is no excuse for this thievery since Giant Clams have shown themselves very suitable for farming. Poachers are occasionally caught and their boats confiscated, but many avoid capture. The degradation of the reefs they have raided is all too obvious to a diver.

Conditions: Partly sheltered – Goodenough Island is so high it produces its own weather. Best diving conditions are when a slight current moves over reef.
Typical visibility: 30–40m (100–130ft); sometimes reduced if local rainfall heavy
Minimum depth: 5m (16ft)
Maximum depth: 50m (165ft)

The best canyon is between the western bommie and the next reef. The canyon is 40m (130ft) deep at its shallowest, and you can sit down in the middle and see both reefs, plenty of sea life, and Grey Reef and maybe Silvertip Sharks swimming overhead. The canyon walls have sea fans and whips and large stands of Green Tree Coral. The water is thick with small fish.

You can find other dives if you re-anchor the boat on the reefs' eastern side.

For snorkellers, the tops of the two larger reefs have excellent hard coral and plenty of fish in shallow water.

10 SEE AND SEA PASSES

★★★★★

Location: Dart Reefs, 5 n. miles (9.3km) southwest of Taleba Point, Goodenough Island.
Access: Anchor in sand patches on reefs in pass.
Conditions: Exposed to strong winds, but can usually be dived early in morning in any weather.
Typical visibility: 40m (130ft) plus
Minimum depth: 8m (26ft)
Maximum depth: 60m (200ft)

A long narrow reef is broken by three short passes; you can anchor on the two reef 'islands' they create. The side of the reef you dive depends on whether the current is moving east or west, as all the fish migrate to the side of the reef receiving the current. You can dive each of the passes, which all have large schools of fish, plus sharks cruising about. The 'islands' have excellent hard-coral growth and, on top, Giant Clams. The passes are 25–30m (80–100ft) deep.

Although this site is exposed, should the weather deteriorate there is an excellent anchorage at Galaiwa Bay, only 30min away. Inland from the anchorage is a large, shallow mangrove-lined lagoon, full of bird-life – and, villagers report, crocodiles.

11 ANNE LEA REEF

★★★★★★★

Location: The western tip of Dart Reefs.
Access: Anchor on ridge in 5m (16ft). Take care: there is a very shallow reef nearby.
Conditions: Calm weather required. Little current on reef.
Typical visibility: 30–40m (100–130ft)
Minimum depth: 5m (16ft)
Maximum depth: 50m (165ft)

The reef is the end part of a ridge that runs for several kilometres. Its western side is a very deep dropoff, its eastern a shallower dropoff into a lagoon. The ridge widens at this point to form a plateau (at about 15–20m; 50–65ft), bordered on its south by a shallower ridge just before the lagoon dropoff. Giant Clams of different colours lie scattered on the reef, and the coral growths are impressive. In calm weather this is an easy, relaxed dive.

Snorkellers on the reef can also see the clams.

12 KEAST REEF

★★★★★

Location: In open ocean 3 n. miles (5.6km) west of Dart Reefs.
Access: Anchor on reeftop at southeast end.
Conditions: The reef is exposed, and requires calm weather; sometimes prone to strong currents. Best conditions are calm seas with slight current from southeast.
Typical visibility: 40–50m (130–165ft)
Minimum depth: 5m (16ft)
Maximum depth: 50m (165ft) plus

With the boat anchored close to the drop, experienced divers can descend quickly to the reeftop, then pull/swim to and over the drop, where the current's effects are avoided. Soft corals bloom all along the dropoff and great schools of fish swarm around. Grey Reef and Silvertip Sharks are frequent. Shark-feeding has been attempted here, with mixed results; even without it this is an exciting and beautiful dive. The reeftop is relatively barren, having been cleaned out by Crown-of-Thorns Starfish around 1989, but is recovering, and young corals can be found scattered around. The fantastic soft corals appeared after a rare cyclone swept through the area in May 1993.

13 B17 BOMBER AIRCRAFT BLACKJACK

★★★★★

Location: In front of Boga Boga village, at Cape Vogel.
Access: Small boats may anchor in a natural cove in the reef, very close to the dropoff that leads down to the wreck. Larger boats may anchor in deep water near (but not on!) the wreck or, in southeast winds, on the reef immediately in front of the wreck in 23m (77ft), hanging back over the wreck. A partial guide-line runs from the dropoff in front of the village towards the wreck.
Conditions: Exposed to strong southeast and northwest winds. Often current over site from southeast. Do not attempt except in calm conditions. This deep dive requires decompression stops, often in current, and should not be attempted by inexperienced divers.
Typical visibility: 40m (130ft) – sometimes reduced
Minimum depth: 40m (130ft)
Maximum depth: 48m (158ft)

The best plan is a direct descent to the aircraft, then a single slow pass over the wings, nose and cockpit areas, finishing at the tail. The starboard tailplane is bent upwards and points to the dive's exit, a reef-slope at about 45° leading to a vertical wall (rising to 3m; 10ft) – ideal for a slow, safe ascent. The wreck is exceptionally intact, with guns and other artefacts to see. Resist the temptation to penetrate the fuselage, where many loose wires hang around. The cockpit may be viewed and photographed through the open side-windows. A machine-gun at the tail still swivels in its mount. Since 1993 the aircraft has been adorned in a colourful array of soft corals. A Giant Grouper is occasionally seen.

There are excellent reef dives near the wreck, particularly at the southeast entrance to the channel in which the wreck lies; or you can dive the wall by the wreck. The usually clear water provides opportunities for wonderful wide-angle photographs of the whole aircraft, though the depth means light is limited – fast film is useful.

The shallow reef nearby has excellent snorkelling and many turtles. A movie describing the aircraft's exceptional war history and its eventual discovery, 'Black Jack's Last Mission', was produced in 1988.

Opposite: *Leaf Scorpionfish, Taenianotus triacanthus.*

The Louisiade Archipelago

From China Strait to Rossel Island, a distance of some 500km (300 miles), the reefs and islands of the Louisiade Archipelago, exposed much of the year to the Southeast Trades, separate the Coral and Solomon seas. The prevailing current, from the southeast, brings clear, cool water from the Coral Sea. The Southeast Trades build up large ocean swells, which batter the southern barrier reefs and make diving these areas difficult much of the year. Even when the winds are low the swells can crash: only when both swells and wind have calmed can you dive – but on those rare days it can be fantastic! The many reefs and islands do give some shelter, and there is always somewhere to dive. Much exploration still has to be done: the archipelago is regarded as one of PNG's last diving frontiers.

BASILAKI ISLAND (SITES 1–4)

Many interesting sites can be found on the northern side of Basilaki Island and in the Engineer Group. Currents can be strong (spring tides should be avoided) and visibility may not be as clear as elsewhere; however, most reefs are very rich, and on days of clear water the diving is exceptionally fine. A beautiful wreck – a P38 Lightning aircraft in near perfect condition – can be dived in sheltered water year-round (Site 3).

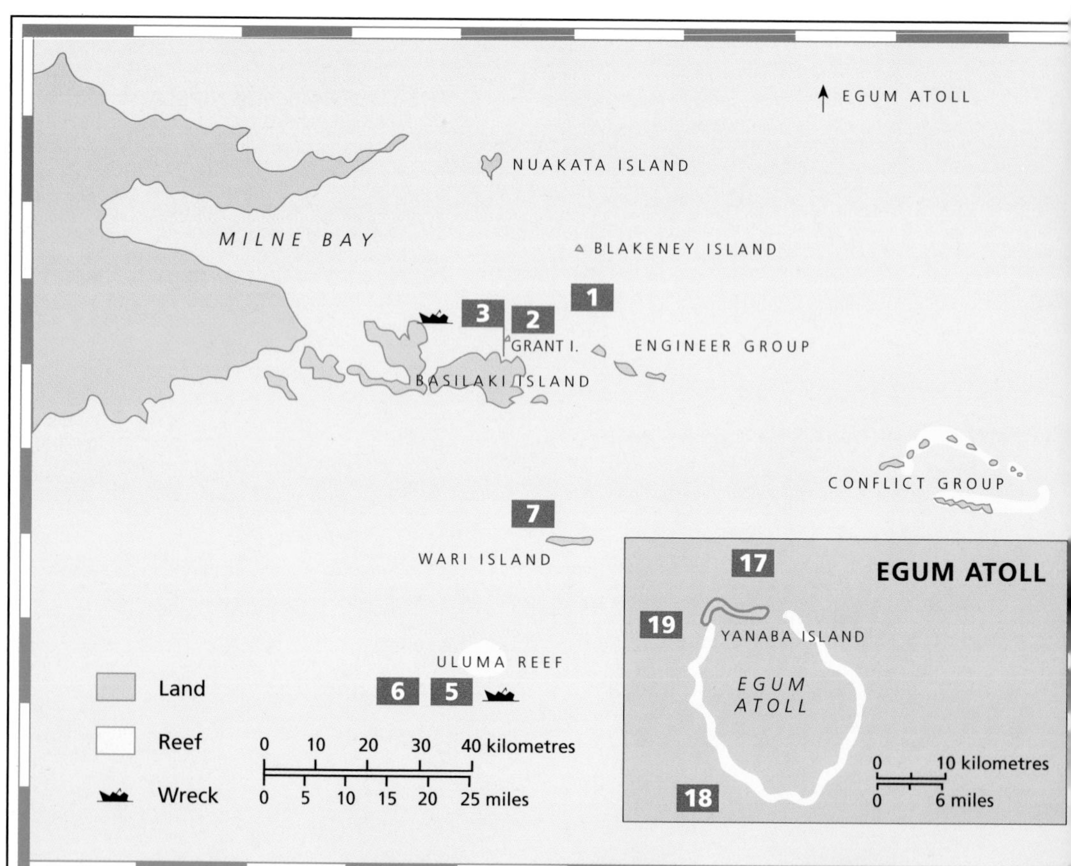

WARI ISLAND (SITES 5–7)

To the southeast of Milne Bay, Wari Island is a hilly, ribbon-shaped island with a sheltered lagoon in which boats can anchor. The eastern entrance is the easier; the western, which threads through shallow reefs, should be attempted only with local knowledge. The friendly islanders have a famous history of skilled boat-building. Wari was visited by seafarers long before Captain Moresby discovered the nearby China Strait in 1873.

During the calmest months (Nov/Dec and Apr/May) anyone cruising in the area should visit Wari, as there are some excellent dives to be made. Good weather and some luck are needed for these, but they are certainly memorable. Water temperature at the best diving times is usually about 27–28°C (80–82°F).

MISIMA ISLAND (SITES 8–10)

There is a steep dropoff all around Misima Island. The outfall from an open-cut goldmine on the southern side has not affected the diving very much: the narrow fringing reefs were poorly stocked with fish and coral anyway – except at Bagga Bagga Point, which juts out into the coastal current and is alive with fish and soft corals.

Good reef diving is found near Misima at the Renard Islands (Site 10), just a 1hr cruise away from the harbour at Bwagaoia, and a well preserved wreck of a Zero fighter lies in Deboyne Lagoon, 25 n. miles (46km) to the west (Site 9).

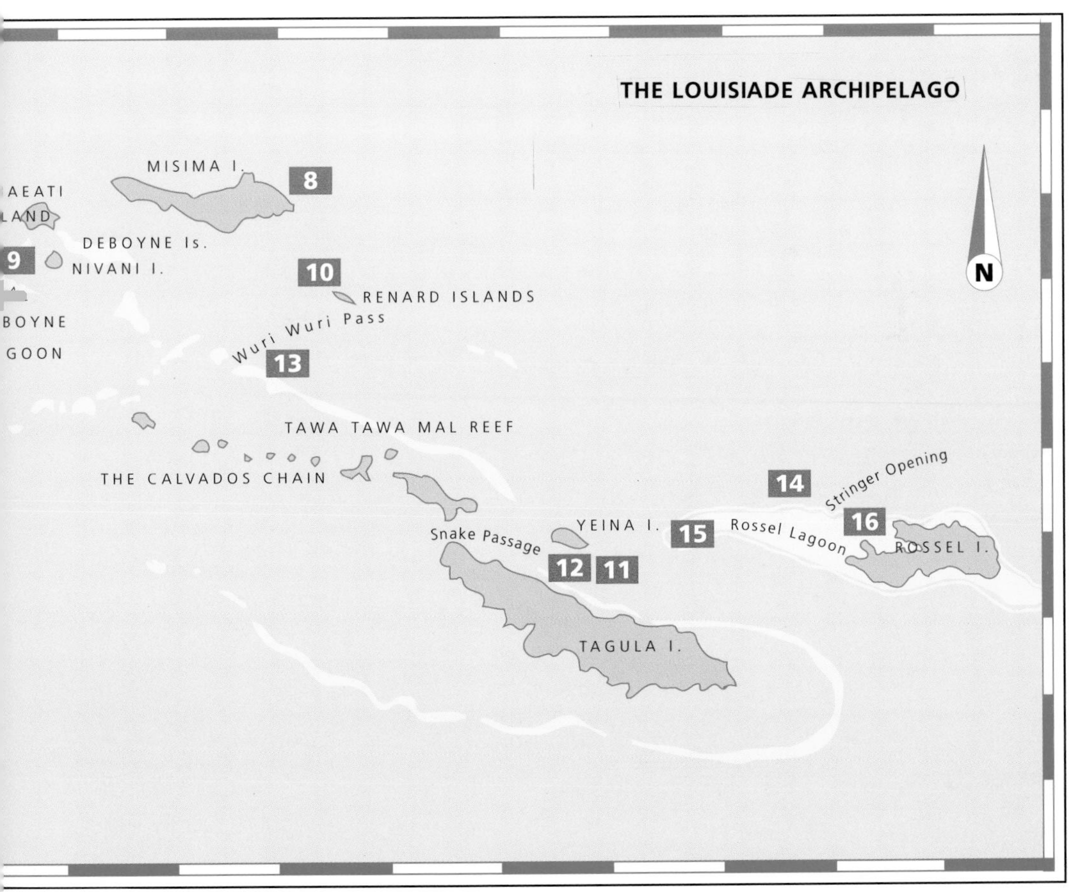

Tagula and the Calvados Chain (Sites 11–13)

A glance at the chart is enough to get your heart pumping – a lagoon over 225km (140 miles) long filled with islands and reefs and an outer barrier sliced with passes, one of which is the winding Snake Passage (Site 12), over 4km ($2^1/2$ miles) long with sheer sides and a bottom 50–60m (165–200ft) deep. Few divers have visited this fascinating area, only a 24hr cruise east of Alotau and much exploration remains to be done. However, some good dive sites have already been located and, just as important, some areas with poor diving have been identified.

The lagoon's southern side is exposed to the winds and swells of the Southeast Trades, which blow most of the year. Although it is often inaccessible, there is some excellent diving along this southern reef. The northern side is protected and mostly calm but, since waves are continuously breaking on the southern reef, the prevailing current is northwards: at the many reef passes the continuous outgoing flow of water brings with it reduced visibility. When the tide is sufficient for current to flow into the lagoon on its northern side, visibility improves dramatically and the diving in some of the passes is first-class. The northwest side of the lagoon is the best.

Near Tagula and the other larger islands the lagoon is shallow and the visibility very poor. Cyclones have been known to affect Tagula Island during the Northwest season, so take care if cruising in the area during Jan/Apr.

Water temperatures vary from 25°C (77°F) in Aug to 28°C (82°F) in Dec. There can be very strong currents in the lagoon passes. The islands are interesting, and many beautiful anchorages may be found. Fishing is excellent, and the people are very friendly and willing to trade.

Rossel Island (Sites 14–16)

The seafaring Rossel Islanders, living at the remote southeast tip of the Louisiade Archipelago, are also fine jewellers, being the principal manufacturers of Bagi, a type of colourful shell necklace made from carved, drilled and threaded discs of a Rock Scallop shell, *Chama imbricata*. Bagi is used in traditional ceremonies like Kula Ring, but is also made to sell and commands a high price.

To the west is a lagoon, 60km (37 miles) long, and to the east a very shallow reef and a small island with a light at its eastern tip. This marks the end of the Louisiade Archipelago and the first open sea east of the PNG mainland. Quite a few ships trying to sail around the Rossel Spit have miscalculated and ended on the reef. Some are high and dry, others smashed beyond recognition.

The Kula Ring

While many clans in PNG were in a constant state of war with their neighbours, the islanders of Milne Bay Province formed an elaborate and magical club bonding them to each other. Their beautiful ocean-going canoes, with planked hulls, are superbly seaworthy but are also decorated with carvings and shells to make them works of art. The canoes sail between islands in a ring – the Kula Ring – formed by the Trobriand, Marshall Bennett, Woodlark, Misima, Panaeate, Engineer, D'Entrecasteau and Amphlett islands. They carry fantastic shell jewellery – necklaces known as Soulava and armbands known as Mwali. The necklaces are passed clockwise around the ring, the armbands anticlockwise. Each recipient is forever bonded with the giver but is only a guardian of the jewellery, which he must eventually pass on around the ring. Being guardian brings a man great prestige, but also an obligation to reciprocate with the person who passed it to him. In such a way the various clans, although separated by hundreds of kilometres of ocean, have formed lasting friendships and secured important trading partners.

Kite Fishing

One of the most fascinating methods of fishing is that practised by the islanders of the Marshall Bennett Group, Milne Bay Province. The fisherman first goes into the forest where, on a cane loom, he collects spider's webs. The mass of webs is gathered and rolled into a lure about the size of half a pencil, and attached to a thin line. The line is attached to a kite which is flown behind a canoe; no hook is used. The kite causes the lure to skip along the surface of the water and this attracts Longtoms (Needlefish; *Tylosurus crocodilus*). The Longtom, a long skinny fish growing to over 1m (40in), has needle-shaped jaws with many sharp teeth. The teeth get tangled in the spider's webs, and the fisherman is able to pull the fish to his canoe.

Rossel Island's southern side and the lagoon have clear water and a steep dropoff, but this is virtually impossible to dive because of the swells. The reefs on the island's northeast are sheltered, but the water is not clear and the corals poor. However, there are some excellent sites along the lagoon's northern side to the west, and at the western end.

Rossel Island is subjected to cyclones in the season Jan/Mar, so avoid this time. There are no scheduled dive cruises, but you can charter a boat from Alotau to explore the area. Egum Atoll (Sites 17–19) is a perfect coral atoll in the Solomon Sea about 90 n. miles (170km) northeast of Alotau; the only way to get there is by boat, as there is no airstrip. Its nearly circular lagoon is 18 n. miles (33km) across, and there are islands both on the fringing reef and in the centre. The best anchorage is among the islands in the centre; a less sheltered anchorage is available south of Yanaba Island, the largest of the fringing islands on the lagoon's northern side.

The island's friendly people are part of the Kula trading ring, so you often see magnificent decorated sailing canoes pulled up on the beaches before the distinctive village houses. This is among the few remaining Melanesian Islands where a traditional lifestyle has been maintained.

Squarespot Anthias

1 DOUBILET REEF

★★★★★

  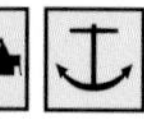

Location: 2$\frac{1}{2}$ n. miles (4.6km) southwest of Blakeney Island.
Access: Anchor carefully on sand patches on eastern end of reef.
Conditions: Requires calm weather and slight currents. Snorkelling usually difficult because of current running over reef.
Typical visibility: 30m (100ft)
Minimum depth: 8m (26ft)
Maximum depth: 40m (130ft)

The reef is too large to swim around on a single dive. The best dive is always on the side of the reef receiving current, and the eastern end is most popular. The reeftop has many large plate corals and soft corals, but do descend the sloping dropoffs, where hundreds of sea fans line up with scattered trees of black coral and clumps of sea whips. On the current side huge schools of fusiliers and other fish swarm at the reef-edge. Sharks and large groupers are sometimes seen down the slopes. On a sunny day in clear conditions this reef has countless great opportunities for wide-angle photography.

2 WATERMAN RIDGE

★★★★

Location: Southeast fringing reef of Grant Island.
Access: Anchor in sand patch on reeftop.
Conditions: Requires minimum current and light winds.
Typical visibility: 30m (100ft)
Minimum depth: 6m (20ft)
Maximum depth: 40m (130ft)

When there is a slight current from the southeast, this reef comes alive with an almost unbelievable abundance of fish. Start into the current, then descend over the front of the reef and down the steep dropoff. Next, turn your left shoulder to the wall until the end of the reef. Swim back to the boat along the reeftop, where there are tree corals and Giant Clams.

Other sites with similar features are nearby.

3 P38 LIGHTNING AIRCRAFT

★★★★

Location: Large bay on northern side of Basilaki Island.
Access: Local knowledge necessary to find wreck. Boats can anchor in 8m (26ft) on a ridge of reef in the bay. Wreck is in 27m (90ft) on sand/silt bottom off ridge's northern tip.
Conditions: Sheltered in all weather.
Typical visibility: 10–18m (33–60ft)
Minimum depth: 25m (80ft)
Maximum depth: 27m (90ft)

This aircraft's call-sign was 2–66869, but all flight details are apparently lost. A villager told me the pilot ditched the aircraft in the bay and came ashore on a liferaft. The wreck is upright and intact except for the two propellers, broken off on impact and in 1994 recovered by Telita Cruises divemaster Chris Carney, who placed them near the wreck. The rest is untouched – the nose still has guns and the cockpit controls are still in place, as is the armour-plating used to protect the pilot's back. The engines and turbochargers are clearly visible, although a large anemone has taken up residence on the starboard side. Sweetlips and crocodilefish are common, although otherwise the wreck has little marine growth. The nose points to the reef, so dives usually end with an ascent up the reef, which has interesting growths of fan sponges. Use wide-angle and natural light for best photographs of the whole aircraft. The water is always slightly green, so a film that produces stronger blues is preferable to Kodachrome; good images have been achieved using Kodak's Underwater film in natural light. As with all PNG wrecks, souveniring is illegal: please leave the wreck as you found it.

4 JEREMY'S REEF

★★★★

Location: Hull Island; exact location withheld because of shark-finners.
Access: Refer to Telita Cruises.
Conditions: Calm conditions and light current required.
Typical visibility: 30m (100ft)
Minimum depth: 6m (20ft)
Maximum depth: 40m (130ft)

The reeftop is quite barren, but down the reef-slope are sea fans and soft and hard corals. On the southeast corner, a ridge continues from the reef down to 25m (80ft), then rises to a coral bommie. A current generally flows over the ridge, and this is the site of a shark-feeding station. Sharks generally appear very quickly here; Grey Reef Sharks are usually first, although there have been sightings of Silvertips and Whitetip Reefs. Do not dive this reef unless feeding the sharks . . . since the sharks are expecting to be fed. Telita and Tiata lead dives to this reef.

Opposite: *Dinah skilfully manoeuvres a school of Chevron Barracuda, Sphyraena putnamiae, to circle around her.*

5 PRESIDENT GRANT, ULUMA REEF

★★★★★★★★

Location: On reef's south side. Parts of wreck are visible at low tide.
Access: About 1½hr cruising from Wari. Anchor close to wreck in 8m (26ft).
Conditions: Requires calm seas, no swells.
Typical visibility: 50m (165ft)
Minimum depth: as shallow as you like
Maximum depth: 12m (40ft)

The wreck is exposed to the Southeast Trades and to swells, and has been salvaged so that it is completely broken up. Nevertheless, this is a fascinating dive. A 4in (10cm) gun still stands photogenically upright among twisted steel plates and giant engine parts. Dozens of machine-guns lie rusted and useless on the surrounding reef, and the many artefacts on view include old bottles and portholes. A healthy fish population inhabits the site, although there is little coral growth. The water is usually very clear, and the shallowness makes long bottom-times possible.

In suitable conditions there is excellent snorkelling on the wreck.

6 SOUTHWEST POINT, ULUMA REEF

★★★★★★★★

Location: On reef's southwest corner.
Access: About 1½hr cruising from Wari. Difficult anchoring because of shallow reef.
Conditions: Requires calm seas.
Typical visibility: 50m (165ft)
Minimum depth: 2m (6½ft)
Maximum depth: 50m (165ft) plus

Most of Uluma Reef slopes to deep water, but at the western side there is a steep dropoff. The most exciting part of the wall is right at the southwest corner. There are big cuts, overhangs and crevices to explore, and a constant stream of large pelagics cruise by. A big school of Hammerheads has been seen deep down the wall, and other sharks, particularly Silvertips and Grey Reefs, are common. As to small fish, this is the first place we found the beautiful Hawk Anthias (*Serranocirrhitus latus*), rarely seen further north in PNG.

Experienced snorkellers will find it hard to beat the excitement of going along the edge of the dropoff, with its splendid formations, great coral growth and occasional sightings of sharks and big fish.

Opposite: *Telita divers prepare to experience the thrilling big fish action at Egum Rock.*

SKULL CAVES

Milne Bay villagers have an ancient tradition of storing skulls. The modern villagers claim no knowledge of the practice – it was just something that happened long ago. Originally we thought the skulls must have belonged to relatives who had died, but we recently had some examined by a neurosurgeon, who concluded they must have been the skulls of enemies slain in battle. He pointed to a healed fracture on one skull, together with another very obvious fracture which had probably killed the owner.

The skulls are stored in caves or ledges close to villages. The villagers place no particular value on them, and there are no taboos relating to who can see or touch them – indeed, we have found village children playing with them. The best skull caves are awe-inspiring, especially where stalactites have formed down over the skulls.

7 DAISY'S DROPOFF

★★★★

Location: Wari Rock, 1 n. mile (1.85km) west of Wari Island.
Access: Two possible anchoring sites, the better being on northeastern side.
Conditions: Partly sheltered but difficult in strong wind conditions. Usually a strong current over site.
Typical visibility: 30m (100ft)
Minimum depth: 5m (16ft)
Maximum depth: 40m (130ft)

A large, steep-sided rock. The wall starts at about 9m (30ft) and drops vertically to over 40m (130ft). It is entirely covered with a brilliant display of soft corals and yellow *Tubastraea faulkneri*, full of colourful anthias and other reef fish. There are soft corals growing on top of soft corals – you can't see the wall for this fantastic display! Sharks and larger fish patrol in deeper water.

This is an exciting dive for those who can handle currents (in slack current the soft corals shrivel). The water is not always as clear here as at Sites 5 and 6, but can be good enough for excellent photography.

8 SKULL CAVE

★★★

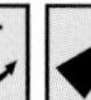

Location: Misima's northeast shore.
Access: Usually by road, a short drive from Bwagaoia.
Conditions: Completely sheltered.
Typical visibility: 40m (130ft)
Minimum depth: as shallow as you like
Maximum depth: 40m (130ft) plus

Obtain permission from the villagers before making this

dive. Enter the pool and, ignoring the several side passages, descend by the main tunnel (where there is always light) to about 20m (65ft). Here it becomes horizontal for a short distance, leading out to the open sea. The tunnel exit is on a wall; note its position as you emerge – otherwise, to end the dive, you might have to swim into a nearby bay. The outer reef is pleasant but has little marine life. The cave and tunnel are clear and free from silt, though mainly coated in algae. There is not a lot of obvious marine life in the tunnel, but you might find unusual species of small creatures by careful searching.

9 ZERO FIGHTER

★★★★★★★

Location: Near Nivani Island's northern tip, Deboyne Lagoon.
Access: Anchorage in shallow water to northwest of Nivani Island; site can be found from beach or boat – a dinghy is useful. Wreck can often be seen from surface; if not, the very friendly villagers will show you.
Conditions: Sheltered all year.
Typical visibility: 15m (50ft)
Minimum depth: 4m (13ft)
Maximum depth: 4m (13ft)

Mainly of interest to wreck fanatics, and usually snorkelled rather than dived. The aircraft is reported to have belonged to the *Shoho*, a Japanese aircraft carrier now lying north of Misima in 2000m (6600ft) of water; when the ship sank the *Zero* was forced to ditch in the sea. The wreck is upright and largely intact, although some guns and instruments have been salvaged. The propeller is in place and makes an excellent subject for photographs; wide-angle and natural light recommended. Sea-grass surrounds the wreck, but there is little marine growth actually on the plane.

The wreck of a US B24 has been reported from Deboyne Lagoon; its position was described by villagers in 1994 as being inside the barrier reef about 2$\frac{1}{2}$ n. miles (4.6km) south of Panniet Island's western end. I have not verified this.

10 RENARD ISLANDS

★★★★★★★★

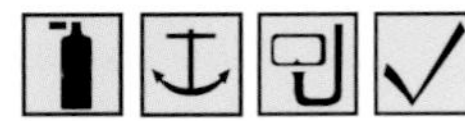

Location: Around the bay on the northwest side of the Renard Islands.
Access: By boat.
Conditions: Sheltered in Southeast season. Currents light.
Typical visibility: 40m (130ft)

Minimum depth: as shallow as you like
Maximum depth: 50m (165ft) plus
Various different sites are available for exploration. The bay has several islands; there is a continuous fringing reef with a couple of shallow passages between the islands. The passes have good fish-life and coral growths, with sea fans and soft corals. Giant Clams are common. The best wall is on the northern side; sea whips, small sea fans and soft corals decorate it. The sites' clear water and sheltered nature make them very attractive to any boats cruising in the area.

Many shallow sites in the bay are unaffected by current and have excellent coral growth, interesting scenery and healthy populations of reef fish – perfect for snorkelling.

11 CHASM REEF

★★★★★★★★

Location: Offshore north of Tagula Island, 4 n. miles (7.4km) southeast of Snake Passage.
Access: You cannot anchor on this reef so drift-diving is usual.
Conditions: The reef provides its own shelter whatever the wind direction.
Typical visibility: 40m (130ft)
Minimum depth: as shallow as you like
Maximum depth: 50m (165ft)
The reef may be dived all around its circumference. The choice of entry depends on current and wind direction: choose the sheltered side, preferably with a current running along the wall, then drift/swim in the direction of the current. The dropoff is immediate and dramatic, with beautifully sculptured reef formations often decorated with soft corals and sea fans. There are schools of fish all along the reef, plus occasional sharks, including large Hammerheads. You can explore the depths, but the best action is in the first 20m (65ft).

The edge of the reef may be snorkelled, with a stunning view of a well sculptured dropoff.

12 SNAKE PASSAGE (YUMA PASSAGE)

★★★★★★

Location: Between Tagula and Yeina islands.
Access: Anchoring difficult (because of shallow reef) but drift-diving easy.
Conditions: Passage is sheltered by its surrounding reef, but often has current through it.
Typical visibility: 25m (80ft), sometimes much reduced
Minimum depth: as shallow as you like
Maximum depth: 50m (165ft)
Snake Passage, over 4km (2½miles) long, leads from the outer deep-water dropoff into the lagoon near Tagula Island; it is easily navigated, even though a tidal current runs through it. The reef at the sides of the passage is very shallow, but then drops vertically for the first 20m (65ft) before sloping to the bottom of the passage. It may be dived anywhere along its length; the best method is to drift-dive along the wall at a curving section of the pass. There are interesting reef formations, plenty of sea fans and large sponges, and excellent fish-life, including sharks and Giant Groupers. The only problem is the visibility: when I last dived here it was only 8m (26ft), though it is reportedly clear at other times.

Snorkelling is easy along the edge of the passage, with plenty to see.

13 NORTH PASS

★★★★

Location: Western side of pass in Tawa Tawa Mal Reef, 5 n. miles (9.3km) southeast of Wuri Wuri Pass.
Access: Anchor on reef ledge in 8m (26ft), close to dropoff.
Conditions: Reef provides shelter from southerly winds and swells, but it is important current is running into lagoon from north.
Typical visibility: 40m (130ft)
Minimum depth: 6m (20ft)
Maximum depth: 50m (165ft) plus
You work into the current or are dropped off, up-current, from an inflatable, then descend the steep dropoff working east (right shoulder to wall) towards the passage entrance. The wall is covered with gorgeous growths of soft corals, sea whips and sea fans. Schools of fish (including resident barracuda) mill around along the edge of the dropoff, and large Dogtooth Tuna and Spanish Mackerel hunt among them. You can proceed into the passage entrance, but the reef-edge close to the pass has the most action. Grey Reef and Silvertip Sharks inhabit the dropoff.

Other sites with similar features are nearby.

14 LORI'S CAVE

★★★★★★★

Location: Northwest point outside Rossel Lagoon.
Access: By boat; anchor on ledge outside main reef near point.
Conditions: Sheltered from southeast swells; slight currents.
Typical visibility: 40m (130ft)
Minimum depth: 3m (10ft)
Maximum depth: 50m (165ft) plus

Next to the shallow barrier reef of the lagoon are a couple of coral bommies rising from a sculptured ledge before the main dropoff. One bommie has a wide tunnel through it, at 20m (66ft), leading to the dropoff. The whole area has excellent coral growths with areas of sponge, soft corals and sea whips. In the cave is the only colony of Lori's Anthias (*Pseudanthias lori*) I have found in PNG. This exquisite fish alone makes the dive worthwhile, but there is plenty of other marine life and the underwater scenery is gorgeous.

The edge of the reef is shallow and perfect for snorkelling. With the typical clear water, the deeper views of the reef are easily seen.

15 FISH CITY

★★★★★★★

Location: Western entrance to Rossel Lagoon.
Access: By boat.
Conditions: Partly sheltered inside lagoon; can sometimes be currents.
Typical visibility: 30m (100ft)
Minimum depth: 5m (16ft)
Maximum depth: 30m (100ft)

On the southern side of the entrance, just inside the lagoon, a sausage-shaped patch reef has grown across the direction of current, providing an ideal place for fish to congregate and feed. Too far from Rossel Island to have regular visits by village fisherman, this is therefore virtually untouched. Giant schools of fusiliers, surgeonfish, trevally, barracuda and Rainbow Runners surge around. Coral Trout, grouper, Spanish Mackerel, Dogtooth Tuna and reef sharks prey on the multitudes, while Manta Rays glide overhead. The reef has a healthy cover of hard and soft corals. The best diving is in the shallow water around the edge of the reef.

In manageable currents the reef and fish-life can be enjoyed snorkelling.

The Lacy Scorpionfish, Rhinopias aphanes, rare elsewhere, is often found in Port Moresby and Milne Bay.

16 STRINGER OPENING

★★★★★★★

Location: Inside Stringer Opening, on north side of Rossel lagoon.
Access: By boat; anchor on patch reef to east of entrance once inside lagoon.
Conditions: Partly sheltered. Possibly currents.
Typical visibility: 25m (80ft)
Minimum depth: as shallow as you like
Maximum depth: 40m (130ft)

The wide entrance to Stringer Opening has good deep diving on its northern side and some very interesting diving inside the lagoon. You need good light to pilot the diveboat through the many shallow reefs, and several are too shallow for anchoring; however, others can be conveniently dived and have good growths of soft corals and gorgonians, plus hard corals. Excellent night-diving is possible on these reefs, and all have a healthy reef-fish population. Visibility, though not as clear as outside the lagoon, is still good – better on an incoming tide.

These shallow reefs offer excellent snorkelling. Take care when any current is running – although several reefs are little affected by the current.

17 EGUM ROCK

★★★★★★★★

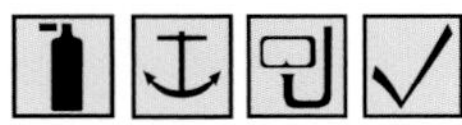

Location: 4 n. miles (7.4km) north of Yanaba Island.
Access: By boat, 40min from Egum Lagoon. In calm weather you can anchor on a ledge next to the rock.
Conditions: Requires calm seas. Often slight current around rock.
Typical visibility: 40m (130ft)
Minimum depth: 5m (16ft)
Maximum depth: 50m (165ft) plus

When I first noticed this rock on the chart I thought it was a speck of dirt and tried to brush it away. An opportunity to explore the rock came in 1981 when I took a group of adventurous Australians out to Egum. This turned out to be among the most spectacular dives I have ever made.

The rock rises vertically from the sea and has been undercut by wave action around its base. Underwater, a ledge runs completely around the rock, with a width ranging from 20m to 50m (65–165ft) and an average depth of 10m (33ft); beyond the ledge depths plunge to over 600m (2000ft). You can swim right round the rock at its base in about 20min. Although you can dive deep, most of the action takes place in the first 20m (65ft), and the important thing is to try to get as much bottom-time as possible. A big school of barracuda is always present, as are large schools of Bigeye

18 HOLLIS REEF

★★★★★★★★

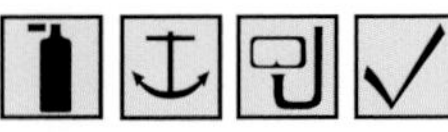

Location: Outside Egum lagoon on southwest side.
Access: Anchor on sand patches on reeftop.
Conditions: Requires calm seas. Can be a current over reef.
Typical visibility: 50m (65ft)
Minimum depth: 5m (16ft)
Maximum depth: 50m (165ft) plus

This patch reef is separated from the main fringing reef. It has a dropoff around it. The southeast side has an unusual formation of sea fans, which grow horizontally, rather than being vertically orientated to catch the prevailing currents. The reason is that, for most of the year, large swells make water move vertically up and down the reef-face. The coral growth is excellent; there are many schools of reef fish and plenty of Grey Reef Sharks.

There is good snorkelling (not for beginners) on the reeftop.

19 NORTHWEST PASS

★★★★

Location: Northwest entrance to Egum Atoll.
Access: Anchor in 10m (33ft) right on edge of dropoff.
Conditions: Requires an incoming tide. Partly sheltered from wind.
Typical visibility: 40m (130ft)
Minimum depth: 10m (33ft)
Maximum depth: 50m (165ft) plus

This current-dive is more suited to experienced divers. You must time the dive for an incoming current, when the fish action is greatest and the water clearest. The pass's top is quite barren, but the wall outside has many large fish: Giant Grouper and sharks along with schooling reef fish. You often see rays swimming through the pass.

How to Get There

Visiting divers fly into Gurney Airport, the gateway to the provincial capital, Alotau. At time of writing work is underway to upgrade the airstrip to international standards for direct jet flights from Cairns. Already Air Niugini (seven flights per week) and Milne Bay Air (nine flights per week) provide connecting flights to Alotau from Port Moresby (flight-time 1hr 15min) for overnight Air Niugini flights from Hong Kong, Manila and Singapore. You can hop on a flight one evening in these cities and be diving the next day in Milne Bay. Free airport transfers in Milne Bay are provided by the dive operators. The Masurina Lodge (see below) provides comfortable accommodation in Alotau, but day-dives from Alotau are not usually available since the best diving (except for the Muscoota wreck – see page 36) is at the mouth of the Bay, 3hr away.

Air Niugini PO Box 3, Alotau
tel 675 641 1100
Milne Bay Air tel 675 641 1591
fax 675 641 1559

Where to Stay

Masurina Lodge PO Box 5, Alotau
tel 675 641 1212 fax 675 641 1406/1286
A 40-room guesthouse offering clean and comfortable accommodation in air-conditioned en suite rooms. Airport transfers and all meals are included in the room rate, and the lodge can organize car hire and local tours. The evening meals are very good; they often feature beautifully cooked local foods along with Western dishes in a generous buffet. There are plans for a beach-front hotel in Alotau in the near future and Masurina Lodge is helping establish village guesthouses in several locations in Milne Bay, so visitors will be able to experience a night or two actually living in a village. They are also working to provide a day-diving service out of Alotau. Most of these developments depend on the completion of work on the new international airstrip that will enable direct flights from Cairns into Alotau.

Village Accommodation
Milne Bay Air provides scheduled services to the many islands in Milne Bay Province. Some of the centres, such as Cape Vogel, have village guesthouses and even if there is not an established guesthouse it is possible to find accommodation with villagers. The adventurous traveller will enjoy the warm hospitality of village life and the superb snorkelling available off most beaches. Villagers are also very happy to take visitors out in their canoes for a modest price and excellent offshore reefs may be visited. Unfortunately none of the islands have facilities for scuba divers.

Live-Aboard

Telita
This was PNG's first purpose-built live-aboard diveboat, and has achieved a reputation as one of the world's finest; she has five double cabins for 10 guests. Construction was completed in Dec 1986, and since then the 20m (66ft) *Telita* has explored nearly all of PNG's coastal provinces. Since 1992 she has been permanently based in Alotau, Milne Bay, her home port. This quiet and comfortable boat was designed so that divers can dive directly from her. In 1994 she underwent a complete refit and overhaul, replacing much of the original machinery and adding a water-maker and top-deck sunshade.
Telita Cruises PO Box 141, Earlville, Cairns, Australia 4870 tel 61 (0)70 545 401
fax 61 (0)70 547 436

Chertan
The *Chertan*, an 18m (60ft) fibreglass diveboat, started operation in 1992. The vessel is owned by Rob Vanderloos, an Alotau businessman and qualified diving instructor. The *Chertan* has a very broad beam of 6.7m (22ft) making the inside spacious. There are six guest cabins for a total of 12 passengers.
Milne Bay Marine Charters
PO Box 176, Alotau tel 675 641 1167
fax 675 641 1291

Telita Cruises also takes bookings for the *Tiata* – see New Ireland directory (page 147) for further details. Niugini Diving runs the *Barbarian II* – see Lae directory (page 99) for further details.

Local Highlights

Milne Bay has a history of building small but seaworthy diesel-powered wooden boats 6–9m (20–30ft) long. This was popularized in the 1930s by a young naval architect, Arthur Swinfield, employed by the then Governor-General, Sir Hubert Murray. Swinfield worked at the Kwato Mission near Samarai, renowned for its enlightened approach to missionary work, emphasizing the teaching of practical skills as well as Christianity. (In 1985 Swinfield came out of retirement to draw the plans for the diveboat Telita, which was built by the grandchildren of the boat-builders he trained.)

There are many small boats carrying passengers and cargo throughout the province. An adventurous traveller can turn up at the wharf at Alotau and find a boat to take a ride to virtually anywhere in the Milne Bay region. Schedules are vague, but if you have time on your hands and do not mind putting up with some discomfort and noise, the boats can take you to Samarai, where there is a guesthouse, or to other more remote islands.

John Kailaga's Guest House at East Cape (see box on page 40).

PORT MORESBY AREA

PNG's capital city, Port Moresby, is situated on a splendid natural harbour on the south coast of the mainland. Backed by the Owen Stanley Mountains and with beaches and hills looking out to several islands and the surf of the barrier reef, Port Moresby could be a very attractive place, but it has become a city of litter, armed guards, razor wire, chaotic services and outrageous prices. Fortunately you can enjoy the fine diving around the Port Moresby area without spending time in the city.

The Southeast season brings constant Trade Winds and clear cloudless skies. It is not uncommon to go for seven months with no significant rain; when the rain does come, in Dec/Apr, there is great rejoicing. When the Trade Winds let loose they cause rough seas, frustrating for diving but wonderful for sailing – indeed, the occasional sailing-canoe races along the coast are among the most incredible sights to be seen from the city.

Air temperatures are pleasant all year, though it gets hot in town because of all the tarmac and concrete. Water temperatures vary from a comfortable 28°C (82°F) in Jan/Feb to lows of 24°C (75°F) in Aug/Sep. For year-round Port Moresby diving, wetsuits and hoods are required.

Starting just west of Port Moresby and continuing for 1000km (620 miles) to the southeast is the Papuan Barrier Reef. Most of its length is completely unexplored, and only the 60km (37-mile) section from just west of Fisherman's (Daugo) Island east to Round Point is dived regularly. In this section the outer reef is only 6–8km (4–5 miles) offshore, beyond which the ocean bed plunges to the depths of the Coral Sea.

There are three main diving locations within the Port Moresby area: the sites along the barrier reef to the southwest and west of Port Moresby which are reached from the capital; dives out of Bootless Inlet, to the southeast of the city; and the Eastern Fields and Porlock Reef, a reef system 90 n. miles (165km) southwest of Port Moresby, out in the Coral Sea.

If you want to know more about the diving around Port Moresby, Neil Whiting has written a fascinating book entitled *Wrecks and Reefs* – published in 1994 – exploring the history of diving in the area with detailed descriptions and maps of the best dive sites.

Opposite: *Tahira Marina, Bootless Inlet. The red dive boat Solatai is in the foreground.*
Above: *Scalloped Hammerhead Sharks, Sphyrna lewini, are regularly seen by divers in PNG.*

Port Moresby

1 BASILISK PASSAGE AND THE FINGER

★★★★★★★

Location: Basilisk Passage.
Access: By boat, 30–40min from Port Moresby.
Conditions: Inside barrier reef is sheltered in most conditions, but outside is difficult in strong Southeast Trades. Early-morning dives preferable when Southeast Trades blowing.
Typical visibility: 30m (100ft) – can be much less
Minimum depth: 5m (16ft)
Maximum depth: 40m (130ft) plus

Basilisk Passage, the main shipping channel through the barrier reef to Port Moresby, is steep-sided and drops away to very deep water, particularly at its southeastern end. When large southeast swells are breaking on the outer reef, the passage may be dived at its northeastern end and near the navigational beacon, an area known as The Fishtrap, but in calm weather the whole passage is accessible. Clarity is best with an incoming tide, and the current can be quite formidable. The passage's eastern side drops away vertically with many cracks, overhangs and swimthroughs. Gorgonians are common. Large schools of fish are here, particularly at the southern end.

Continuing about 1 n. mile (1.85km) past the passage's mouth at the southeast end, you find The Finger – comprising sand and coral outcrops – jutting from the outer reef-wall. This exceptional site captures a

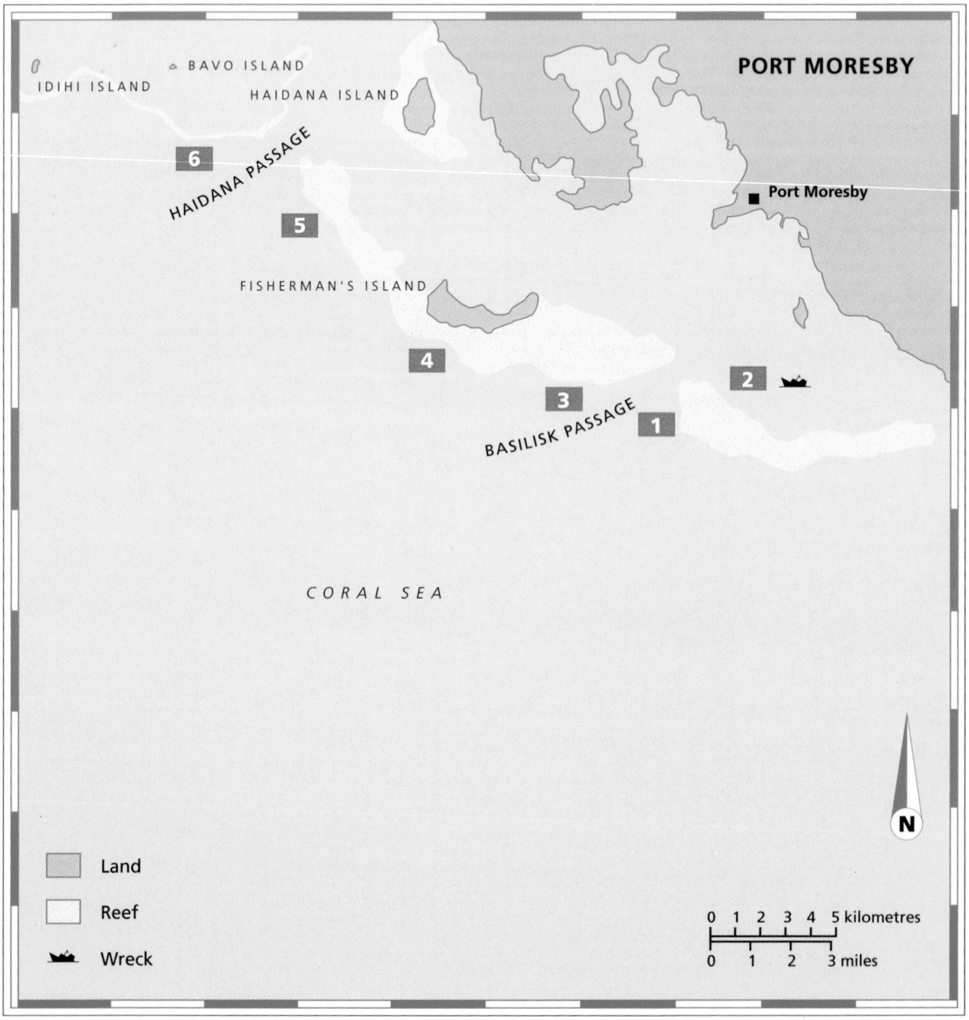

PORT MORESBY
BAVO ISLAND
IDIHI ISLAND
HAIDANA ISLAND
HAIDANA PASSAGE
Port Moresby
FISHERMAN'S ISLAND
BASILISK PASSAGE
1
2
3
4
5
6
CORAL SEA
N
Land
Reef
Wreck
0 1 2 3 4 5 kilometres
0 1 2 3 miles

massive amount of fish-life; large pelagics and sharks are frequent (including resident Hammerheads). A small swimthrough on the eastern side of The Finger is marked by a large derelict mooring-chain and Admiralty anchor. When the current and seas are right, The Finger is the best dive close to Port Moresby – though it can be hard to get to.

In calm conditions the shallows on top of the barrier reef, either side of the passage, afford good snorkelling.

2 NEW MARINE #7

★★★

Location: Inside eastern end of Basilisk Passage.
Access: By boat, 30min from Port Moresby.
Conditions: Sheltered by barrier reef. Slight currents only.
Typical visibility: 20m (65ft)
Minimum depth: 5m (16ft)
Maximum depth: 25m (80ft)

This 30m (100ft) fishing vessel is among the small ships sunk in the Port Moresby area as artificial reefs and dive sites. Its sheltered position was chosen to offer a convenient and interesting dive in conditions when it is difficult to get to the outer passage. Soft corals and sponges have grown and lionfish hunt the many baitfish attracted to the wreck. Shovelnose Sharks (*Rhinobatos* spp) are sometimes seen resting on the surrounding sand, and there is a resident Wobbegong Shark. The wreck is near the reef-slope, which you can ascend at the end of the dive to see the shallow reef.

A second vessel, the *MV Kukipi*, has more recently been sunk very close by, facing the opposite way. It has seen very rapid coral growth, and the fish-life is prolific.

3 OWEN STANLEYS

★★★★

Location: Outer reef, 3 n. miles (5.6km) west of Basilisk Passage.
Access: By boat, 40min from Port Moresby.
Conditions: Exposed in Southeast Trades. Requires calm seas.
Typical visibility: 25m (80ft)
Minimum depth: 5m (16ft)
Maximum depth: 40m (130ft) plus

This section of the outer reef – not far from Fisherman's Island (Site 4) – has an unusual seascape comprising deep valleys and rolling coral hills leading down to a square-edged dropoff at 40m (130ft); this then plunges vertically to the depths of the Coral Sea. Schools of fish and large pelagic species, along with sharks, are often met at the edge of the dropoff. The shallows abound with all kinds of marine life. This spectacular site can, if conditions are right, be dived either from an anchored boat or by drifting along the reef in the slight currents that sometimes occur.

GUBAS

The weather in Port Moresby can be frustrating for divers. The biggest challenge comes during the Northwest, rainy season from January until March. The day can start out calm and inviting, but then change with sudden ferocity when a Guba strikes.

A Guba is a rain-squall blowing from the northwest. It can occur at any time of day or night, and can last for several hours, causing seas to build rapidly. Wise divers always keep an eye on the western horizon for any low dark clouds, and make sure their boats are anchored securely, with a boat-handler aboard. Of course, these problems are soon forgotten on thoses perfect calm sunny days, when Port Moresby shows that it has probably the finest diving of any capital city in the world.

LIONFISH

Lionfish are among the most dramatic of the fishes found in PNG. They are scorpionfishes, and pack a powerful sting in their dorsal spines. Divers in PNG should be able to recognize five species. The largest and most common is *Pterois volitans*, easily distinguished by the separate plumes formed by the pectoral fins. The pectoral fins of *P. antennata* end in long white filaments. The three smaller species of lionfish are *Dendrochirus zebra*, which has continuously webbed pectoral fins, *D. brachypterus*, with continuously webbed pectoral fins again, but this time distinctly banded, and *D. biocellatus*, which has two or three very obvious eye-spots on the soft part of the dorsal fin behind the spines.

4 FISHERMAN'S ISLAND (DAUGO ISLAND)

★★★★★★★

Location: On outer barrier reef west of Fisherman's Island.
Access: By boat, 45min from Port Moresby.
Conditions: Difficult in strong Southeast Trades, though slightly protected. Early-morning dives preferable in Southeast season.
Typical visibility: 30m (100ft), but highly variable
Minimum depth: 5m (16ft)
Maximum depth: 40m (130ft) plus

Three different sites are usually dived here. Three Crack Bommie features a picturesque entry through one of three cracks in the reeftop to a depth of 15m (50ft), then on to the face of an overhanging wall covered with pink soft corals. At 27m (90ft) are two deep coral pinnacles and the start of the deep dropoff. The Twin Peaks starts on a steep coral-covered wall that merges into a large sand basin, where three spectacular coral pinnacles rise almost to the surface. Turtles are common on both sites; pelagics and sharks, including the beautiful Leopard Shark (*Stegostoma fasciatum*) are always present, and rays are frequent. At the third site, The Sandy Patch, a steep wall leads to a white sandy plateau and an area of caverns and swimthroughs, home to Tawny Nurse Sharks (*Nebrius ferrugineus*) and Stingrays. When visibility is good this is an excellent area to dive.

In calm conditions there is very good snorkelling on the reeftop.

5 LAGAMARA

★★★★★★

Location: Eastern side of Haidana Passage.
Access: By boat, about 1hr from Port Moresby.
Conditions: Partly sheltered.
Typical visibility: 20m (65ft), sometimes reduced
Minimum depth: 5m (16ft)
Maximum depth: 40m (130ft) plus

The reef-wall has a maze of cracks and caverns full of interesting creatures: lobsters and shrimp, nudibranchs and shells, weird worms and small fish hide among the coral-encrusted walls and overhangs. Explore the many swimthroughs and isolated coral towers. If you want some big-fish excitement, Eagle Rays and Grey Reef and Silvertip Sharks patrol a deeper dropoff into the passage. There are great opportunities for macro photography, and the shallow reef has good snorkelling.

BOTTLE DIVES

Although PNG does not have a long history of European trade, there are areas near main wharves throughout the country that were used in early years as rubbish dumps. The degradable rubbish soon disappeared; the only remains now are the glass and ceramic containers of the time. These are of course buried under layers of silt or sand, but patient divers are still finding beautiful artefacts, like torpedo-shaped glass-stoppered bottles and ceramic beer bottles.

Port Moresby has a couple of excellent sites in the harbour, but visibility is poor and the bottles are mingled with apparently live artillery shells from the war. Samarai Island (in Milne Bay) has masses of bottles in clear water buried beneath hundreds of modern beer bottles thrown from the wharf.

6 BAVA 98

★★★

Location: Outside reef past Bavo Island, 12 n. miles (22km) west of Port Moresby.
Access: By boat, 50min from Port Moresby.
Conditions: Calm weather and clear water required.
Typical visibility: 20m (65ft), often reduced
Minimum depth: 5m (16ft)
Maximum depth: 40m (130ft) plus

This outer wall has a healthy population of sharks of several different species: Silvertips, Grey Reefs, Whitetip Reefs, Blacktip Reefs and Bronze Whalers. The dive is not suitable for novices, particularly if clarity is below par, although visibility is sometimes better deeper down. Simply descend the wall to about 30m (100ft) and see what turns up.

Bluefaced Angelfish, Pomacanthus xanthometopon.

Bootless Inlet

PNG still has no official National Marine Parks, even though it has some of the finest reefs and richest marine life in the world. I look forward to a time when the reefs and islands in the Bootless Inlet and other areas are officially protected. As Port Moresby itself becomes more and more industrialized, Bootless Inlet could become the key to recreation on the sea near the capital.

There are three islands close to Bootless Inlet. One, known as Lion Island because of its distinctive shape and colour during the dry season, is uninhabited but makes an ideal picnic spot and can be dived in all weather conditions (Site 1). Nearby Loloata Island Resort has a Boston A20 Havoc aircraft wreck from World War II in 18m (60ft) on its fringing reef (Site 2). The third island, Motupore, is the site of a marine research station for the University of Papua New Guinea.

The best dive sites on the barrier reef out of Bootless Bay all have tidal currents, so require caution, but the bonus is that the currents bring a bountiful supply of food to the reefs, which thus support large populations of fish.

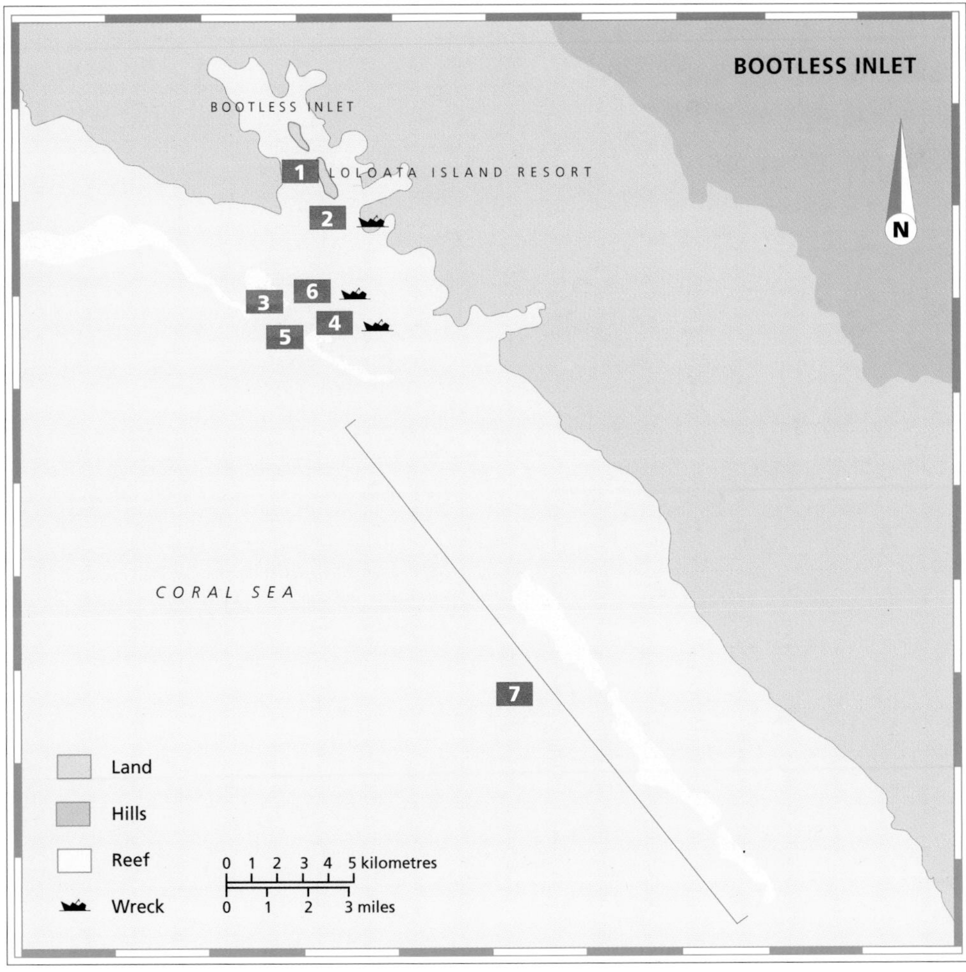

1 LION ISLAND

★★★★★★

Location: Lion Island, Bootless Inlet.
Access: By boat, 15min from Tahira Marina.
Conditions: Sheltered all year.
Typical visibility: 15m (50ft), often less
Minimum depth: as shallow as you like
Maximum depth: 25m (80ft)

Lion Island is always sheltered, no matter what the weather. Several dives are possible. On the south side is a reef with black corals, gorgonians and the wreck of a small tugboat, with growths of soft corals. A wall to 20m (65ft) runs along the eastern side, and a large fishing trawler has been sunk about halfway along. At the northern end is a sandy slope with sea-grasses, reef patches and the wrecks of a coastal trading barge and a small yacht. Many interesting shells can be found (particularly on night-dives) on the sand slope, which changes to silt deeper down. There is a fascinating array of unusual marine creatures, including ghost pipefish, Flying Gurnards, Dwarf Lionfish and crocodilefish. Great macro photography is possible.

The island's fringing reef offers sheltered and interesting snorkelling.

2 BOSTON HAVOC A20 AIRCRAFT

★★

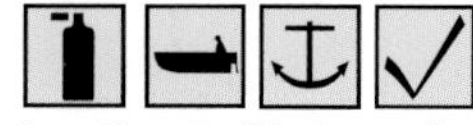

Location: On fringing reef south of Loloata Island.
Access: By boat, 5min from Loloata Island Resort, 20min from Tahira Marina.
Conditions: Calm weather (any season) essential.
Typical visibility: 12m (40ft)
Minimum depth: 12m (40ft)
Maximum depth: 18m (60ft)

A shallow reef with several Giant Clams and surprisingly good coral growth surrounds this wreck, which sank into a silty hole in the reef. The aircraft is in good condition, with only the nose gunner's section broken off; this section, 20m (65ft) or so directly behind the rest, was the first part seen when Dik Knight, who operates the Loloata Island Resort, discovered the wreck. The cockpit cover can be opened, and all the controls are in place. The lack of current has prevented much growth, and the water is usually dirty (a challenge for photographers), but this is a notably fine example of a World War II aircraft wreck.

The surrounding reef is good for snorkelling.

Opposite: *An incredible array of sea fans and whips decorated with featherstars.*

GHOST PIPEFISH

These fabulous little fish can make themselves invisible (hence 'ghost') by adjusting their colours and body appendages to suit their habitats. Many live in crinoids, whose feathery arms they mimic, and can be black, red, yellow or whatever the crinoid colour is. Others live in black corals, soft corals, sea-grasses or algae, and imitate them – even to the extent of turning from green to brown for dead sea-grass, or to white for dead Halimeda algae. Males are about 5cm (2in) long, and females about twice that size with a pouch to carry their developing eggs. Ghost pipefish typically occur in pairs, though I have seen groups of up to a dozen; they swim vertically with their heads down. Two species are regularly seen in PNG: *Solenostomus paradoxus* and *S. cyanopterus*. However, a rarer 'hairy' variety is sometimes encountered, and I recently collected a specimen to confirm its identification. It turns out that it is indeed a new species, not just an exotic variety.

3 BIG DROP, SUNKEN BARRIER

★★★★

Location: Eastern end of Sunken Barrier, 4 n. miles (7.4km) south of Bootless Inlet.
Access: By boat, 35min from Tahira Marina; anchor in rubble at reef's southeast corner so divers can proceed south and over vertical dropoff.
Conditions: Exposed to southeast swells, requires calm weather. Often currents. Best with calm seas and slight incoming tide.
Typical visibility: 25m (80ft)
Minimum depth: 8m (26ft)
Maximum depth: 40m (130ft) plus

The dropoff here (unlike the case for most of the outer barrier reef) does not reach a sandy slope, but at 35m (115ft) actually undercuts and drops vertically out of sight. Gorgonians grow from the wall at 40m (130ft), and among the large fish often seen are Spanish Mackerel, Hammerhead and Silvertip Sharks and Manta Rays. There are healthy growths of coral all down the wall and on the reeftop. Schools of fish congregate at the reef-edge. This exciting dive is a great introduction to wall-diving if you haven't tried it before.

4 PAI II

★★★★★★★★

Location: Horseshoe Reef, 5 n. miles (9.3km) south of Bootless Inlet.
Access: By boat, 40min from Tahira Marina.
Conditions: Partly sheltered but not possible in strong Southeast Trades and Gubas.
Typical visibility: 25m (80ft)

Minimum depth: 3m (10ft)
Maximum depth: 30m (100ft)
Horseshoe Reef, a part of the outer barrier reef, has a wide deep passage on its west side. The reef's lagoon side, within the passage, is sheltered from the large southeast swells common in the Coral Sea, and makes a dive site accessible most of the year in all but extreme conditions. The fishing trawler *Pai II* was sunk upright on the reef-slope with its keel in 30m (100ft) and the masts reaching up to 10m (33ft). There used to be fish-feeding in the area, so many of the fish – including 'Gobbler', a large Malabar Grouper (*Epinephelus malabaricus*) – will approach you closely. Soft corals grow on the wreck, and the surrounding reef is very healthy and has abundant fish-life. Lacy Scorpionfish are often found in the shallows, and many other interesting creatures have been seen following the passage from very deep water into the lagoon. Large visitors include Whale Sharks, Orca, Hammerheads and Manta Rays. This is among the most pristine local dives.

There is excellent and varied snorkelling along the edge of the reef, over pretty coral gardens.

5 THE END BOMMIE

★★★★★★★★★

Location: Horseshoe Reef, 5 n. miles (9.3km) south of Bootless Inlet.
Access: By boat, 40min from Tahira Marina; anchor in shallow water at western end of Horseshoe Reef.
Conditions: Sheltered in all but extreme Southeast Trades and Gubas.
Typical visibility: 30m (100ft), often less
Minimum depth: 3m (10ft)
Maximum depth: 40m (130ft)
You swim west from the boat, either down the dropoff on the lagoon side or along the reef-slope on the south side, until you reach a saddle. Cross the saddle, which often has a current flowing through it, until you come to a large bommie rising from deep water to 9m (30ft). As you circumnavigate this you see many colourful sea fans and other gorgonians festooned with crinoids, plus schools of fusiliers and feeding sea perch. Sharks and pelagics are common. The area is bursting with life: there is always plenty to enjoy. Juvenile Whitetip Reef Sharks are often found under plate corals on the reeftop, and there is a resident Lacy Scorpionfish. Hammerheads, Whale Sharks and Manta Rays have been encountered. Greatest numbers of fish are seen when the current is running out of the lagoon. A large colonial anemone, with hosts of anemonefish, is on the main reef just before the saddle. This is an excellent night-dive, too: you might see sleeping turtles.

There is good snorkelling in sheltered water around the boat. More adventurous snorkellers can try the reeftop when there are southeast swells running and breaking there.

Tassled Wobbegong, Eucrossorhinus dasypogon, are found in southern PNG.

6 PACIFIC GAS

★★★★

Location: 1km (1100yd) north of Horseshoe Reef.
Access: By boat, 35min from Tahira Marina.
Conditions: Sheltered except in strong Southeast Trades and Gubas.
Typical visibility:: 25m (80ft)
Minimum depth: 14m (45ft)
Maximum depth: 43m (140ft)

This is the largest of a series of boats sunk as artificial reefs in the waters near the capital. The vessel's two huge gas tanks were removed; it was cleaned and then anchored on site. Explosive charges were used to blow small holes in its bottom. It sank in an upright position in only 9min, with the bow at 14m (45ft) and the propeller in 43m (140ft). The wreck was placed close to very deep water, with partial shelter from Horseshoe Reef but where tidal currents would run over it. The results of this care are obvious: the wreck is covered with luxuriant growths of soft corals and a multitude of fish make it their home. The bridge – at 25m (80ft) – crew-quarters and engine-room can all be easily penetrated. A Queensland Grouper often guards the propeller, at the deepest part of the wreck. A wonderful site for both experienced and first-time wreck-divers.

7 BARRIER REEF, BOOTLESS INLET TO ROUND POINT

★★★★★★★★

Location: Barrier reef from Horseshoe Reef southeast to Round Point.
Access: 1–3hr cruising (depending on site) in *Solatai* from Tahira Marina.
Conditions: Not accessible in strong Southeast Trades or Gubas, but most sites are calm in early morning. Sometimes strong currents at best sites.
Typical visibility: 30m (100ft), often less
Minimum depth: 1m (40in)
Maximum depth: 40m (130ft) plus

The several sites along the barrier coincide with passes through the reef where water from the Coral Sea flows in and out of the lagoon. The sites are always at their clearest when the current flows in from the south, although an outgoing tide sometimes produces more fish-life. One pass – **The Pumpkin Patch** – has scattered coral bommies, prolific fish-life and a unique field of soft corals growing from a sand patch at 30m (100ft). Another, **The Pinnacles**, is a series of coral peaks, covered with sea fans and abounding with fish, rising in a deep pass to under 7m (23ft). **PJ Passage** starts at an outer wall and is often the site of exciting pelagic encounters. **Sandy Passage** may be drift-dived and is the home of several Eagle Rays.

All the reef passes have excellent hard-coral growths, large numbers of reef fish (including schools of Goldman's Sweetlips and barracuda), and soft corals and gorgonians growing deeper in the passages. These sites are not often visited because of the distances involved and the necessity of good weather, but are world-class when the conditions are good. Big animals, including Killer Whales, Manta Rays and Hammerhead Sharks, are regularly encountered.

Current permitting, there is excellent snorkelling on top of the barrier reef.

The most elusive lionfish species in PNG is the Ocellated Lionfish, Dendrochirus biocellatos.

Eastern Fields

Ninety nautical miles (170km) southwest of Port Moresby in the Coral Sea is a magnificent reef complex comprising Eastern Fields and Porlock Reef – a true Coral Sea reef system surrounded by deep water. The Australian Coral Sea reefs are often devastated by cyclones, but Eastern Fields is too far north to suffer the storm effects. This is an absolutely stunning, pristine diving area, abounding with fish and beautiful coral formations, and typically blessed with water of exceptional visibility. A marvellous live-aboard cruiser, the elegant *Golden Dawn* captained by Craig De Wit, runs seasonal cruises from Port Moresby. The *Golden Dawn* also runs cruises along the Papuan coast to Mailu Island where the 14,000 ton logging ship, the *Maritime Hibiscus,* lies with its stern at 46m (155ft) and its mast tips at 10m (33ft). Sunk in 1991 after hitting a nearby reef, the ship still carries a cargo of hardwood logs.

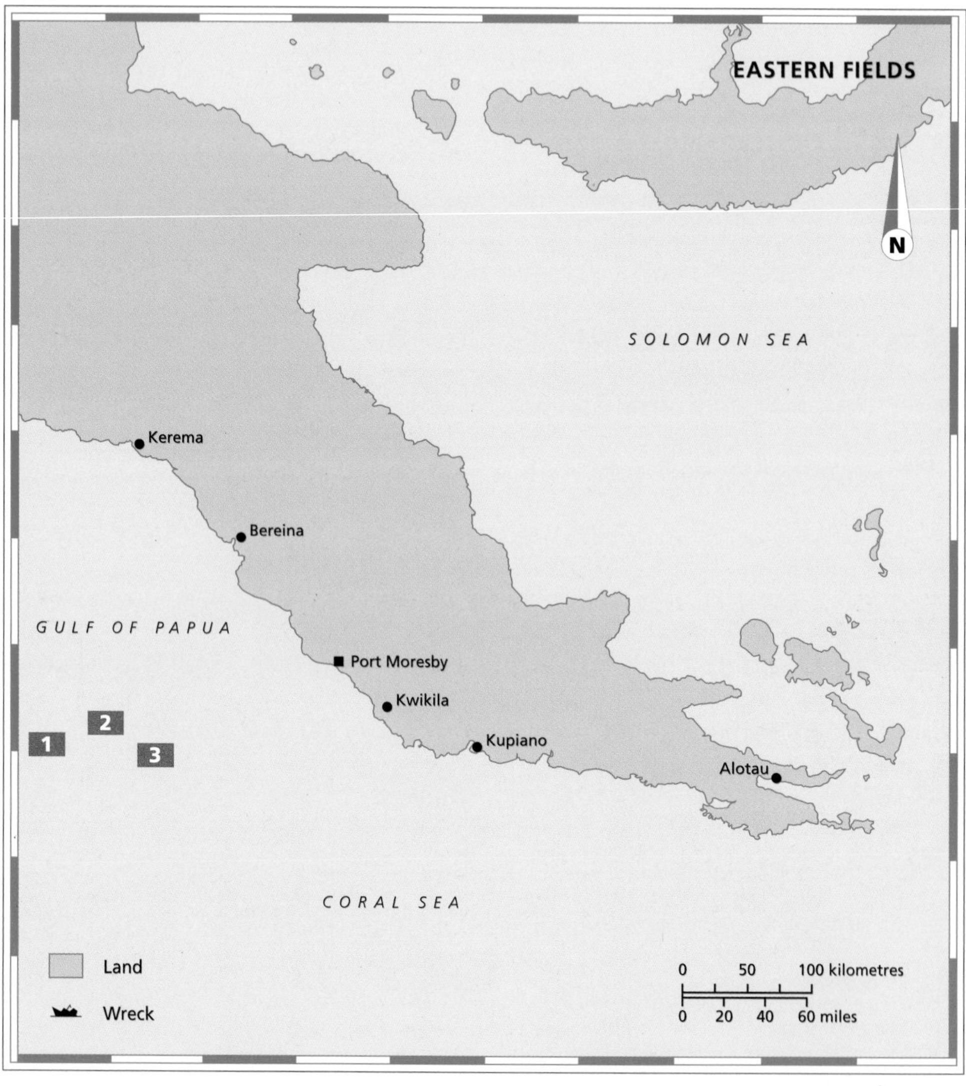

1 JAY'S REEF

★★★★★

Location: Porlock Reef. Precise location withheld because of shark-finners.
Access: By *Golden Dawn*, 15hr from Port Moresby.
Conditions: Sheltered in most conditions; slight current.
Typical visibility: 60m (200ft)
Minimum depth: 3m (10ft)
Maximum depth: 50m (165ft) plus

A spur of reef at 20m (65ft) on the outer dropoff is the site for a tremendous shark-feeding station. Over 20 Silvertips and an equal number of Grey Reefs come to baits placed on a bommie that rises conveniently from the spur; a large Moray Eel joins in. You can position yourself slightly below the sharks, making conditions ideal for photography – particularly as the water is usually incredibly clear. Afterwards you ascend the reef-wall to a saddle where the boat is anchored.

2 CRAIG'S ULTIMATE

★★★★★★★★

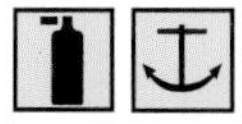

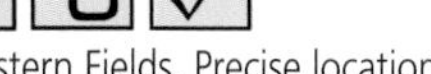

Location: Eastern Fields. Precise location withheld because of shark-finners.
Access: By *Golden Dawn*, 10hr from Port Moresby.
Conditions: Sheltered; slight current usual.
Typical visibility: 60m (200ft)
Minimum depth: 5m (16ft)
Maximum depth: 50m (165ft) plus

A drift-dive on a smaller reef on the western side of Eastern Fields, with a dramatic wall on its eastern side. You pass caverns, cracks and overhangs decorated with soft corals – one formation, where light streams through a hole, has a cathedral effect. Fish-life gradually increases until, back near the anchored boat, you discover a mass of fish feeding in the current. Small groups of Scalloped Hammerhead Sharks (*Sphyrna lewini*) swim past and pairs of the much rarer and fantastic Great Hammerhead (*Sphyrna mokarran*) are regularly encountered.

The reeftop is suitable for snorkelling, with shark sightings likely.

3 CARL'S ULTIMATE

★★★★★★★★

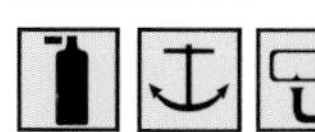

Location: Eastern Fields.
Access: By *Golden Dawn*, 10hr from Port Moresby.
Conditions: Sheltered, but with tidal current.
Typical visibility: 60m (200ft)
Minimum depth: 5m (16ft)
Maximum depth: 50m (165ft) plus

A sausage-shaped reef just inside the lagoon entrance at a reef pass. At the lagoon end of the reef, where the boat anchors, is a small rubble patch, but the rest of the reef is completely carpeted with an unbelievable display of soft and hard corals, sea fans, whips and sponges. You descend to about 27m (90ft) on a reef-spur that points into the incoming tide, where you can watch an incredible congregation of marine animals in fabulously clear water: sharks, turtles, huge schools of trevally, barracuda and reef fish, Dogtooth Tuna and a rare family of Potato Cod (*Epinephelus tukula*). You then slowly ascend the spur and drift along the reeftop back to the boat. When the current is going out there is the added excitement that Silvertip Sharks appear.

Among the world's great dives, this was named for Carl Roessler, who declared it the richest reef he had seen. You can snorkel on the reeftop at slack tide.

Shoaling Bigeye trevally, Caranx sexfasciatus.

ANCHORING AT DIVE SITES

All divers and diveboat operators are very concerned about anchor damage to reefs. Putting down moorings is, unfortunately, not the complete answer to this problem. In certain circumstances moorings may actually cause worse damage to the reefs than careful and consistent anchoring.

Disadvantages of Moorings

Fishing is a vital part of the lifestyle of coastal villagers in Papua New Guinea, and the villagers' traditional fishing rights to the reefs near them are protected by law. It is vital that all diveboats visiting an area both respect the fishing rights of villagers and at the same time make it clear to village people that sport divers are not involved in the removal of any living creatures from the reef.

One of the many ways villagers fish involves paddling out to the reef in canoes laden with a cargo of small rocks, each about the size of a child's fist. A palm leaf is tied around the rock, and the baited hook of the fishing line is pushed through the loose end of the palm leaf 50cm (20in) or so from the rock. The rock is then lowered over the side taking the baited line with it. When the rock hits the bottom the line is given a jerk, so that the hook is freed from the palm frond, the length of the frond ensuring that the hook is left hanging clear of the coral and doesn't snag. In the course of a night's fishing a single canoe may drop a hundred or so rocks around the reef. If you place a mooring on the reef, this becomes a favourite spot for the fishermen to tie up their canoes and fish from, so the reef around it soon becomes littered with rocks, and the coral gets badly damaged.

Operators have tried to solve this problem by placing the moorings underwater, so that tying up necessitates the use of a diver and in many instances the ploy has been successful. However, manoeuvring a large boat with a diver in the water is a hazardous exercise. Moreover, the rope and chain used for underwater moorings are prized by villagers.

Moorings are nevertheless used on certain dive sites in Papua New Guinea, particularly those not close to villages, but they require constant attention and monitoring.

Selecting Anchorages

Happily, reefs damaged by Crown-of-Thorns starfish or anchors, for instance, will recover in a surprisingly short length of time if left alone. Thus a usual method used by diveboats is to anchor close to the best dive site on an area on the reef that is naturally less 'alive' than the rest.

In the site descriptions given in this book the anchoring positions for the various sites are given, but local operators must be contacted to ensure the correct anchorages are used and the valuable coral the operator has been protecting is not damaged.

'Live' Boats and Other Approaches

On some reefs the coral growth is so prolific that it is nowhere possible to anchor without doing some damage so diving is arranged with a 'live' boat. This necessitates a competent and safety-conscious boat captain, or minced diver may be the result. Further situations requiring a 'live' boat are where the reef along a dropoff is too shallow to anchor, or where a drift-dive is planned. Whenever a 'live' boat is used divers should depart and approach the boat on the surface, so the captain can see them clearly and manoeuvre appropriately.

Because of the steep slopes characteristic of many anchorages, another technique used is to lower the anchor down the slope, then swing the boat around and tie the stern to a tree ashore. Permission to do this should always be sought from the local villagers – it is usually cheerfully granted.

When diving is not taking place live-aboard boats typically use sheltered anchorages in bays close to shore. In Papua New Guinea this generally means they are anchoring in a mud or sand bottom, so there is no possibility of doing any damage, however much the boat might swing about.

Anchoring correctly - in the sand.

Port Moresby

How to Get There

Various air services come to Port Moresby from overseas. Air Niugini in conjunction with Philippine Airlines runs two flights weekly from Hong Kong via Manila (flight-time 6½hr). In conjunction with Singapore Airlines, Air Niugini has two flights per week from Singapore (flight-time 6hr 25min). Air Niugini in conjunction with Qantas runs six flights per week from Sydney, Australia, via Brisbane (flight-time 4½hr), and nine flights per week from Cairns, Australia (flight-time 1hr 25min). Domestic services are run by Air Niugini and by Milne Bay Air.

Air Niugini
PO Box 7186, Boroko
tel 675 325 9000
tel 675 327 3444 (bookings)
fax 675 327 3482/327 3550

Milne Bay Air
PO Box 170, Boroko
tel 675 325 0555
fax 675 325 2219

Where to Stay

Loloata Island Resort
PO Box 5290, Boroko
tel 675 3258590/3251369
fax 675 3258933
The ideal location for visitors wishing to dive the Port Moresby area. Just a 15min drive and 10min boat ride from Jackson's International Airport, Loloata avoids the city and all its problems. This long narrow island has a high ridge running down its 1.5km (1-mile) length; the resort is tucked away at the northern end, near a sandy beach. Most of the island is thus in its natural state, ideal for walks – which present beautiful views of the surrounding reefs and islands and the Owen Stanley Mountains. The island itself is surrounded by fringing reefs, and the sheltered waters make an ideal site for snorkelling and other water sports such as windsurfing. Diving and fishing trips are offered to the outer barrier reef only 6km (4 miles) away. The resort has 20 rooms, including several new units built right over the water's edge. It provides free airport transfers for guests and, in conjunction with the Dive Centre (see below), provides day trips or single-dive trips for up to 20 divers. Diving and snorkelling gear available for hire; instruction can be arranged. The manager, Dik Knight, is a very experienced diver, a gracious host and longtime resident of PNG.

Alternatives
If you plan more than a single night in Port Moresby, the Loloata Island Resort is the place. However, for an overnight stay before connecting with other centres or a live-aboard diveboat, there are several hotels of international standard.

For the convenience of being at the airport the **Gateway Hotel** (tel 325 3855/fax 325 4585) is a popular and comfortable choice. The **Airways Motel** (tel 325 7033/fax 325 0759), nearby, has excellent lounging and swimming facilities and more modest accommodation.

In downtown Port Moresby, with fine views of the town and barrier reef, the **Port Moresby Travelodge** (tel 321 2266/fax 321 7534) provides the city's most luxurious accommodation – although, being on a hill, it has been known to suffer from the town's periodic failure of water supply.

Also offering a high standard of service, and with an attractive pool area, is the **Islander Travelodge** (tel 325 5955/fax 321 3835), near the Government and University buildings at Waigani.

The **Ela Beach Hotel** (tel 321 2100/fax 321 2434), right on Ela Beach, is particularly convenient for divers in that the Dive Centre (see below) operates its dive shop from the hotel lobby. Although attractively sited, the hotel itself is not very glamorous – but it does boast a swimming pool.

For budget accommodation you cannot beat the **Amber's Inn** (tel 325 5091/fax 325 9565), a spotless and pleasant guesthouse in Boroko.

Where to Eat

There are several very good restaurants in Port Moresby, though unfortunately you always have to worry about security when venturing out of your hotel at night. With local knowledge or guidance advised, the following are among the most popular establishments, and provide their own security guards:

Daikoku Japanese Restaurant
Taurama Supermarket Building
Hubert Murray Highway
tel 325 3857
Excellent Japanese fare cooked at your table in pleasant surroundings.

Seoul House
5-mile, Hubert Murray Highway
tel 325 2231
Excellent Korean food. Private rooms available. Good drive-in security.

The Galley Restaurant
Aviat Club
Aviat Street
Konedobu
tel 321 2167
Very good mixed menu. Good service.

The Kwantung Village
Boio St
East Boroko
tel 325 8997
From the outside – and for that matter the inside – you might never expect it, but this restaurant serves very good Chinese food!

Dive Facilities

The Dive Centre
PO Box 1488, Port Moresby
tel 675 3201200
fax 675 3201257
Run by PADI instructor and longtime PNG resident John Miller. Based at the Ela Beach Hotel, a retail dive store stocks and services diving gear by Scubapro, US Divers, Sherwood, Tusa, Suunto, SeaQuest and other brands. Instruction is available from one-day 'Discover Diving' courses to Open Water Certification and other courses up to DiveMaster. Scuba-gear servicing is available, as are air-fills and day- and night-dive trips on two diveboats. The *Stinger*, a fast outboard-powered boat with a sunshade, can handle up to eight divers and operates out of Port Moresby. The *Solatai* is an 11m (36ft) diesel-powered diveboat, which provides day trips out of Bootless Inlet to the southeast of Port Moresby. *Solatai* is fitted with a compressor and can handle 16–20 divers for multiple dives. Both vessels have safety equipment, including oxygen. The *Solatai* also runs dive trips for Loloata Island Resort (see above) when required.

Dive-Co
PO Box 1786, Port Moresby
tel 675 325 4466
fax 675 325 4418
Specializes in organizing helicopter transport to some of the most remote areas in PNG, and can combine visits to remote villages with scuba diving and snorkelling on reefs accessible only by helicopter. Accommodation is provided in coastal villages and plantation houses. Although the company is based in Port Moresby, the diving expeditions are typically to New Ireland Province.

Port Moresby Sub Aqua Club
PO Box 6362, Boroko
(tel/fax depends on current officers)
This active club has its own boat and runs regular weekend boat dives for its members out of Port Moresby to the best local sites.

Live Aboard

MV Golden Dawn/Dolphin Enterprises
PO Box 1335, Port Moresby
tel 675 325 6500
fax 675 325 0302
The elegant and spacious 25m (80ft) *Golden Dawn* operates from Port Moresby to the best sites along the Papuan Barrier Reef and out into the PNG Coral Sea to Eastern Fields and Porlock Reef – some of the best diving in the world. The captain, Craig de Wit, has pioneered diving at Eastern Fields and

knows more than anyone about the incredible dive sites there; the cruise to it comprises a short overnight crossing of the 90 n. miles (165km) of open sea which *Golden Dawn*, fitted with stabilizers, handles comfortably. During the part of the year when the weather is less suitable for expeditions to the Coral Sea, *Golden Dawn* operates as a mother ship for river barramundi and bass fishing expeditions and also makes occasional cruises along the Papuan Coast to dive the wreck of the *Maritime Hibiscus* (see page 82). She accommodates up to 10 passengers in twin cabins, plus eight crew.

Specialist Travel Agents

South Pacific Tours
PO Box 195, Boroko
tel 675 321 3500
fax 675 321 3136
Owen Coney has worked for many years – first in Sydney and now with his own business, South Pacific Tours, in Port Moresby – to promote PNG diving. His knowledge of the nation's diving opportunities is excellent, and he also has very close working relationships with Air Niugini and other airlines.

Local Highlights

The **Varirata National Park**, situated in the mountains behind Port Moresby, is a 42km (26-mile) drive along a narrow but scenic route. The park, at an elevation of about 600m (2000ft), is pleasantly cool after the tropical heat of Port Moresby, visible as you look down from the steep cliffs along the park's southern boundary. There are many walking trails through the park's grassland and rainforest areas, and there is the opportunity to hear and possibly see the Raggiana Bird of Paradise. For security reasons you are advised not to travel to the park without a guide. Information can be obtained from the Park Ranger on tel 675 325 9340.

Just out of Port Moresby, on the way to the park, an interesting stop can be made at **Moitaka Wildlife**, where for a few Kina entrance fee you can see a crocodile farm, with some very large crocodiles, and other wildlife.

PNG is justly famous for its visual arts, and many visitors wish to return home with examples of the fantastic wood carvings and other artworks. However, there are few carvers in the main areas you are likely to go to, unless you also take a cultural tour. The Sepik River is one of the principal carving areas, the Trobriand Islands another – although most of the best carvings from the Trobriand area are exported and not available in the islands themselves. Carvings are often available at the hotels, particularly at Madang and Wewak, and the beautiful Tami bowls are available in the Tami Islands. Fortunately there is in Port Moresby an excellent warehouse of PNG artefacts, with a huge selection and fair prices. This is PNG Arts, run by Joe Chan, who seeks out the best examples of the different art forms. His is a very efficient business, and he can pack and freight artefacts to anywhere in the world. PNG Arts is open 7 days a week:

PNG Arts
Spring Garden Road
PO Box 9264, Hohola
tel 675 325 3976
fax 675 325 7803

The Golden Dawn and the Tiata meet to exchange diving stories.

TUFI

Cruising northwest along the coast of the mainland from the flat peninsula of Cape Vogel, it is something of a shock to see Tufi loom ahead. Mount Victory, at about 2000m (6600ft), and Mount Trafalgar, only slightly smaller, are perched right at the coast. Over 30 fiords, up to 8km (5 miles) long, cut into the base of the mountain; they provide calm refuge for ships and excellent anchorages, though boats must steam right up into the fiords to find shallow-enough water.

Tufi was a US PT boat base during World War II, and the wrecks of two PT boats are right at the wharf; since they are in 50m (165ft) of water and the timber hulls have been largely eaten away, they are seldom dived. However, Tufi is an ideal base for diving some excellent reefs just a few minutes offshore. Only a few have been accurately charted, though some are conveniently marked with navigation lights. Many remain to be explored and, judging by the standard of those so far dived, this will be a very exciting adventure.

Most of the diving is to the east and southeast of Tufi although other reefs exist further to the north and the incredible wreck of the *S'Jacob* (Site 6), usually dived by means of the live-aboard *Barbarian II* out of Lae, is just a few hours away to the northwest. This does make the diving somewhat dependent on the weather although, because of the mountains, land breezes tend, even in the middle of the Southeast season, to produce calm weather in the mornings. During the late Southeast season there is a run of Spanish Mackerel through the reefs.

The Southeast Trades blow about May/Nov, and this is Tufi's dry and cooler season, with water temperatures going as low as 26°C (78°F). Good diving is still available in the wet season, Jan/Mar, with water at a very pleasant 28°C (82°F). Wet-season runoff, as elsewhere, makes the surface waters dirty, but there is usually clear water and good visibility just a few metres down.

Tufi is a very small centre with only a few hundred residents. However, there is a government station, some village guest houses and also a hotel which has recently been renovated into the 'Tufi Dive Resort' by diving instructor Ken Weaving.

Opposite: *Coastal views in the Tufi region are some of the most attractive in PNG.*

Above: *The Hawkfish Anthias, Serranocirrhitus latus, is found in the southern provinces of PNG.*

1 STEWART REEF

★★★★★★★

Location: 5 n. miles (9.3km) southeast of Tufi.
Access: By boat, 20min from Tufi. Reef bears a red navigation light, so is also convenient for night-diving.
Conditions: Exposed to strong Southeast Trades, but often accessible in early morning. Best when slight current from east (usually is).
Typical visibility: 40m (130ft)
Minimum depth: 6m (20ft)
Maximum depth: 30m (100ft) plus

A wall runs along the reef's east side, and a slope on its west side. Schools of fish mill around the front of the wall. There are soft corals, sea fans and whips and excellent hard-coral growths. At night the reef is alive with Epaulette Sharks (*Hemiscyllium* sp.), Decorator Crabs (*Dromidiopsi edwardsi*), octopus and Morays.

Although snorkelling is good on this and nearby reefs, sharks can come up from deep water, so this is recommended only for experienced snorkellers.

2 PAUL'S REEF

★★★★

Location: 300m (330yd) north of Stewart Reef.
Access: 20min by fast boat from Tufi.
Conditions: Exposed to strong Southeast Trades, but usually accessible in early morning.
Typical visibility: 40m (130ft)
Minimum depth: 6m (20ft)
Maximum depth: 35m (115ft)

A small patch reef loaded with marine life, especially when a slight current is running. You don't need to dive deep, as the saddle, which goes to 18m (60ft), is the best spot, with sharks, turtles, barracuda and Spanish Mackerel common. Moray Eels and Spiny Lobsters are found on the reeftop, where staghorn-coral growths are prolific. There are soft corals and fans on the reef-wall and -slopes.

3 TONY'S BOMMIE

★★★★

Location: 8 n. miles (15km) southeast of Tufi.
Access: 25min by speedboat from Tufi.
Conditions: Exposed in strong Southeast Trades, but often accessible in early morning.
Typical visibility: 40m (130ft)
Minimum depth: 5m (16ft)
Maximum depth: 40m (130ft) plus

You can make several dives on this reef, which is covered with good coral growth and has excellent fish-life. The best, suitable for more experienced divers, is to a saddle in the reef at 40m (130ft): a large school of

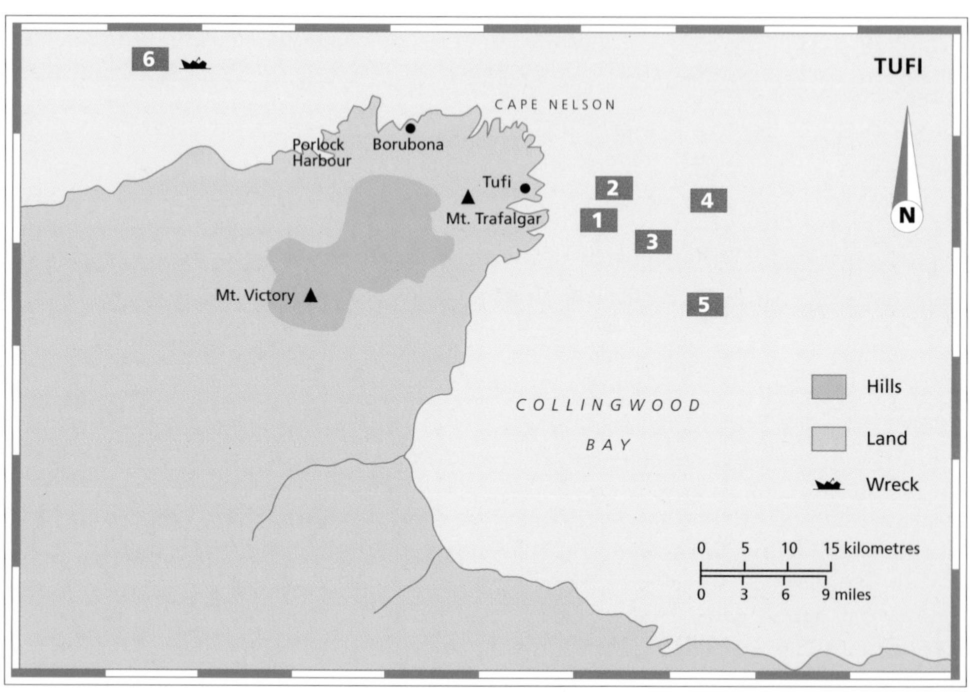

barracuda circles above while sharks and pelagics swim through the saddle, and there is a huge colony of garden eels in the sand nearby. A special feature is the regular appearance of Manta Rays and Giant Groupers. There is always something happening on this dive.

4 CYCLONE REEF

★★★★★★★

Location: 11 n. miles (20km) east of Tufi.
Access: About 35min by fast boat from Tufi.
Conditions: Exposed in Southeast Trades, but usually accessible in early morning.
Typical visibility: 40m (130ft)
Minimum depth: 4m (13ft)
Maximum depth: 40m (130ft)

Several different dives can be made on the reef

PHOTOGRAPHING MANTAS IN PLANKTON

We mostly encounter Manta Rays after a plankton bloom. Plankton, the favourite food of these beasts, is typically thickest near the surface. Manta Rays will enter a particularly thick patch of plankton then perform a series of loops, mouth agape, continually scooping up as much food as they can.

Photographing them can be difficult. A flash light on the camera is useless, as it lights up all the suspended plankton particles, but natural light can likewise create problems unless you ensure the sun is behind the camera. In shallow water and bright sunlight the solar rays produce flare if you aim the camera in even the general direction of the sun. With the sun behind you, however, the water appears much clearer and you should be able to get sharp images of the Manta Rays.

At the edges of the reef, swarms of Anthias feed on current-borne plankton.

surrounding the cay. For the most fish action, dive the part of the reef receiving any current; here Dogtooth Tuna and sharks patrol among the many schools of fish. There is a good wall dive on the edge of the reef. The shallow water near the cay is ideal for beginners, with beautiful reef patches on a sandy bottom, and this is also very good, safe snorkelling.

5 VEALE REEF

★★★★★★★★★

Location: 12 n. miles (22km) southeast of Tufi; white navigation light on reef.
Access: About 45min by fast boat from Tufi.
Conditions: Requires calm weather, but usually accessible in early morning. Often a current, typically from southeast.
Typical visibility: 50m (165ft)
Minimum depth: 5m (16ft)
Maximum depth: 50m (165ft) plus

An excellent reef perched on the edge of very deep water. The eastern side has a steep wall, plunging from 5m (16ft) to 600m (2000ft). Along the wall are seen Hammerhead Sharks, Dogtooth Tuna, Spanish Mackerel, other sharks and schools of smaller fish. The reeftop is carpeted with staghorn and plate corals in excellent condition. The whole eastern side of the reef offers excellent diving; probably the favourite end is the northern, where cuts and crevices sculpture the dropoff. Soft corals and fans are uncommon, but there are some giant sponges. The water is usually exceptionally clear.

The reeftop has lovely snorkelling for the experienced.

6 S'JACOB

★★★★★

Location: Offshore, approximately 6 n. miles (11km) northwest of Porlock Harbour on Tufi Peninsula. (Exact location guarded to prevent vandalism.)
Access: *Barbarian II* makes regular expeditions. Suitable only for advanced divers.
Conditions: Exposed to strong southeasterly and to northwesterly winds, but during Apr/May and Nov/Dec there are often flat, calm conditions perfect for diving. It may be possible to dive the wreck at other times of year, particularly early morning, when land breeze from high coastal mountains keeps sea calm. A manageable current often flows over site.
Typical visibility: usually 30m (100ft) or more, though runoff from a large swamp 20km (12 miles) southwest can cause dirty water to 25m (80ft) – visibility rarely poor on wreck itself

PHOTOGRAPHING DEEP WRECKS

I have seen many poor photographs of deep shipwrecks. The usual mistake is to rely too much on flash lights (strobes) because the background light is low. Cameras on automatic settings are particularly at fault for, although the wreck itself may be well lit, the surrounding water appears black as night.

You should consider the background light the most important. It may be you have to use a fast film, like Kodachrome 200, or slow shutter speeds of 1/30th or even 1/15th sec, but the camera must be set to expose the background correctly. (Sometimes you need an upward view to accomplish this.) You then have to calculate the distance and flash settings to give the correct subject exposure while maintaining the right background exposure. If the aperture is wide, you may have to reduce strobe power. Insufficient strobe power is rarely the problem.

Minimum depth: 35m (115ft)
Maximum depth: 56m (185ft)

The five stars above are an underestimate! This 3000-ton shipwreck has been neither fished nor salvaged. An oasis of life far from any reefs, it is a haven for hugely varied and prolific fish-life, from Manta Rays and Giant Groupers to sparkling baitfish and colourful Redbar Anthias (*Pseudanthias rubrizonatus*). The batfish are so fearless you have to chase them away if you want clear photographs of the wreck! Tiger Sharks have been reported.

The ship is upright, the funnel rising to 35m (115ft) and, like the rest of the wreck, covered with soft and black corals. Artefacts scattered about include lanterns, binnacles, guns and even an anti-mine paravane. Some easy penetrations are possible, particularly into the bridge. The pristineness of the wreck and the unbelievable marine life make this undoubtedly the finest wreck-dive I have ever made. The wreck was discovered through the efforts of Rodney Pearce, who has left everything in place for others to enjoy. Do not remove anything. For photographers, fast film is recommended.

Tufi

How to Get There

Milne Bay Air runs three flights per week from Port Moresby, with a flight-time of 45min (relevant contact details for Milne Bay Air are in the Port Moresby directory – see page 86). Alternatively, planes are available for charter from Port Moresby.

You are advised not to travel to Tufi via the Oro provincial capital, Popondetta, which is one of the most unattractive and lawless places in the whole of PNG.

Where to Stay

Tufi Dive Resort
c/o Tufi Post Office
Oro Province
tel 675 611438
fax 675 611438
Owned and operated by PADI instructor Ken Weaving, with over 20 years of diving experience. He has renovated the old Laki Hotel to make a clean and comfortable guesthouse with a variety of rooms suitable for families, couples or singles. The rooms are basic but pleasant with fans for cooling.

Diving is made from a twin-outboard-powered 'banana' boat fitted with a sun-roof and safety gear, including first-aid kit, oxygen and radio contact with base. A back-up boat is available. The boat enables fast access to the main dive sites, which are a 15–50min ride from the resort. Six full sets of hire gear are available, and there are two Bauer Capitano compressors to fill the tanks. The resort can handle a maximum of 12 divers, but usually has fewer. Instruction and day- and night-dives are offered. Fishing trips, village tours, trips to the fiords and freshwater prawning are also available.

Alternatives
Several village guesthouses are available for visitors who would like to sample the village lifestyle. They have a reputation for providing good seafood meals – much more interesting than the usual village fare. It is difficult to book these before arrival, but local people are very friendly and helpful and will direct visitors to somewhere suitable. The villagers are also able to take you on walks through this very scenic fiordland area.

Dive Facilities

Tufi Dive Resort
c/o Tufi Post Office
Oro Province
tel 675 611438
fax 675 611438

Live-Aboards

Tufi is not on any regular itineraries, but is dived occasionally by the live-aboards listed below, usually as a part of expeditions to dive the wreck of the *S'Jacob*:
Barbarian II (out of Lae)
and, more rarely,
Tiata (out of Alotau – usually based in Kavieng)
Telita (out of Alotau)
See relevant directories (pages 71, 99 and 147) for contact details.

Local Highlights

Tufi's people are among the friendliest in Oro Province, and have a unique culture. Their traditional dress utilizes their speciality – the making of Tapa cloth from the bark of a mulberry tree. The cloth's basic colour is an unassuming olive-brown, but it is decorated with beautiful designs and may be used as a stunning wall-hanging. Hard to find elsewhere in PNG, Tapa cloth is easy to buy – at very reasonable prices – in Tufi and Cape Vogel.

The fantastic wreck of the S'Jacob teems with marine life.

LAE

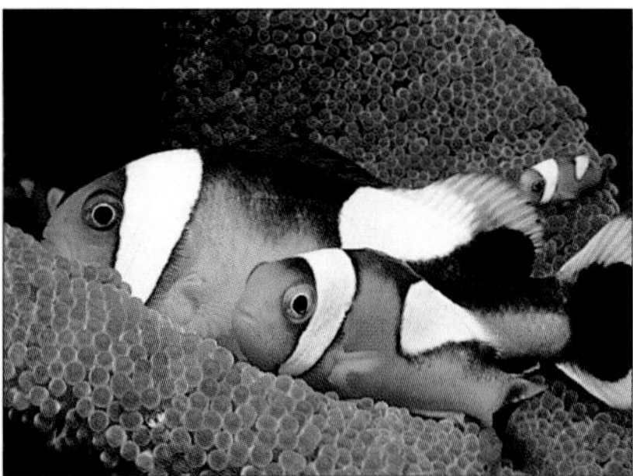

Lae is perched on the edge of a great submarine cliff. Huon Gulf, over 1000 fathoms (1.83km) deep, is just a few kilometres away. The Markham River spews a continuous flood of muddy fresh water into the Gulf, but this stays mostly on the surface; a few metres down, clear water flows.

Some 30km (20 miles) south of Lae is the Salamaua Peninsula. Blessed with clear water all year round, this is the main destination for Lae divers. The peninsula itself has reefs around much of its length – like the spectacular soft-coral gardens of Sheila's Reef (Site 6) – and other attractions are the several offshore seamounts, like Shepparton Shoals (Site 9) and the uncharted Halfway Reef (Site 2), discovered by Rodney Pearce. The big dive at Salamaua is an incredible World War II shipwreck, the *Yokohama Maru* (Site 3).

Excellent diving can be found a little further from Lae at the Tami Islands, to the east (Site 10) and the Siassi Islands in the Vitiaz Strait to the northeast of the Huon peninsula. At Tami I have dived several reefs which are as good as any in PNG.

Lae has a heavy annual rainfall, with the wettest period being May/Oct; however, this has little effect on the diving. The water temperature is noticeably warmer than in Milne Bay, at 27–29°C (80–84°F), warmest during Jan/Feb.

Historically Lae has been the gateway to the Highlands of PNG but it was not until the 1930s that Europeans first walked inland up the valleys behind Lae to discover more than a million people who were unaware of any outside world. They are very aware now and the Highlands Highway – a road linking the major Highlands centres with the coast at Lae – is the busiest commercial road in the country, carrying agricultural produce from the fertile Highlands valleys to be shipped around the world. The road carries people too, and Lae is a bustling and dynamic city with PNG's most cosmopolitan population and a 'rascal' problem that rivals that of Port Moresby.

The old airport in the centre of town facing the sea is not used these days. Flying into Lae, passengers will find themselves at the rebuilt airstrip of Nadzab, 45km out of town, and have to face a drive which generally takes longer than the flight from Port Moresby!

Opposite: *Sea whips have a more flexible body structure than sea fans.*
Above: *Panda Clownfish, Amphiprion polymnus, favour sea grass beds.*

1 TENYO MARU

★★

Location: ½ n. mile (930m) east of Lae Yacht Club at Voco Point.
Access: By boat or by swimming 100m (110yd) from shore.
Conditions: Calm conditions with offshore winds necessary; best season therefore Nov/Jan.
Typical visibility: 12m (40ft) at depth, less near surface
Minimum depth: 2m (6½ft)
Maximum depth: 40m (130ft)

The wreck is upright on a steep slope, with its bow just beneath the surface. Quite a big ship (5400 tons), it is still largely intact and has 5in (130mm) guns aboard. The biggest problem is the nearby river, which continually flushes out very muddy water. Although the water usually clears as you descend, very clear water is uncommon, and there is a lot of silt inside the wreck (penetration is not recommended). Marine growths are sparse, and there are few fish on the wreck. Nevertheless, this is an interesting dive, particularly if you do not have time for a day trip to the offshore reefs and wrecks. You can get interesting photographs using natural light or shooting macro.

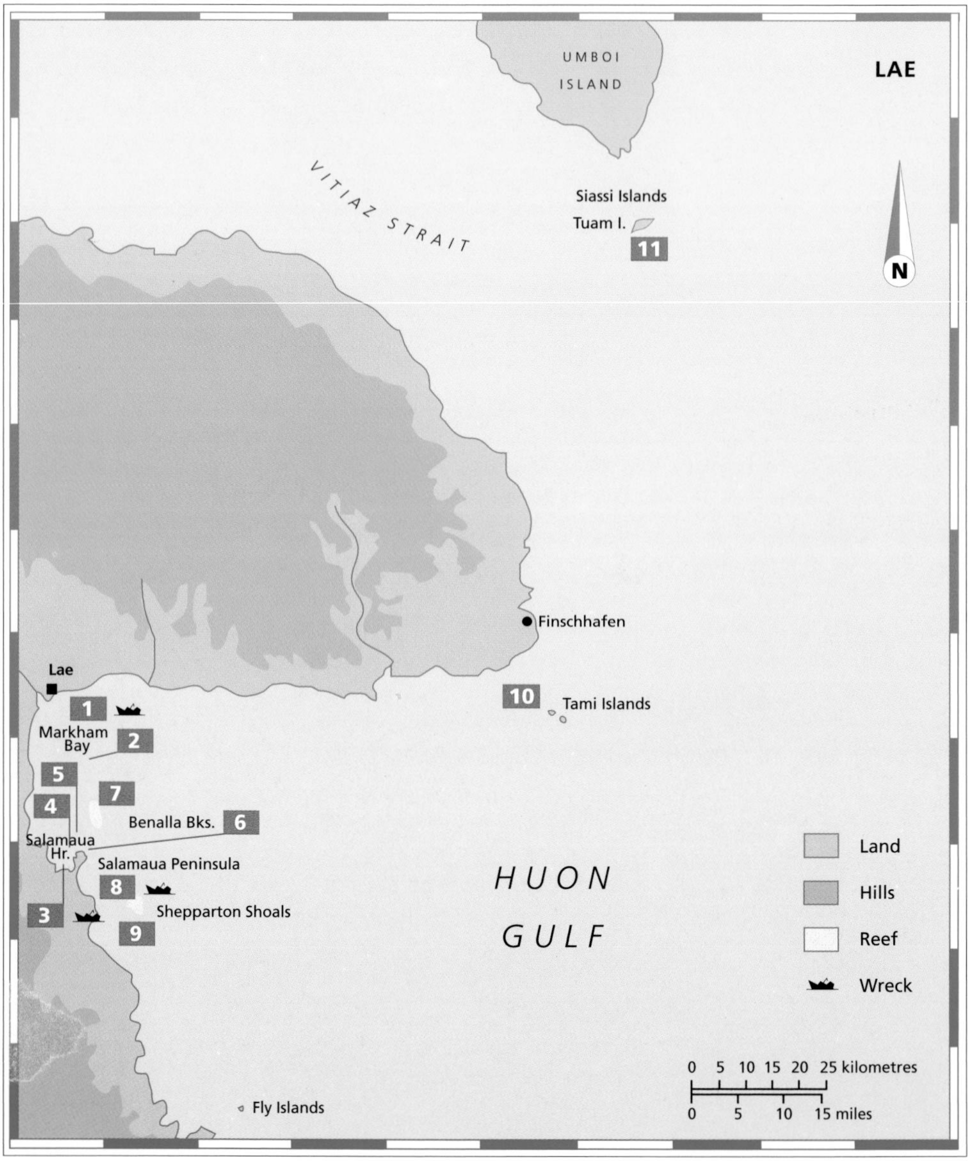

LAE
UMBOI ISLAND
VITIAZ STRAIT
Siassi Islands
Tuam I.
11
N
Finschhafen
10
Tami Islands
Lae
1
Markham Bay
2
5
4
7
Benalla Bks.
6
Salamaua Hr.
Salamaua Peninsula
8
3
Shepparton Shoals
9
HUON GULF
Land
Hills
Reef
Wreck
0 5 10 15 20 25 kilometres
0 5 10 15 miles
Fly Islands

2 HALFWAY REEF

★★★★

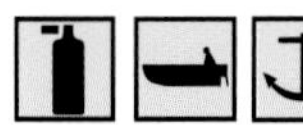

Location: Halfway between Lae and Salamaua.
Access: Local knowledge and echo sounder necessary to find reef, which is uncharted and at its shallowest 25m (80ft).
Conditions: The reef is exposed and cannot be dived in rough conditions, though these are rare.
Typical visibility: 40m (130ft) at depth; may be much reduced on surface
Minimum depth: 25m (80ft)
Maximum depth: 40m (130ft) plus

A beautiful and dramatic site. Follow the anchor-line down to the reef, which is covered with massive soft corals, black corals, gorgonians and sponges. Some barrel sponges are big enough to contain a diver! (Don't be tempted to get inside them as this damages the sponges.) Coral overhangs deeper down the reef are festooned in soft corals. Fish congregate on the reef, and Whale Sharks are sometimes seen. Because of the depth and temptation to overstay, take care over air-supply and decompression requirements.

3 YOKOHAMA MARU

★★★★★

Location: Salamaua Harbour. The wreck is usually marked with buoys.
Access: By boat. Only dinghies should tie to the buoys.
Conditions: Calm all year round. Little current. Only for the highly experienced: really requires technical diving training, redundant air supply and decompression-gas mixtures.
Typical visibility: 40m (130ft) plus
Minimum depth: 55m (180ft)
Maximum depth: 75m (250ft)

A fantastic dive. The ship is upright in calm, clear water with minimum currents. You cannot cover the whole ship in one dive, so must choose which buoy to descend. If descending in the midships area, the shallowest part of the ship (excluding the mast-tops) is the framework of the bridge, festooned in white soft corals and black corals with white polyps. These give the wreck a ghostly appearance. Schools of trevally and batfish swirl around the masts. At an original 6143 tons, this is probably PNG's biggest divable World War II shipwreck. It is a challenge to photographers to capture the magnificent spectacle – fast film is useful. The buoy lines have been in place for quite a time so some photographers, after a brief look at the wreck, concentrate while decompressing, on the excellent macro opportunities among the growths on the lines.

4 THE BEACON, SALAMAUA

★★★★★★★

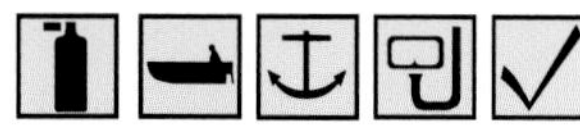

Location: Salamaua Harbour.
Access: By boat.
Conditions: Sheltered most of year.
Typical visibility: 30m (100ft)
Minimum depth: 1m (40in)
Maximum depth: 50m (165ft)

The best diving is in shallow water – to 18m (60ft) – where the ideal conditions make for a relaxing dive pottering among the corals. This is a perfect night-diving spot. Other nearby sites have similar features.

Excellent, easy snorkelling is possible in the calm shallow waters, where you can see a great variety of marine life.

5 AQUARIUM

★★★★

Location: Off northern tip of Salamaua Peninsula.
Access: By boat.
Conditions: Often current on site. May be dived in calm to moderate seas. A difficult dive because of current and depth – should be attempted only by experienced divers. Pick-up boat at surface essential.
Typical visibility: 40m (130ft)
Minimum depth: 27m (90ft)
Maximum depth: 40m (130ft)

Descend the anchor-line to a gently sloping plateau adorned with giant sponges and black coral trees. Crinoids abound, and an immense amount of fish-life congregates, probably because there is often a moderate current. Grouper, sharks, Spanish Mackerel, Dogtooth Tuna, barracuda and Oceanic Triggerfish are common.

6 SHEILA'S REEF

★★★

Location: Off Salamaua Peninsula's northwestern tip.
Access: Careful navigation needed to find ascent-line; to avoid damage to corals, a buoyed line is often used as a reference for the divers, who are dropped in and picked up from a 'live' boat.
Conditions: Partly sheltered, but cannot be dived in rough conditions.
Typical visibility: 40m (130ft)
Minimum depth: 18m (60ft)
Maximum depth: 40m (130ft)

The site is at 18m (60ft) on a gently sloping sandy plateau. A slight current flows over it, and you can see many very large sea fans and sponges.

7 BENALLA BANKS

★★★

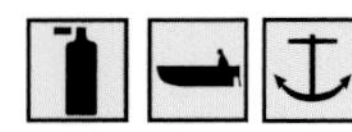

Location: 5 n. miles (9.3km) northeast of Salamaua Peninsula.
Access: By boat.
Conditions: Exposed to weather, so calm conditions necessary.
Typical visibility: 40m (130ft)
Minimum depth: 18m (60ft)
Maximum depth: 40m (130ft) plus

This is a big reef area, and many different dives are possible. There is a steep dropoff on the eastern side and the rest of the reef slopes away with a shallow average of 22m (70ft). Sharks are frequent.

8 KOTOKO MARU

★★★★★★★★

Location: Southeastern side of Salamaua Peninsula.
Access: By boat – although close to shore, access from beach is difficult.
Conditions: Cannot be dived in strong southeast wind conditions, but accessible most of year.
Typical visibility: 25m (80ft)
Minimum depth: 1m (40in)
Maximum depth: 20m (65ft)

The ship is quite broken up but parts of it, particularly the bow area, are quite recognizable. Coral has grown so prolifically that it is difficult to decide in some areas what is wreck and what is natural coral growth! These corals are alive with fish and other marine creatures.

Since the wreck is mostly in shallow water it makes an excellent snorkel dive. The surrounding reef is interesting and full of life.

9 SHEPPARTON SHOALS

★★★★★★★

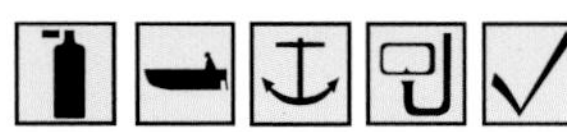

Location: 4 n. miles (7.4km) southeast of Salamaua Peninsula.
Access: Anchor in rubble patches on reeftop in 8–10m (25–33ft).
Conditions: Calm to moderate seas required. Current not a problem.
Typical visibility: 40m (130ft)
Minimum depth: 7m (23ft)
Maximum depth: 30m (100ft) plus

A large reef – 1¼ n. miles (2.3km) long – so several dives are possible. Although there are not usually strong currents on the reef, if you detect any you should dive on the side receiving it. There are barren patches on the reeftop, but it is always possible to find areas of good coral and fish action. There is a dropoff on either side of the reef.

The site offers excellent snorkelling for the more experienced.

10 TAMI ISLANDS

★★★★★★★★

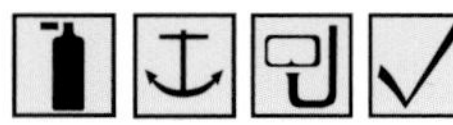

Location: 50 n. miles (90km) east of Lae.
Access: Only small boats with shallow draft and people with local knowledge should attempt to anchor inside Tami Lagoon.
Conditions: Best time of year Oct/Apr, but can be dived all year round.
Typical visibility: 30m (100ft)
Minimum depth: 2m (6½ft)
Maximum depth: 40m (130ft) plus

Many different sites are in the area but I have found the reefs to the north of the group the most rewarding. Several patch reefs a couple of kilometres offshore rise to 5m (16ft) or so, sloping away to 40m (130ft). The reeftops have good growths of hard corals, including large stands of cabbage coral, and the slopes are covered with sea fans and sea whips. There is often current in the area, and many schools of fish swarm the front of the reefs to feed; sharks are frequent. Beautiful wide-angle photography is possible.

At times of slack current you can snorkel on the outer reefs; there is excellent snorkelling in shallow water around the islands.

11 SIASSI ISLANDS

★★★★★★★★

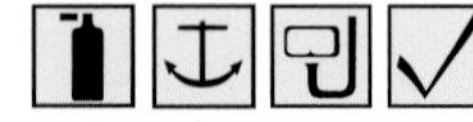

Location: South of Umboi Island in the Vitiaz Strait.
Access: By boat.
Conditions: Calm conditions essential.
Typical visibility: 50m (165ft) – exceptionally clear
Minimum depth: 2m (6½ft)
Maximum depth: 50m (165ft) plus

Many different sites are possible around these islands and their reefs. The sausage-shaped Tuam Island, the largest, is surrounded by a vertical dropoff. Its best diving areas are its tips; since it is impossible to anchor except with a very shallow-draft vessel, drift-diving is normal – it's also a good idea because there are quite often currents along the walls. Very little diving has been done in the area, so expect to see pristine reefs and large and plentiful marine life. A plague of Crown-of-Thorns Starfish invaded Tuam in 1990, but went unnoticed at other Siassi islands.

There is excellent and safe snorkelling in the shallows close to shore.

Lae

How to Get There

Air Niugini runs 5–7 flights daily from Port Moresby to Lae (flight-time 1/2hr).

Air Niugini
PO Box 237, Lae
tel 675 42 4744 (international)
tel 675 42 3111 (domestic)
fax 675 42 4758

Where to Stay

Lae International Hotel
PO Box 2774, Lae
tel 675 42 2000
fax 675 42 2534

This large hotel situated in 9 acres of tropical gardens, 2min walk from the centre of Lae, has over 100 deluxe rooms and all the amenities you would expect from a world-class international hotel.

Melanesian Hotel
PO Box 756, Lae
tel 675 42 3744
fax 675 42 3706
Very close to the centre of Lae town, this international-standard hotel has 68 rooms, swimming pool, good restaurant and bars.

Klinkii Lodge
PO Box 192, Lae
tel 675 42 6040
Acceptable budget accommodation. Most rooms have shared bathrooms; two have private bathrooms.

Where to Eat

The two hotels have the best dining-rooms in Lae, but it is certainly worth going to the **Lae Yacht Club** (tel 675 42 4091) for a drink and a very reasonably priced hearty meal. You will see all the fascinating activity around the waterfront and probably meet fellow-divers resident in the Lae area. The Yacht Club is built on the waterfront at Voco Point, a tiny spur behind which is Lae's only small-boat anchorage.

Live-Aboard

Barbarian II
Designed by owner and operator Rodney Pearce as an affordable live-aboard for budget-conscious divers, *Barbarian II* is small – 13m (43ft) long – but has all the facilities necessary for a successful cruise for six passengers, accommodated in three cabins. The vessel has a steel hull and timber superstructure, beautifully fitted out in PNG rosewood. A feature is the large portholes, salvaged by Rodney from a sunken wreck.

At the *Barbarian II* base in Lae is a small dive shop, New Guinea Diving, which is also owned by Rodney Pearce; it specializes in Mares dive equipment and SSA dive skins.

Barbarian II/Niugini Diving
PO Box 320, Lae
tel 675 42 5692
fax 675 42 2455

Local Highlights

Morobe Tours operate bus tours round the Lae township and can take visitors to the **War Cemetery**; this is situated in the splendid Botanical Gardens, which have an excellent display of orchids.

Morobe Tours
PO Box 245, Lae
tel 675 42 3647
fax 42 5788

Rodney Pearce's expedition live-aboard, the much-travelled Barbarian II.

MADANG PROVINCE

Madang boasts one of the best natural harbours in the whole of PNG, and is built around lakes and waterways which have all been beautifully landscaped. Just north of the entrance to the main harbour is a beautiful lagoon with an outer barrier reef, and several islands with exciting diving in the passes between them, as well as some interesting wrecks. The inner harbour is not clear enough to dive, but the lagoon has interesting diving with healthy coral reefs and plenty of sea fans and marine animals.

To the north of Madang can be found some remarkable shore dives, including the wreck of the *Boston* (Site 2). Further along the North Coast Road (5hr drive), at Hansa Bay, lie many sunken Japanese ship and aircraft wrecks. The offshore volcanic islands of Karkar and Bagabag (see page 106) are a few hours' cruising from Madang and, though seldom visited, have very good diving. Bagabag in particular is famous for its pelagic action. Crown Island, Long Island and Hankow Reef take about 9hr cruising, so require a live-aboard, but in fair weather are well worth the trouble.

Madang and the North Coast Road

There is a wealth of marine life to be seen in the passages between the islands outside Madang's main harbour. Three wrecks are also regularly dived. The *Henry Leith* (Site 4) is an old iron tugboat sunk by Kevin Baldwin and myself near Wongat Island because we thought it would be nice to have a wreck-dive there ... only to discover a year later there was a World War II B25 Mitchell aircraft wreck (Site 5) just 200m (220yd) away! The *Coral Queen* (Site 7) was deliberately sunk by one-time local dive operator Bernie Grayson, and is now famous as a night-dive because of its incredible population of flashlight fish. But most of my best memories of Madang diving are of Magic Passage (Site 9). On an incoming tide this narrow channel just north of Kranget Island is a truly magic dive.

About a 1hr drive from Madang, along the North Coast Road, will bring you to more

Opposite: *Snorkelling over shallow reef off a beach on the North Coast Road, near Madang.*
Above: *This species of Anglerfish, Antennarius striatus, prefers sandy habitats close to shore.*

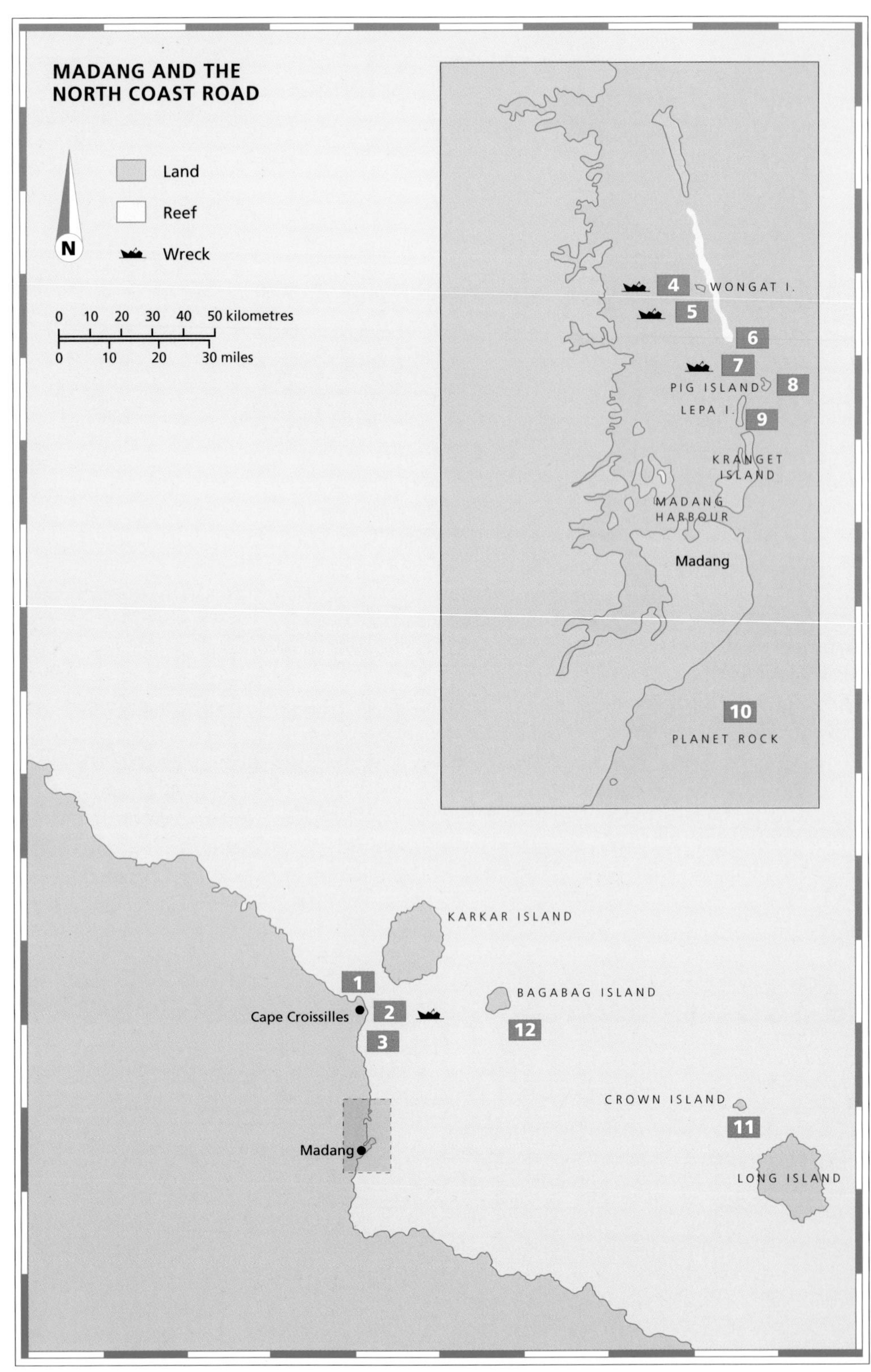

MADANG AND THE NORTH COAST ROAD
Land
Reef
Wreck
N
0 10 20 30 40 50 kilometres
0 10 20 30 miles
WONGAT I.
PIG ISLAND
LEPA I.
KRANGET ISLAND
MADANG HARBOUR
Madang
PLANET ROCK
KARKAR ISLAND
BAGABAG ISLAND
Cape Croissilles
CROWN ISLAND
LONG ISLAND
1
2
3
4
5
6
7
8
9
10
11
12

excellent diving. The Waterhole (Site 1) is a unique all-weather dive, since the beach is completely protected from the ocean dropoff by a raised reef enclosing a tiny lagoon. Nearby, The Quarry (Site 3) is another excellent dive with many sea fans and soft corals.

OUTLYING ISLANDS

67 nautical miles (124km) east of Madang and accessible only by sea, Crown Island is rarely visited – a pity, because there is fantastic diving on its surrounding reefs, which are undisturbed and bursting with marine life. The diving is all around the island, so it is just a matter of choosing the sheltered side and picking a likely reef. The water is apparently always clear, although quite often currents run over the best reefs. A live-aboard is necessary, but you should be able to charter one out of Madang. The best time of year is probably Oct/Nov, at the end of the Southeast season, but you can dive whenever the weather is reasonably calm, as there is some shelter at the island.

Bagabag Island is an old volcano whose caldera has breached to the sea, forming a perfectly sheltered anchorage (entrance on southeast side), New Year's Bay, which cuts right into the heart of the Island. On the western side is the smaller Christmas Bay, which provides sheltered anchorage in the Southeast season only. Bagabag has a fringing reef with surprisingly good diving around it; a surrounding barrier reef, about 4km ($2^1/2$ miles) offshore, has several passes through to the lagoon.

LOOTING WRECKS

If you found it in your back yard it would be junk — but if you find it underwater it is treasure. I never cease to be amazed at the stuff brought up by divers.

Unfortunately, some divers effectively vandalize a perfect time capsule by taking artefacts from a wreck. These are useless above water, but their absence near the dive is spoiled for those that follow.

On 19 September 1992 a ban was imposed under the Papua New Guinea War Surplus Materials Act to prevent the removal and/or export of war relics from their resting place without specific Government authority. This means that divers can see and photograph war relics, such as sunken ships and aircraft, but may not remove any artefacts or souvenirs. The penalties are severe: the law allows for fines of up to K10,000.

1 THE WATERHOLE

★★★★★★★★

Location: On coast about 5km (3 miles) west of Cape Croissilles.
Access: You can drive right up to this site (about 1hr from Madang on North Coast Road).
Conditions: May be dived in all conditions.
Typical visibility: 40m (130ft)
Minimum depth: as shallow as you like
Maximum depth: 40m (130ft) plus

A small lagoon with a white sand beach is completely protected from the open sea by a sharp rocky shore, which often has surf breaking against it. After a beach entry into the lagoon, you descend and swim towards a large tunnel at 6m (20ft) which leads through the rock to the open ocean. Looking up, you see the surf smashing against the rocks, but are deep enough to have no difficulty moving through the surf zone into a beautiful coral garden, then down a steeply sloping dropoff. You must be able to find the tunnel again if you're to make a safe exit, so take care navigating once through the tunnel.

On calm days divers with local knowledge can enter the water at a blowhole about 600m (660yd) east. Here the wall is vertical and very dramatic. Swimming along the wall, you eventually end up at The Waterhole and can exit through the tunnel. Ideally the current should help you drift along the wall, but it is hard to predict and can often be running the opposite way – since the only easy exit is through The Waterhole, this is a problem! Big fish and turtles are often encountered, and the wall is alive with soft corals, sponges and sea whips.

The lagoon makes pleasant, easy snorkelling – ideal for novices. On calm days good skin divers can dive through the tunnel.

2 BOSTON

★★★★

Location: About 4km ($2^1/2$miles) south of Cape Croissilles.

Access: Usually from shore (50min drive on North Coast Road from Madang). Can be dived by boat (1hr from Madang).
Conditions: For experienced current-divers only, but well worth the effort. Very difficult in Southeast season. Strong currents flow over site. Diving from boat straightforward, but take great care if diving from shore, which consists of sharp rocks. If any waves breaking on shore this entry not recommended.
Typical visibility: 40m (130ft)
Minimum depth: 22m (70ft)
Maximum depth: 45m (150ft)
You can drive a car right to the entry point off the North Coast Road. Enter by jumping from the rocks. Descend immediately down the steep slope, then let yourself be pushed north by the prevailing current. At about 30m (100ft) you come to the stern of the wreck, which – intact and upright – is a beautiful sight, being covered with soft corals and fish. A gash in the hull at the port stern shows where the propeller reportedly sliced the hull after becoming tangled in mine-sweeping cables. A school of barracuda hovers above the wreck, and large pelagics, sweetlips, trevally and cod are resident.

After drifting over the wreck, make a direct ascent across the current and then, when back in shallow water, return south to the exit point: the current in the shallows is much reduced, so you can return without much effort. (Return at depth is very difficult, and could easily result in your running out of air before reaching the exit.)

3 THE QUARRY

★★★★

Location: About 4km (2½miles) south of Cape Croissilles.
Access: Usually from shore (about 50min drive from Madang on North Coast Road).
Conditions: Difficult in strong southeast winds with surf breaking on shore. Can be strong currents.
Typical visibility: 40m (130ft)
Minimum depth: as shallow as you like
Maximum depth: 40m (130ft) plus
Among the best of all shore dives. You can drive right to the site and gear up on the beach next to the entry. This can be tricky if there are any waves. Almost immediately there is a steep dropoff, and you should swim slightly northwards to a descending ridge covered with sea fans, sea whips and soft corals. Schools of batfish and trevally will come to greet you, and pelagics, turtles and sharks are frequently met. A large Tiger Shark has often been seen, but has never bothered divers. The soft corals are spectacular and colourful. Take care with the current, particularly over the ridge, but otherwise this dive is straightforward.

FLASHLIGHT FISH

A light on a boat at night soon draws clouds of plankton. One smart fish has developed its own light to attract plankton and thus save itself the trouble of having to swim around in search of a meal. Flashlight fish have evolved a luminous organ below the eye, powered biochemically by bacteria that live within the light organ. The fish are otherwise completely black. They are, for obvious reasons, nocturnal.

The lights can be turned on and off either by rotating the organ or by using a flap of skin to cover it, and are thought to be used to see and to signal as well as to attract plankton. The flashlight fish most common in PNG is *Photoblepheron palpebratus*, which grows to about 10cm (4in). These can be seen in water as shallow as 2m (6½ft). During the day they hide deep within crevices in the reef.

4 WONGAT ISLAND AND HENRY LEITH

★★★★★★★

Location: Off white sand beach west of Wongat Island.
Access: 5min by boat from Jais Aben Resort. Wreck easily located by swimming directly down sand slope at northern end of Wongat Island beach.
Conditions: Sheltered in all weather. A great wreck-dive for beginners.
Typical visibility: 20m (65ft)
Minimum depth: 10m (33ft)
Maximum depth: 20m (65ft)
The boat was purchased for K1 by Kevin Baldwin and sunk by Kevin and myself to make an interesting dive near picturesque Wongat Island. The wreck is upright and has a slight current flowing over it; within months it was covered with soft corals. Lionfish are common on the wreck, as are many other fish and invertebrates.

In shallow water around Wongat Island there is excellent, safe snorkelling.

5 MITCHELL B25 AIRCRAFT

★★★

Location: On reef 200m (220yd) southwest of Wongat Island.
Access: By boat – 15min from Madang Resort Hotel, 5min from Jais Aben Resort.
Conditions: Usually calm. An easy dive.
Typical visibility: 15m (50ft)
Minimum depth: 12m (40ft)
Maximum depth: 22m (70ft)
The aircraft was ditched after losing its port engine, but is otherwise intact. It lies upright on a reef-slope, with its port wingtip up the slope. The wreck is covered with a rich growth of soft corals and sponges. It was discovered

by David Pennefather, and I was fortunate to be able to dive it that same day and photograph it – within a few days vandals had removed the side swivel-guns and other artefacts, even though they were worthless away from the wreck. (This act prompted concerned divers to push the Government into legally protecting all World War II relics.) Some of the guns and other artefacts are still there, and you can see the cockpit controls, especially if you have a torch. The tail area, with its twin fins and machine-gun, is particularly photogenic. Complete the dive by ascending the nearby reef, whose top, in 5m (16ft), has anemones and their fish. This is an excellent night-dive.

Although the wreck is just too deep for snorkelling, the reef next to it offers plenty to see. Competent skin divers can reach the wreck.

6 RASCH PASSAGE

★★★★★★★

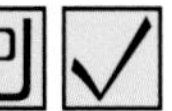

Location: First passage north of Pig Island.
Access: 10min by boat from the Jais Aben Resort.
Conditions: Exposed to southeast winds. Often current in passage. Can be done either by anchoring at front (eastern end) of pass and diving dropoff, or by drifting through pass. Should only be done with an incoming current, when visibility is at best and big schools of fish gather at mouth of passage.
Typical visibility: 40m (130ft)
Minimum depth: 5m (16ft)
Maximum depth: 40m (130ft) plus

Good hard- and soft-coral growths line the passage, and black corals grow down the slopes. There is a resident school of barracuda. Sharks are sometimes seen. You can snorkel along the shallow edge of the passage.

7 CORAL QUEEN

★★★★

Location: In lagoon behind barrier reef north of Pig Island.
Access: 15min by boat from Madang Resort Hotel.
Conditions: Sheltered all year. Dark night required.
Typical visibility: 25m (80ft) – but variable
Minimum depth: 15m (50ft)
Maximum depth: 30m (100ft)

The wreck is upright, with its deck at 24m (75ft), and has been taken over by a huge colony of flashlight fish, making this one of PNG's most spectacular night-dives. The fish are most abundant on very dark nights with little moon. The flashlight fish are so numerous that, once on the wreck, you can continue your dive without a torch. A unique, diving experience.

8 BARRACUDA POINT

★★★★★

Location: Eastern side of Pig Island.
Access: 10min by boat from Madang Resort Hotel.
Conditions: Not comfortable in strong southeast winds. Can be current running over site. Can be done as a drift-dive, depending on current.
Typical visibility: 40m (130ft)
Minimum depth: 5m (16ft)
Maximum depth: 40m (130ft) plus

The point of the reef gradually drops off into the depths of the Bismarck Sea. The current often flowing over the point attracts schools of fish including barracuda, trevally, sea perch and fusiliers. Big Coral Cod and sweetlips are common. Large sharks are regular visitors, particularly Hammerhead, Grey Reef and Silvertip. Although the main attraction is the fish-life, the corals are well formed, with a mixture of hard and soft corals and gorgonians. The reef dropoff steepens away from the point until nearly vertical.

There is perfect snorkelling from the beach of nearby Pig Island.

9 MAGIC PASSAGE

★★★★

Location: Between Kranket and Lepa Islands, Madang Harbour.
Access: 10min by boat from Madang Resort Hotel.
Conditions: Usually calm. Requires incoming current for best visibility and action – very disappointing if current flowing out of lagoon.
Typical visibility: 30m (100ft)
Minimum depth: 5m (16ft)
Maximum depth: 40m (130ft) plus

The boat is usually anchored on the northern side, close to the passage's entrance. You then descend into the current down the side of the passage, past excellent growths of hard and soft coral. The passage's bottom, at about 35m (115ft), has a couple of coral bommies covered with superb white sea fans, black coral sea whips and colourful soft corals. Surrounded by shy garden eels, groups of Painted Sweetlips (*Diagramma pictum*) sit facing the incoming tide; they allow you to get very close. Above, a school of barracuda wheels around a school of Bigeye Trevally. From the middle of the passage you can see both walls, with stands of Green Tree Coral and some giant barrel sponges. Sharks, including Great Hammerhead and Whale, have been seen at the entrance. A brilliantly coloured scarlet and purple stonefish (*Synanceia verrucosa*) has been photographed on the reeftop.

10 PLANET ROCK

★★★★

Location: 4 n. miles (7.4km) south of Madang Harbour entrance.
Access: 20min by boat from Madang Harbour.
Conditions: Requires calm seas. Usually current running.
Typical visibility: 40m (130ft) – sometimes reduced on surface
Minimum depth: 4m (13ft)
Maximum depth: 40m (130ft) plus

This seamount rises from 600m (2000ft) to a small patch reeftop you can easily swim around in a few minutes. There is usually a current over the reef, so you can simply move to the side of the reef receiving the current and watch all the fish milling around. Big schools of barracuda and trevally mingle with sea perch and fusiliers. Hammerheads are fairly common, and Dogtooth Tuna hunt among the baitfish. Evening dives here can be exciting as the predators feed. There are some good coral formations on the reeftop. Sometimes the surface water looks dirty because of river runoff, but there is always clearer water below.

11 CROWN ISLAND - SOUTH REEF

★★★★★

Location: South side of Crown Island.
Access: Anchor on reeftop in 5m (16ft).
Conditions: Calm seas required. Usually current. Not a dive for the inexperienced, because of current and fearless behaviour of predators.
Typical visibility: 50m (165ft)
Minimum depth: 5m (16ft)
Maximum depth: 50m (165ft) plus

One of several sausage-shaped reefs next to the dropoff fringing Crown Island. Anchor at the end of the reef facing into the current. The front slope of the reef gradually drops to deep water, with no wall. Down the slope are many sea whips and fans, barrel sponges and black corals. Schooling reef fish buzz everywhere, chased by Dogtooth Tuna, Spanish Mackerel and Giant Trevally. Sharks are common, and Hammerheads are sometimes seen. The action is quite exceptional.

12 BAGABAG ISLAND

★★★★★★★★

  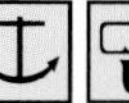 

Location: 32 n. miles (60km) northeast of Madang.
Access: 4hr cruising from Madang.
Conditions: Calm weather advised for crossing to Bagabag; shelter available after arrival. Some currents on outer reefs.
Typical visibility: 40m (130ft) plus
Minimum depth: as shallow as you like
Maximum depth: 50m (165ft) plus

The inner fringing reefs have steep dropoffs to the lagoon floor at 40m (130ft). The highly sculptured walls have caverns and crevices and are rich in surface marine life, with healthy populations of invertebrates like nudibranchs and flatworms. The usual reef fish are found, though not in great numbers.

The outer barrier reefs and passes have some of the most dynamic pelagic diving in the Madang area. Sharks are frequent, as are Dogtooth Tuna, Spanish Mackerel, barracuda, Bigeye Trevally and others. Soft corals and sea fans decorate the walls and great clouds of fish feed in the currents. Very little diving has been done here, as is obvious from the reefs' pristine quality.

There is excellent, easy snorkelling in the shallows of the fringing reefs. Only experienced snorkellers should try the outer barrier.

Sea whips, which can occur in dense gardens on ridges, framing a diver.

Hansa Bay

Hansa Bay is reached by a 230km (140-mile) drive from Madang along the scenic North Coast Road; in the dry season the journey takes under 4hr. In the bay's centre is Laing Island (Site 3), home of the Belgian King Leopold III Biological Research Station.

About 34 reported World War II Japanese wrecks lie in relatively shallow water in the bay. The positions of only a few are commonly known. This presents a wonderful opportunity to dive wrecks that have rarely been dived before – and even to discover undived wrecks.

Diving at Hansa Bay will always be seasonal. To the northwest, within 50km (30 miles) of the bay, are the mouths of two large rivers, the Ramu and Sepik, both spewing mud into the sea. In Jan/Mar, the rainy season, the prevailing currents from the north sweep the mud into the Bay. So diving is possible only from about May through Nov, when the prevailing current is from the southeast, and even then unseasonal rains can sometimes flood the small rivers that empty into the bay. However, when the water is good the diving is exceptional.

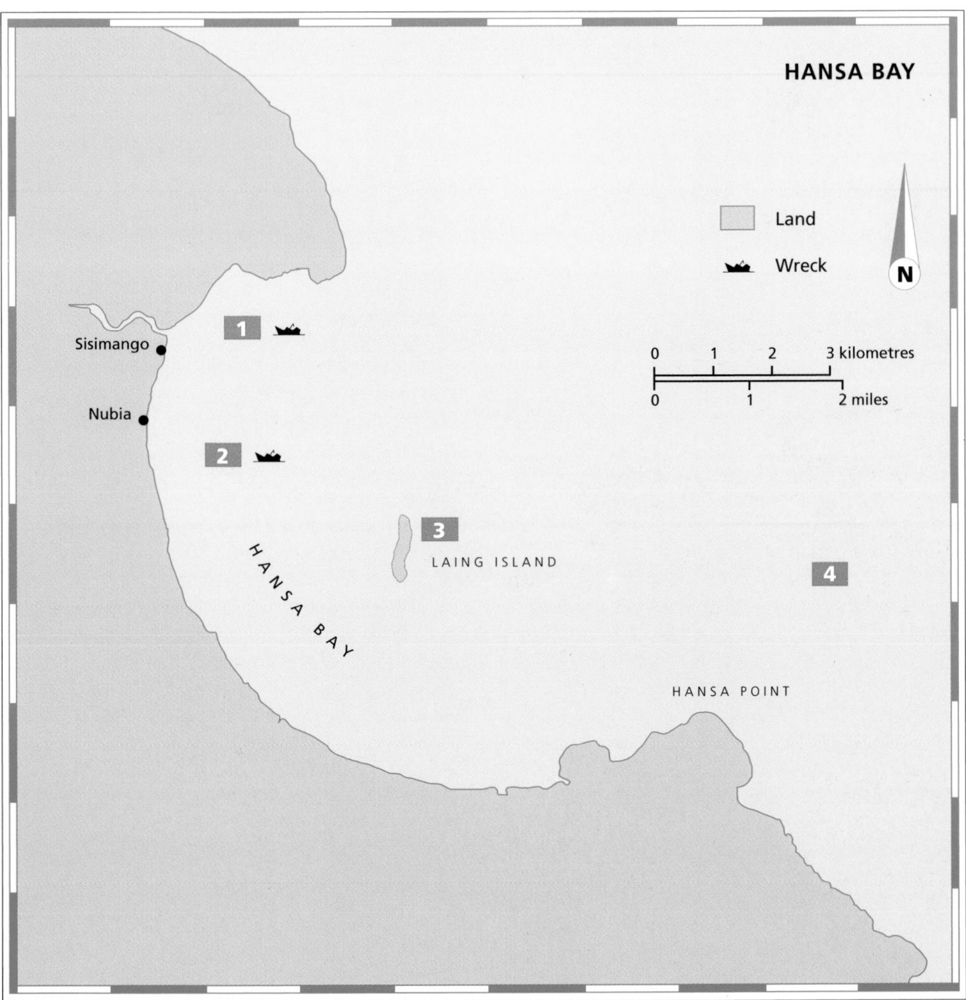

1 DAVIT WRECK (AND OTHERS)

★★★★★★

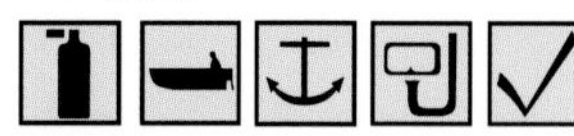

Location: Northeast of river mouth near Sisimango.
Access: 5min by boat from Awar Plantation.
Conditions: Avoid Jan/Mar. Mostly sheltered.
Typical visibility: 20m (65ft) – can be much less
Minimum depth: as shallow as you like
Maximum depth: 15m (50ft)

A medium-sized freighter. For many year a davit from the wreck could be seen above the surface; its remains are now awash at low tide. The ship has good coral growth – though not as luxuriant as on the *Sushi Maru* (Site 2) – and plenty of interesting swimthroughs. Off its stern lies, about 20m (65ft) away, the wreck of a twin-screw wooden boat: the wood has long disappeared, but the engines and other machinery can be seen.

Three further wrecks are nearby. The Mast Wreck, similar to the Davit Wreck, lies to the southwest, only 100m (110yd) off the beach. Another wreck lies directly at the river mouth, further to the southwest. An Air Cobra aircraft wreck is in 27m (90ft).

The shipwrecks may be easily snorkelled in clear conditions; the Mast Wreck is particularly convenient, being accessible from the beach.

2 SUSHI MARU

★★★★★★★

Location: 500m (550yd) from beach in front of Nubia Village.
Access: 10min by boat from Laing Island or Awar Plantation.
Conditions: Avoid Jan/Mar. Mostly sheltered.
Typical visibility: 25m (80ft) – can be much less
Minimum depth: 8m (26ft)
Maximum depth: 24m (75ft)

A large (over 5000 tons) armed Japanese transport sunk in an upright position in 1943. The marine growth on this wreck is exceptional. Its large size and shallow depth mean you can make several dives, exploring different parts of the ship. The anchor and chain are in the sand off the bow, where a large winch can also be seen. Two anti-aircraft guns, originally on the bow, have fallen onto the sand. The forward hold has sake bottles, shells and a trailer, but the next hold is the most interesting (the aft hold is empty), with trucks and a fire engine inside. The bridge and superstructure are badly damaged, but the wreck has many interesting swimthroughs – though care must be taken with deteriorating steel plates: a collapse is always possible.

In clear conditions this is a good snorkel, especially if you can skin dive down to the wreck.

3 LAING ISLAND

★★★★★★

Location: Laing Island.
Access: 10min by boat from Awar Plantation. Permission is required to land on the island, but visitors are usually welcome.
Conditions: Avoid Jan/Mar. Always sheltered. The island provides good anchorage.
Typical visibility: 25m (80ft) – sometimes less
Minimum depth: as shallow as you like
Maximum depth: 40m (130ft) plus

The best diving is probably on the eastern side, where the reef drops to deep water, but this is not always accessible. The sheltered western side has some good coral growth and a barge wreck in only 5m (16ft). The reef on this side gradually slopes away, with some patches of soft corals and fans.

There is good snorkelling, particularly on the sheltered western side. The barge wreck is visible from the surface. Snorkelling conditions here are generally better than those closer to shore.

4 ENCOUNTER REEF

★★★★

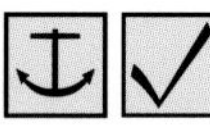

Location: Between Manam Island and the PNG mainland, about 2 n. miles (3.7km) northeast of Hansa Point.
Access: By boat – 15min from Laing Island, 30min from Awar Point Plantation jetty.
Conditions: Requires calm weather. Reef is completely exposed and may have strong currents.
Typical visibility: 40m (130ft)
Minimum depth: 5m (16ft)
Maximum depth: 50m (165ft) plus

This reef is small enough to be circumnavigated on a single dive, so you should move around the reef to find the side with the most action. There are many pelagics, plus resident schools of barracuda and trevally. Sharks are common; Tiger Sharks have been seen. The reef is steepest and deepest on its northeast side, but the whole reef has excellent coral cover, with many soft corals and sea fans. Giant Clams, uncommon elsewhere in the Madang region, are found here.

Some of the several other seamounts off Hansa Bay have yet to be explored.

Madang

How to Get There

Air Niugini runs 2–4 flights daily from Port Moresby to Madang (flight-time 1hr); many more flights come via Lae or Goroka.

Air Niugini
PO Box 140, Madang
tel 675 82 2255

Where to Stay

Madang Resort Hotel
PO Box 111, Madang
tel 675 82 2655
fax 675 82 3325
Beautifully landscaped grounds contain an orchid garden and a large swimming pool. Great variety, from five-star accommodation to backpackers' bunk rooms. Offers harbour cruises, village tours, nature walks, plus diving and snorkelling under auspices of Niugini Diving Adventures (details below). Game fishing can be arranged. Owned by Melanesian Tourist Services, who can provide a complete travel itinerary within PNG including cruises aboard the *Melanesian Discoverer* (details below) and accommodation at the Pine Lodge (at Bulolo), Kiburu Lodge (near Mendi) and Malagan Lodge (at Kavieng).

Jais Aben Resort
PO Box 105, Madang
tel 675 82 3311
fax 675 82 3560
16km (10 mile) from Madang along the North Coast Road. A harbour within a harbour, Nagada is the perfect site for Jais Aben Resort. Boats go from the sheltered lagoons and within minutes are at any of Madang's major dive sites. 18 rooms, some with full self-catering facilities, plus restaurant, bar, swimming pool. Village tours offered. Jais Aben has waterskiing, surf skis, catamaran, paddle boards and windsurfing, in addition to diving and snorkelling. Harbour cruises and visits to the Madang islands can be made.

In the resort's attractive grounds is a biological research institute:
Christensen Research Institute
PO Box 305, Madang
tel 675 82 3011
fax 675 82 3306

Malolo Lodge
PO Box 413, Madang
tel 675 83 7462
fax 675 52 2470
Trans Niugini Tours
PO Box 371, Mount Hagen
tel 675 52 1438
fax 675 52 2470
42km (26 miles) from Madang north along the scenic North Coast Road; owned by Trans Niugini Tours, one of PNG's largest and longest-established tour companies; also owns the Karawari Lodge and *Sepik Spirit* riverboat on the Sepik River and the Ambua Lodge in the Southern Highlands. The Malolo Lodge, rebuilt in grand Colonial style on site of old Plantation Hotel, has 14 rooms, and offers cultural and nature tours plus a diving and snorkelling service (see below).

Smuggler's Inn
PO Box 303, Madang
tel 675 82 2744
fax 675 82 2267
Beautifully sited on Madang coast and popular with visitors. Part of Coral Sea Hotel chain, as are Gateway Hotel (Port Moresby), Highlander Hotel (Mount Hagen) and Melanesian Hotel (Lae), all of high standard.

The Coastwatchers Hotel
PO Box 324, Madang
tel 675 82 2614
fax 675 82 2716
Offers deluxe and budget rooms, a restaurant, bar, swimming pool and day tours. The rates are generally cheaper than the other hotels in Madang, but it does not have a beach frontage.

Dive Facilities

Niugini Diving Adventures/Melanesian Tourist Services
PO Box 707, Madang
tel 675 82 2766
fax 675 82 3325/3543
A diving service offered by the Madang Resort Hotel (address above). Dive shop in hotel grounds has a selection of gear for sale and hire, and a perfectly located jetty for the three diveboats, a 9m (30ft) jet-boat, an 8m (25ft) centre-console and a 5m (16ft) runabout. These boats and two compressors cater for up to 15 divers at any one time. Instruction usually available.

Jais Aben Resort
PO Box 707, Madang
tel 675 82 2766
fax 675 82 3325/3543
There is a resident diving instructor here for tuition, and full sets of diving gear are available for hire. With two boats and two compressors, dive groups of up to 20 divers can be catered for.

Malolo Lodge
PO Box 707, Madang
tel 675 82 2766
fax 675 82 3325/3543
The lodge offers a divemaster service for up to eight divers. Dive gear available for hire; compressor at lodge. No diving immediately nearby, but conveniently located for dives at Cape Croisilles, a short drive along the North Coast Road.

Live-Aboards

Somona
Tim Rowlands' Aqua Ventures
PO Box 166, Madang
tel 675 82 2037
fax 675 82 3386
Australia fax (0)70 578 164
Tim, a very experienced diving instructor based in Madang for many years, runs the 11m (36ft) *Somona*, a comfortable, shaded, diesel-powered day-boat; specializes in diving around Madang and in expeditions to dive the wrecks and reefs of Hansa Bay, and to the reefs of Bagabag Island, northeast of Madang. The *Somona* is equipped with a compressor and equipment for eight divers; 240V power, GPS navigation and on-board oxygen supply. Tim arranges accommodation ashore then provides full-day diving trips.

Melanesian Discoverer
PO Box 707, Madang
tel 675 82 2766
fax 675 82 3325
Modern 38m (125ft) cruising catamaran with 21 passenger cabins able to carry 42 passengers and 21 crew. Luxuriously appointed, fully air-conditioned, all cabins *en suite*. Famous for her Sepik River cultural cruises; also makes seasonal cruises from Madang to the Trobriands and Alotau, with diving as optional extra.

Local Highlights

The Madang Visitor's Bureau can direct visitors to the local sights. These include a **Cultural Centre** – with artefacts and handicrafts on display – the historical **German Cemetery**, the market and the **Coastwatchers' Memorial**, a beacon 30m (100ft) high with a revolving light on top, used in directing ships to Madang's harbour entrance. The memorial remembers the incredible work done in World War II by the brave men who stayed behind after the Japanese invasion to spy on the enemy's activities.

Madang Visitor's Bureau
PO Box 2025, Madang
tel 675 82 3302
fax 675 82 3540

Beware: Corallimorpharians!

I have always thought of myself as a prudent diver, but I have to admit making one dive which I thought was safe but which turned out to be dangerous, and which caused me a nasty injury. It was a shallow dive in clear, calm, still water. What caused my injury was the same thing that causes most underwater injuries: ignorance.

A beautiful little fairy basslet called the Princess Anthias is uncommon in Milne Bay, where I usually dive. I had just found a mob of them on a reef near Garove Island in the Bismarck Sea. I tried to find a convenient place where I could settle quietly on the reef to take some photographs, but there was not a barren spot to be seen. The reef patches between the live coral had small, olive-brown anemone-like things all over them. I figured (correctly) that I could not do them any harm, and, as I was wearing a lycra suit, which I assumed would protect me, I gently settled in among the 'anemones' and proceeded to make beautiful pictures.

I noticed a slight stinging sensation through the lycra suit, but being a professional tough guy I continued my photography. Not satisfied with the first film through the camera I surfaced, reloaded, and repeated the dive – and realized after a while that I was being stung again. Marine stings have never affected me very much so, since at this stage it was not very painful, I continued to ignore the sensation.

Later, as I was taking my evening shower, I noticed a mass of stings on my left arm and shoulder and elsewhere. They looked and felt rather like sand-fly bites. In fact, I was a mess. Later still my shoulder felt strange and developed a deep ache, and I wondered if perhaps I was suffering the bends – although that did not make much sense considering the depths and times of the dives I had made.

The pain grew much worse over the next week. I tried to exercise the shoulder but it hurt, especially if I moved my arm after it had been resting, and I had great difficulty sleeping. I went to a local doctor, who thought I might have pulled a muscle, and I tried some pills and massage. Nothing helped, and I noticed the arm was getting weaker. Feeling my back I found my left trapezius muscle was atrophying: where I had had a bulging muscle before, now there was a hollow.

I made some phone calls to a diving doctor who suggested that, to eliminate the possibility of a bends bubble causing the problem, I should do a six-hour oxygen therapy. I was glad to receive this advice and spent one morning in harbour sucking on a regulator connected to the ship's oxygen-supply. But it made no difference; and, although I would gladly have felt better, I was also sort of pleased that the bends had probably been eliminated as a suspect.

By this time I was investigating exactly what it was that had stung me, and had found out there was a case history of a person badly stung by fire coral who had exercised after the sting and ended up with neuritis. Neuritis is painful and can cause muscular atrophy. Fire corals are in the same biological phylum as hydroids, sea jellies and anemones – namely the *Cnidaria*.

Searching for more clues, I talked to some of my very experienced diving friends. Valerie Taylor told me of an expedition which had dived the same reef I had; all the divers had ended up in pain after coming into contact with the 'little brown anemones'. Kevin Deacon told me a similar story: after his fiancée Cherie had touched the 'anemones' while modelling for him, she had suffered and her face had swollen up. But very few people knew much about the 'anemones', and certainly I could find nothing in the diving books.

The Culprit Unmasked

The brute turned out to be not an anemone at all, although it is a relative. The proper term is Corallimorpharian, and there are several different species. Corallimorpharians do not catch food with their tentacles, like anemones do: during the day they spread themselves flat (I would guess they need sunlight, as do many

Cnidarians) but in the evenings they curl up into a ball, with a small opening at the top. Whenever any fish or shrimp enters the hole, this causes it immediately to close, trapping them.

If a Corallimorpharian is molested it can produce a mass of special white filaments called acontia. These have huge stinging nematocysts that pack a potent venom. They can easily penetrate a lycra suit. Probably a few stings would not have caused me too much bother, but I had had a large double dose and then exercised, which almost certainly made the problem worse.

The specimen that zapped me was of the genus *Discosoma* (the species is uncertain, possibly undescribed) and is found throughout Papua New Guinea, but usually in small colonies just 1m (40in) or so across; there may be several hundred animals in a colony, since each individual is less than 10cm (4in) wide and they live in contact with their neighbours. But on certain reefs, like the one I'd been diving, corallimorpharians form huge colonies, virtually covering the whole reef suface.

Another species has a larger disc, 20cm (8in) or more across, and is usually found in groups of fewer than 10. A small commensal shrimp lives on this larger species. I have provoked members of the larger species and they do not produce as many acontia as their smaller cousins; as to whether they pack the same punch, I do not know – and I've no intention of testing.

About six weeks after my injury the pain gradually disappeared, but I was left with a very weak left arm; it took a year of working out with weights to get it back to normal. Now I am well – and wiser.

In the good old days of diving we used to say things like 'The More You Know, The Longer You Live'. Somewhere over the years and thousands of dives I must have forgotten, or perhaps I just assumed I knew everything I needed to know. Neptune has a way of dealing with foolish thinking like this.

So don't make the same mistake I did. Ignorance is dangerous. If you don't know, don't touch.

Dinah with large patch of Corallimorpharians

WALINDI AND KIMBE BAY

On the northern side of West New Britain Province, the Willaumez Peninsula, a finger of land 60km (37 miles) long with a string of a dozen extinct volcanic cones on it, has created a wonderland for divers. Snuggled into the shore on the east of the peninsula, is one of the world's greatest diving resorts, perfectly positioned to take advantage of the incredible diving. Walindi is an oil-palm plantation. The owners, Max and Cecilie Benjamin, pioneered the exploration of the reefs in Kimbe Bay, and have established on the plantation's beach a resort dedicated to divers.

A 20min drive south of Walindi is the small town of Kimbe, the trading and administrative centre for the area. A further 25min drive along the coast takes you to Hoskins, with air connections to Port Moresby and Rabaul.

In the bay are several small islands and even more small patch reefs, all rising from water averaging 600m (2000ft). These seamounts, the tips of ancient volcanoes, are blessed with very clear water and visits from big marine animals. Whales are frequent, including Killer Whales, as are various species of dolphins. The reefs are characterized by exquisite growths of sea fans, sea whips, barrel sponges and vibrant shallow coral gardens stacked with fish of great variety.

A recent bonus for Walindi has been the live-aboard diveboat the *FeBrina*, a 12-passenger air-conditioned vessel, based at the resort and skippered by Alan Raabe. The *FeBrina* dives reefs in the bay but also makes longer cruises to the Bali Witu Islands (northwest of Willaumez Peninsula) and to reefs near Lolobau Island (east of Walindi), and in the Northwest season has made some exploratory cruises to the south coast of New Britain.

Although there is year-round diving out of Walindi, the best season is considered to be May/Dec. The water is warm throughout the year, around 28–30°C (82–86°F), so wetsuits are unnecessary – lycra suits with a hood are recommended.

At the Antibes Festival of the Sea in 1992 the Gold, Silver and Bronze medals for underwater photography were all awarded to divers submitting shots taken at Walindi.

Opposite: *A village inside the caldera at Garove Island.*
Above: *The Princess Anthias, Pseudonthias smithvanezi, is abundant north of Walindi.*

1 HANGING GARDENS

★★★★★★

Location: 2 n. miles (3.7km) northeast of Walindi.
Access: Mooring on reef – do not anchor.
Conditions: Usually sheltered all year.
Typical visibility: 20m (65ft)
Minimum depth: 1m (40in)
Maximum depth: 30m (100ft)

A wall dive descending from the surface to a sand and rubble bottom at about 27m (90ft). Along the sheer wall are numerous ledges and overhangs, plus several large cuts back into the cliff. The site is named for the many tangles of rope sponge dangling along the wall, some up to 3m (10ft) in length, with crinoids clinging to them. In the shaded areas beneath overhangs and within the cuts are prolific encrusting communities, dominated by sponges and tunicates. This is an excellent habitat to search for nudibranchs, featherduster worms and living shells, and for macro photography. It is also a productive and easy night-dive, flashlight fish being frequent.

Snorkellers can look down the vertical wall from very shallow water.

2 NUMUNDO REEF (BOB'S KNOB)

★★★★★★★

Location: 4 n. miles (7.4km) south-southeast of Walindi.
Access: Mooring on reef – do not anchor.
Conditions: Usually sheltered.
Typical visibility: 25m (80ft)
Minimum depth: 2m (6½ft)
Maximum depth: 40m (130ft)

The top of this reef is covered with a dense growth of delicate staghorn and other corals, and small fish abound; cardinalfish, squirrelfish and damselfish thrive in the sheltered environment. The reef slopes to deeper water, and a number of coral pillars have resident lionfish and dottybacks. The deeper part of the reef, near rubble patches, has aggregations of the fabulous Filament Wrasse. The males, mating in the evenings, display dorsal fins with long-filament rays. These lovely fish are a real challenge to the underwater photographer as they dash from female to female displaying.

This is an easy and rich site for snorkellers.

MACRO IN MICA

The volcanic sand slopes around PNG harbour some of the most interesting creatures for macro photographers, but two major problems need to be overcome if you are to achieve successful photographs. Luckily they both have the same solution.

- separating the subject from the background – a single flash light (strobe) above the subject forms a dark shadow, so the subject is melded to the dark sand
- the dark sand often has reflective mica particles in it, and these create flare around the subject where the flash light strikes the sand

The solution to both problems is to use two flash lights either side of the camera – not above it – aimed parallel to the bottom.

3 SCHUMANN ISLAND

★★★★★★★

Location: 12 n. miles (22km) north of Walindi.

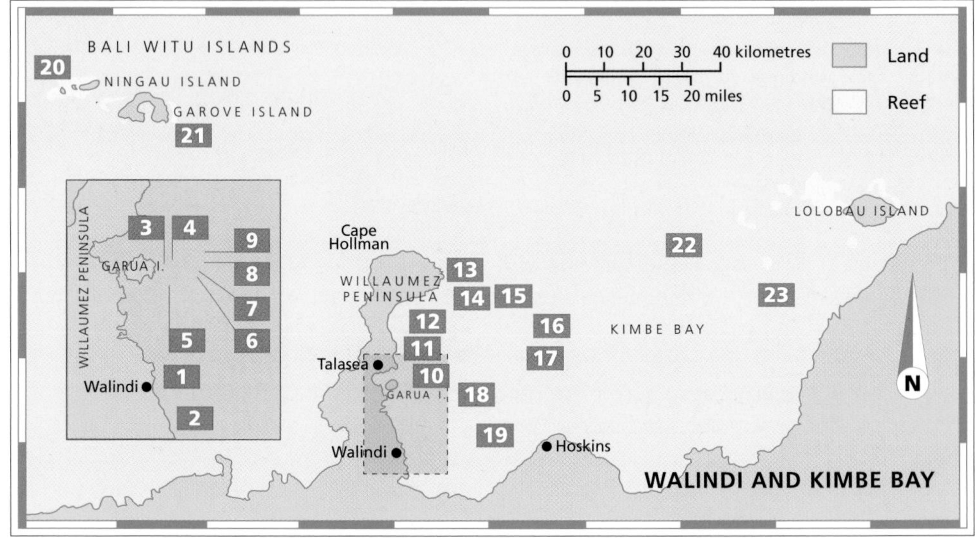

Access: By boat.
Conditions: Usually calm.
Typical visibility: 20m (65ft)
Minimum depth: as shallow as you like
Maximum depth: 10m (33ft)
On the shallow sandy bottom, with coral outcrops, are a multitude of marine animals never seen on classic coral reefs. Panda Clownfish and the very photogenic Porcelain Crab live in sand anemones. Sand Divers and wormfish dwell in the sand, and with care you can approach and photograph them before they dive into it. Banded Pipefish are common on the shallow reef patches, along with many different damselfish and blennies. This site rewards patient observers and macro photographers.

You can snorkel here from the beach of the island.

PHOTOGRAPHING NUDIBRANCHS

Nudibranchs are beautiful shell-less snails. Typically they have two sensing organs (rhinophores) which look like small feelers and which retract into the head; on their backs they have bushy gills, which can likewise be retracted. PNG possesses very many species of nudibranchs, from giant Spanish Dancers – 30cm (12in) or more long – to specimens that can be seen only under a microscope; it is probable that many have yet to be scientifically described and named.

Most are colourful and, because they move very slowly, are deceptively easy to photograph. I say 'deceptively' because, although you can easily get a 'record' of a nudibranch with a camera – particularly if using a Nikonos and framer – it is not very often that you see beautifully composed photographs. Avoid trying to shoot directly down on the nudibranch: use a more interesting angle with a carefully considered background.

4 RESTORF ISLAND

★★★★★★★

Location: Just east of Schumann Island (Site 3).
Access: Mooring at site – do not anchor.
Conditions: Usually calm. Sometimes currents on outer reef.
Typical visibility: 25m (80ft)
Minimum depth: as shallow as you like
Maximum depth: 35m (115ft)
The waters around the island have an incredible diversity of marine life. At least three different dives can be made, depending on your interests.

On the sand between the mooring and the beach are shrimp gobies (at least one being of an undescribed species), garden eels and Titan Triggerfish – who should be avoided when nesting as they ferociously defend their nests and will attack divers. Avoid also the Spiny Devilfish (*Inimicus* spp), a type of scorpionfish common in shallow water. Blue-Spotted Stingrays feed in the sand, and Eagle Rays are sometimes seen. Large Mantis Shrimp burrow in the sand; these amazing creatures have a very effective slashing defence, so don't touch.

On the main reef area, to the northeast, is a profusion of coral growth, especially gorgonians and black corals, alive with different fish. Grey Reef Sharks are frequent.

West of the island the main reef has a number of small coral outcrops, many serving as anchors for gorgonians, black corals, sea whips and sponges, which are home to some of the most beautiful fairy basslets (anthias), Swallowtailed Hawkfish (*Cyprinocirrhites polyactis*) and various invertebrates.

The beach is an ideal picnic and snorkelling area.

5 JOY'S REEF

★★★★★★★

Location: 1 n. mile (1.85km) southeast of Restorf Island (Site 4).
Access: Two moorings on site – do not anchor.
Conditions: Usually calm.
Typical visibility: 25m (80ft)
Minimum depth: as shallow as you like
Maximum depth: 35m (115ft)
A hard-coral reef, exposed at low tide, slopes downward northwesterly to a sandy bottom at about 24m (75ft). Staghorn corals predominate in the shallows, but other species thrive down the slope until the reef breaks up into isolated bommies with gorgonian and sponge growths scattered over the sand. Shrimp and burrowing gobies – like the exotic Crab-eye Goby (*Signigobius biocellatus*) – are in the sand near the reefs. The reef-slope is bounded by vertical walls, the eastern being the lusher; the wall and the floor beneath it are worth a careful search for shells and nudibranchs. This is excellent macro photography.

There is great snorkelling in the staghorn-coral gardens.

6 CHRISTINE'S REEF

★★★★★★★★★★

Location: 12 n. miles (22km) north-northeast of Walindi.
Access: Three moorings on reef – do not anchor.
Conditions: Usually calm.
Typical visibility: 40m (130ft)
Minimum depth: 1m (40in)

Maximum depth: 40m (130ft) plus
A beautiful scenic dive. The best feature is a saddle between the main reef and two smaller, detached reefs. The saddle has large sea fans, Red Sea Whips and giant barrel sponges covered with colourful crinoids. The larger of the two dark red fans at the saddle's southern end is a good place to observe Long-nosed Hawkfish (*Oxycirrhites typus*). Sea anemones are common, and the amazingly well camouflaged crocodilefish (*Cymbacephalus* sp) can be found by carefully searching the reef. Related to flatheads, this fish, up to 50cm (20in) long, is often confused with scorpionfish because of its elaborately frilled body, but is harmless.

This is among the best snorkel dives in the area, offering a large expanse of shallow reef with plenty of live coral and fish.

7 KIRSTY JAYNE'S REEF

★★★★★★

Location: 12 n. miles (22km) north-northeast of Walindi.
Access: 25min by boat from Walindi. Mooring on reef – do not anchor.
Conditions: Usually calm.
Typical visibility: 40m (130ft)
Minimum depth: 4m (13ft)
Maximum depth: 30m (100ft)
Descending at the mooring, you come to an area in 18m (60ft) where soft corals, sea fans and whips are arranged in a picture-perfect garden. A Bulb-tipped Anemone – with attendant Tomato Clownfish – has its home here along with other species of anemones and anemonefish. A school of shrimpfish, very popular with underwater photographers, tries to hide among the sea whips. The reef extends to deep water but the best diving is in the first 18m (60ft) – too deep for surface snorkellers but within the range of competent skin divers.

8 VANESSA'S REEF

★★★★

Location: 13 n. miles (24km) north-northeast of Walindi.
Access: Two moorings on site – do not anchor.
Conditions: Usually calm all year round, can be currents.
Typical visibility: 30m (100ft) plus
Minimum depth: 18m (60ft)
Maximum depth: 35m (115ft)
A ridge extends westwards from a shallower reef at 18m (60ft) or more, with many large sea fans and other gorgonians and a sponge garden. This garden has some huge Elephant-ear Sponges and barrel sponges. Many interesting small creatures live on the fans and sponges, which are also well decorated with crinoids. When current is running, barracuda and Grey Reef Sharks patrol the ridge's edge.

A nearby shallow reef is suitable for snorkelling.

THE RED-LINED SEA CUCUMBER

One of the first creatures I photographed in PNG was a sea cucumber. Unlike the usual rather dull tones of this normally shallow species, this cucmber was a stunning red colour, and lived at a depth below 18m (60ft). When the Australian marine naturalist and photographer Neville Coleman came to dive with us at Port Moresby in 1980, he got very excited when he saw it, as he had never seen anything like it before. It turned out to be a species unknown to science. In 1991 it was 'described' by Claude Massin and David Lane and given the name *Thelenota rubralineata*, in tribute to its wonderfully coloured pattern.

9 SUSAN'S REEF

★★★★★★

Location: 14 n. miles (26km) north-northeast of Walindi.
Access: 35min by boat from Walindi. Two moorings on site.
Conditions: Usually calm.
Typical visibility: 40m (130ft)
Minimum depth: 1m (40in)
Maximum depth: 40m (130ft) plus
Dense growths of Red Sea Whips distinguish this reef from others nearby. The whips are most numerous at the southern end of the reef, between 15m and 22m (50–70ft), as it rises to form a saddle that connects with a much larger reef. Susan's Reef extends northerly with a sheer wall on its east side and a sloping garden of hard corals on the west. There are also some sea fans and, in shallower water, dense growths of staghorn corals with scattered anemones among the branches.

The shallows make pleasant and easy snorkelling.

10 INGLIS SHOAL

★★★★

Location: 17 n. miles (31.5km) north-northeast of Walindi.
Access: 40min by boat from Walindi. Mooring on site – do not anchor.
Conditions: Not accessible in strong Southeast Trades.
Typical visibility: 40m (130ft) plus
Minimum depth: 12m (40ft)
Maximum depth: 50m (165ft) plus

A seamount rising to 12m (40ft) from below 600m (2000ft). The reeftop slopes, but soon changes to a vertical wall. Large pelagics and sharks are frequent. Scalloped Hammerheads visit regularly, particularly if the water is cooler than normal, being usually seen deeper than 30m (100ft). Other big fish are more approachable: you can have close encounters with Dogtooth Tuna, schools of Chevron Barracuda (*Sphryaena putnamiae*) and Bigeye Trevally. The reeftop – plate- and other hard-coral mounds decorated with grey soft corals – is home to a pair of giant Moray Eels. Triggerfish, anemonefish, fairy basslets and others abound. This is a good site for shark and fish photography.

11 SOUTH EMA REEF

★★★★★★★★

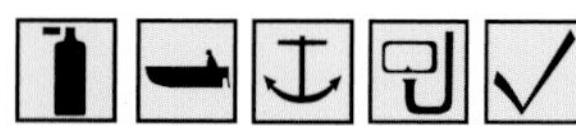

Location: 20 n. miles (37km) north-northeast of Walindi.
Access: 45min by boat from Walindi. Mooring on reef.
Conditions: Not always possible to dive if strong Southeast Trades.
Typical visibility: 50m (165ft)
Minimum depth: 10m (33ft)
Maximum depth: 50m (165ft) plus

The site is down a deep saddle from a shallow reef to a bommie which rises to 10m (33ft). Just off the saddle's west end, where it starts to rise again at about 30m (100ft), are the entrances to a swimthrough cave. Entering the smaller opening on the north side, you can admire the gorgonians and sponges framing the larger, south-side opening. On the bommie's slopes are exceptional growths of soft corals, Red Sea Whips and a cluster of barrel sponges, the largest almost 2m (6½ft) tall. The bommie's crest is covered in hard corals with occasional sea anemones. Fusiliers, batfish, trevally and sometimes barracuda cruise above the bommie, which is alive with many kinds of smaller fish, including dartfish, gobies and hawkfish.

The shallow reef can be snorkelled, but the reef's main features can be seen only by diving.

12 NORTH EMA REEF

★★★★★★★★

Location: 21 n. miles (39km) north-northeast of Walindi.
Access: 50min by boat from Walindi. Three moorings for different wind directions.
Conditions: Can be difficult to dive in strong southeast winds.
Typical visibility: 50m (165ft)
Minimum depth: 1m (40in)
Maximum depth: 45m (150ft) plus

You descend from the shallow main reef down a deep

Clown anemone fish, Amphiprion ocellaris.

saddle to a bommie whose top is at 35m (115ft); even deeper bommies are nearby. The reef-sides drop into very deep water from which Scalloped Hammerheads sometimes appear. The bommie is covered with sea fans, sea whips and soft corals. After a few minutes on the deep bommie, ascend to the main reef, where there are different species of anemonefish, among other reef fish. A wonderful site for wide-angle photographers.

You can snorkel on the shallow main reef.

13 CAPE HEUSSNER

★★★★★

Location: 25 n. miles (46km) north of Walindi.
Access: 1hr by boat from Walindi.
Conditions: Calm except in strong Southeast Trades. Can be strong currents – sometimes best to drift-dive rather than anchor.
Typical visibility: 40m (130ft)
Minimum depth: 1m (40in)
Maximum depth: 25m (80ft)
The reefs around Cape Heussner slope to sand flats at about 20–25m (65–80ft). Pelagics, rays and sharks are seen around the reefs, garden eels and shrimp gobies on the sand flats. Large sponges and gorgonians are plentiful.

14 SOUTH BAY REEF – CECILIE'S WALL

★★★★★★★★

Location: 25 n. miles (46km) north-northeast of Walindi.
Access: 1hr by boat from Walindi. Mooring on reef.
Conditions: Difficult to dive in strong Southeast Trades and northwesterly swells.
Typical visibility: 50m (165ft)
Minimum depth: 1m (40in)
Maximum depth: 50m (165ft) plus
On the northern side the reef-wall drops vertically from very shallow water. At about 18m (60ft) is a profusion of beautiful and delicate lace coral (*Stylaster* spp): take care not to damage these growths. Silvertip Sharks are sometimes seen deeper down, but the top is interesting too, with anemonefish, including White-bonnet Anemonefish. A pod of Spinner Dolphin lives around this reef; although difficult to dive with, they'll come to the moving boat and ride the bow wave.

Snorkellers can easily see the anemonefish among the excellent and varied coral growths.

THE WHITE-BONNET ANEMONEFISH

Amphiprion leucokranos is a beautiful anemonefish described as recently as 1973 from specimens found in Madang. The fish is actually quite common in shallow water throughout PNG; the reason it avoided detection for so long is the fact that a solitary specimen usually shares an anemone with a family of anemonefish of a completely different species. The fish is easy to distinguish, as it has a white blotch on, and another white blotch either side of, its head. The body is yellow-orange, and the blotches are sometimes connected. White-Bonnet Anemonefish have been known to produce hybrids with their 'host' anemonefish. It is an interesting conjecture that this may be because they get confused as to who they really are.

15 BRADFORD SHOAL

★★★★★

Location: 25 n. miles (46km) north-northeast of Walindi.
Access: 1¼hr by boat from Walindi. Mooring on site – do not anchor.
Conditions: May be dived in all but strong Southeast Trades and northwesterly swells. Mild currents sometimes present.
Typical visibility: 50m (165ft)
Minimum depth: 20m (65ft)
Maximum depth: 50m (165ft) plus
A seamount rising from over 600m (2000ft) to 20m (65ft). The reeftop is covered with large plate corals and colonies of leather coral. The reef slopes downward from its twin summits to a lip at about 27m (90ft), after which the drop is almost vertical. The many less common species of fish found on this reef include Burgess's Butterflyfish (*Chaetodon burgessi*), Blackspot Angelfish (*Genicanthus melanospilos*) and Harlequin Grouper (*Cephalopholis polleni*). Above the reef schools of Bigeye Trevally, barracuda, Rainbow Runners and batfish are common, and will swim around you as you make a safety stop on the mooring-line. Grey Reef and Hammerhead Sharks are sometimes seen.

16 KIMBE ISLAND BOMMIE

★★★★★

 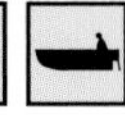 

Location: Close to Kimbe Island.
Access: 1hr by boat from Walindi. Mooring marks site, which cannot be seen from surface.
Conditions: Difficult to dive in strong Southeast Trades or northwesterly swells. Best when slight current running, when all the fish come to feed on pinnacle.
Typical visibility: 50m (165ft)

Minimum depth: 27m (90ft)
Maximum depth: 50m (165ft) plus
The reef abounds with life and is richly decorated with hard and soft corals and gorgonians. Some ridges extend from the pinnacle into water far too deep to dive. This is among the best sites in the area to see schools of big fish, but the current is important – on a still day you'll wonder what all the fuss is about.

17 KIMBE ISLAND

★★★★★★★

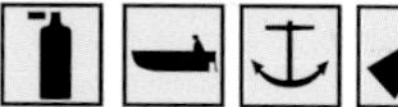

Location: 25 n. miles (46km) northeast of Walindi.
Access: 1hr by boat from Walindi.
Conditions: Difficult to dive in strong Southeast Trades or northwesterly swells.
Typical visibility: 40m (130ft) plus
Minimum depth: as shallow as you like
Maximum depth: 50m (165ft) plus
Although the reef drops off into very deep water the shallows are very interesting, full of common reef species, and make an easy dive. Small Blacktip Reef Sharks are frequent, plus a multitude of tropical fish.

A large pod of Spinner Dolphin (*Stenella longirostris*) resident around the island has become quite used to snorkellers, and will sometimes allow you to approach.

18 OTTO'S REEF

★★★★★★★★

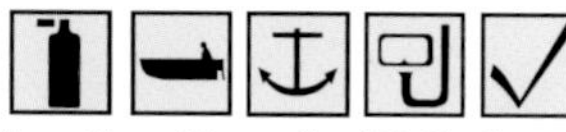

Location: 17 n. miles (31.5km) east–northeast of Walindi.
Access: 40min by boat from Walindi. Two moorings – do not anchor.
Conditions: Difficult to dive in strong Southeast Trades and northwesterly swells.
Typical visibility: 40m (130ft) plus
Minimum depth: 1m (40in)
Maximum depth: 50m (165ft) plus
The best dive is at the northeast end, where the reef forms a point. Many schools of fish congregate here to feed in the slight currents – barracuda, trevally, sea perch, fusiliers and unicornfish are joined by sharks and tuna, and you can get very close to these feeding fish. The wall south of the point, at 5–15m (16–50ft), has many interesting ledges, overhangs and small caves. This area's rich growth of many kinds of sponges, plus black corals, clams and ascidians, makes an ideal habitat for nudibranchs and other invertebrates.

In calm conditions this is an exciting snorkel dive. Dolphins and Pilot Whales are sometimes seen.

Clown triggerfish, Balistoides conspicillium, appear on all open water reefs in PNG.

19 PALUMA REEF

★★★

   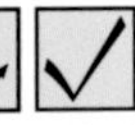

Location: 26 n. miles (48km) east of Walindi.
Access: 1hr by boat from Walindi. Mooring on site – do not anchor. Easily accessible from Hoskins.
Conditions: Can be dived in all but strong Southeast Trades and northwesterly swells.
Typical visibility: 40m (130ft)
Minimum depth: 15m (50ft)
Maximum depth: 40m (130ft) plus

A deep plateau joined to the main reef by a ridge. The primary attraction is the large number of lavender, pink and yellow soft corals (*Dendronephthya* spp), some being 1m (40in) tall. Scattered black-coral bushes, sea fans and whips among these make for one of the most colourful of all Kimbe Bay's reefs. Though not as numerous as elsewhere, fish are still plentiful, and a school of barracuda often visits divers on the mooring-line. The average dive depth is 25–30m (80–100ft), so only relatively short dive-times are possible. A good site for scenic photographs with colourful soft corals.

20 THE ARCH

Location: North side of Ningau Island, Bali Witu Islands.
Access: By boat.
Conditions: Exposed in Northwest season, otherwise partly sheltered. Slight currents.
Typical visibility: 50m (165ft)
Minimum depth: 5m (16ft)
Maximum depth: 25m (80ft) plus

A ridge gradually descends from the main reef. At 25m (80ft) a large archway has soft corals, sea fans and sea whips. A very pretty spot with lots of fish-life, including resident crocodilefish.

21 LAMA SHOAL

Location: 1 n. mile (1.85km) east of Garove Island, Bali Witu Islands.
Access: Mooring on reef – do not anchor.
Conditions: Exposed to strong southeasterly winds, otherwise sheltered. Can be considerable current.
Typical visibility: 40m (130ft)
Minimum depth: 8m (26ft)
Maximum depth: 50m (165ft) plus

An exceptional site for fish action. After descending to the reeftop, make your way against the current to the side receiving the current, where you'll find huge schools of barracuda and Bigeye Trevally. Dogtooth Tuna patrol the dropoff, among schools of other reef fish. Sharks are occasionally seen. Princess Anthias (*Pseudanthias smithvanizi*) swarm over the reef, and lionfish are common. Down the sloping dropoff are many large bushes of black coral, sea whips and barrel sponges.

An unusual feature is that the top and upper slope are carpeted with a small brown anemone-like creature. Beware! This is a giant colony of Corallimorpharians.

22 FATHER'S ARCH

★★★★

  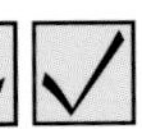

Location: 14 n. miles (26km) west of Lolobau Island.
Access: By boat.
Conditions: Partly sheltered in Southeast season. but exposed to northwesterly winds and swell.
Typical visibility: 50m (165ft)
Minimum depth: 5m (16ft)
Maximum depth: 40m (130ft) plus

A ridge drops from the main reef. Swimming along this, gradually descending, you reach an archway whose top is at 25m (80ft). There are many soft corals and sea fans and whips. Schooling fish are common; a large school of barracuda often circles right over the arch. A favourite site for underwater photographers.

23 FAIRWAY REEF

★★★★★

Location: Lolobau Island.
Access: Refer to *FeBrina*.
Conditions: Partly sheltered in Southeast season, but exposed to northwesterly winds and swells.
Typical visibility: 50m (165ft)
Minimum depth: 8m (26ft)
Maximum depth: 50m (165ft) plus

A main reef with, off its north end, a bommie reached by swimming along a ridge. On the ridge are scattered sea fans and barrel sponges, one bright orange fan being particularly photogenic. At the bommie the fish action starts with a resident school of barracuda and Bigeye Trevally. Sharks, including Silvertip and Grey Reef, are frequent at the site – Alan Raabe of the *FeBrina* is developing this as a shark-feeding station.

Walindi

How to Get There

Air Niugini runs two flights daily from Port Moresby into Hoskins (flight-time 1hr 5min). Some flights into Hoskins are via Lae or other centres.

Air Niugini
PO Box 181, Kimbe
tel 675 93 5287 (international)
tel 675 93 5041 (domestic)
fax 675 93 5669

Where to Stay

Walindi Plantation Resort
PO Box 4, Kimbe
tel 675 935441
fax 675 935638
The Walindi Plantation Resort, the base for Walindi Diving (see below), is owned and operated by Max and Cecilie Benjamin, who have pioneered the diving in West New Britain. The resort has 12 rooms either in the Plantation House or in beautifully landscaped beach-front duplex bungalows. The resort is easily accessible on the Talasea Road (20min drive from main town of Kimbe; 45min from airport at Hoskins) and has a restaurant and bar. It provides land-tours including bushwalks, village tours, tours to the hot springs, island picnics, visits to the crocodile farm and artefact-buying tours.

Palms Resort Hotel
PO Box 10, Hoskins
tel 675 93 5113
fax 675 93 5015
A well established colonial-style hotel situated only 1km (1100yd) from Hoskins Airport. In 1995 it started its own dive operation (details below). It has 15 rooms, a bar, a restaurant and a swimming pool, all in a tropical-garden setting. Aside from diving, game-fishing and land excursions to war relics, the hot springs and villages are on offer.

Dive Facilities

Walindi Diving
Walindi Plantation Resort
(address above)
Snorkellers are extremely well catered for here, with snorkelling tours and opportunities to see and snorkel with whales and dolphins. The scuba diving is first-class, with qualified instructors and divemasters available to cater for a maximum of 18 divers. Two fast diveboats – with radio contact to base – cater for day- and night-diving, and both single-dive and whole-day trips (lunch provided) are available. Two Bauer compressors ensure fast and reliable air-fills, and the resort carries a large stock of dive cylinders and gear for hire. Instruction up to Assistant Instructor level is offered through PADI and NASDS. A retail dive shop sells many major brands, including Tusa. Equipment servicing and repair are available, with a good stock of parts for various brands.

Dive Hoskins
Palms Resort Hotel (address above)
Runs day trips to the reefs just a few kilometres off the resort in Kimbe Bay. Has a 7m (22ft) fast twin-hulled diveboat able to cater for 8–10 divers, and a dive shop where tanks are filled and guests' equipment rinsed and stored. Rental equipment available; equipment servicing; limited supplies of new equipment for sale. NAUI/PADI instruction is offered. The sites are all within 10–25min of the resort.

Live-Aboards

MV FeBrina
PO Box 4, Kimbe
tel 675 935441
fax 675 935638
Based at the Walindi Plantation Resort and operated by Alan Raabe, the *FeBrina* is a comfortable 22m (72ft) steel-hulled, air-conditioned live-aboard for 12 passengers and up to 7 crew. Passenger accommodation consists of 6 twin-bunk cabins. The *FeBrina* runs diving cruises to Father's Reefs (near Lolobau Island; and the Bali Witu Islands (see page 120), and has started running exciting cruises in the Northwest season to explore the south coast of New Britain.

The *Manta*/Frank Butler
For details see the Rabaul directory (page 133).

Local Highlights

The **Crocodile Farm** at Kimbe has 2–300 young crocodiles and is open to visitors for no charge (the animals do not actually breed on site). The Saltwater Crocodile has been protected in PNG for many years, with the result that populations have been steadily increasing. The animal is now managed rather than protected, and young crocodiles with a belly-width under 51cm (20in) may be taken for skins and meat. Larger crocodiles are completely protected as breeding stock. Baby crocodiles are collected by villagers and sold to the farms, which feed them on offal from the local abattoirs. When the crocodiles reach marketable size they are slaughtered, their skins exported and their meat sold to local hotels. Two very big crocodile farms in Lae and Port Moresby have large crocodiles on display, but usually charge for admission.

The highly regarded live aboard dive boat, the FeBrina.

RABAUL

On 18 September 1994 an earthquake shook Rabaul, and the town was ordered to evacuate. The following morning a massive eruption commenced: volcanoes both sides of the harbour started spewing volcanic ash and pumice. After two weeks of continuous eruption, Rabaul had been destroyed by the weight of ash settling on the roofs of buildings and the rivers of mud flowing through the streets. The water in the inner harbour was covered with a solid raft of pumice over 1m (40in) thick. Wonderfully the huge loss of life experienced in an earlier eruption, in 1937, was avoided.

The harbour and surrounding waters contain a fleet of ships and planes wrecked during World War II. Those outside the main harbour were unaffected by the eruption; those within it have inevitably lost some of the marine life reported below and now have a heavy coating of ash. In March 1995 the Royal Australian Navy hydrographic survey vessel, HMAS *Flinders*, reported that a few of the harbour's most popular wrecks may have been flattened and buried by the huge quantities of ash and boulders falling into the harbour. At the time of writing, however, a full survey by divers has yet to be made. Frank Butler has dived the *Manko Maru*, *Italy Maru* and the *Yamayuri Maru* since the eruption and reported a healthy population of fish-life surviving on the wrecks.

Diving Rabaul's wrecks

The wrecks in the harbour are easily accessible by boat, or sometimes even straight from shore. Probably the most famous of these is the *Hakkai Maru* (Site 7), 128m (420ft) long and sitting upright with its bow at 40m (130ft) and stern at 30m (100ft). Some of the Rabaul wrecks are very deep and should be dived with caution. They are not suitable for inexperienced divers – although nearby can be found excellent shallow diving to suit all tastes and abilities. You can penetrate many of the wrecks, though beware: their insides often have a coating of fine silt that can easily obliterate visibility, and hanging cables wait

Opposite: *View near Rabaul before the 1994 volcanic eruption.*

Above: *The beautiful but venomous Blue Ring Octopus, Hapalochlaena sp.*

to snare the unwary. But, for those with the right training and experience, penetrations are entirely feasible and rewarding.

Several shallower wrecks in the harbour are more broken up and make great dives for wreck fossickers, though the rule is: strictly photographs only – no souvenirs. Many of the other vessels sunk were salvaged after the war, but there are still tantalizing rumours of undived wrecks in the harbour – including that of a submarine reportedly glimpsed by a diver at 100m (330ft)! Around the wrecks the bottom is littered with hundreds of artillery shells, often sticking up out of the bottom like so many sailors guarding their ghost fleet.

Outside the harbour a blue-water current sweeps through Saint George's Channel, the passage between New Britain and New Ireland. Here lie two exceptional wrecks in water that is mostly brilliantly clear. George's Wreck (Site 2), named for its discoverer, long-time Rabaul resident and adventurer George Tyers, always amazes me since it hangs bow-up on a steep slope down which it should decades ago have disappeared! Just round the corner the beautiful wreck of a 'Pete' reconnaissance biplane (Site 1) sits perfectly on the bottom at 27m (90ft) and decorated with soft corals. This small but spectacular aircraft wreck is a must for all divers visiting Rabaul.

Photographing Wrecks in Murky Water

It is sad but true that the captains of ships and pilots of aircraft typically wrecked their vessels with complete disregard to the convenience of sport divers. Instead of picking clear water offshore, they mostly opted for murky bays, making underwater photography a challenge. It is generally useless to try to use an underwater flash (strobe), since particles in the water reflect light back, no matter how cleverly you position your lights. Moreover, the water tends to be green. In short, the resulting photographs are useless.

I have found that very interesting and clear photographs can be taken by combining

- very wide-angle lenses
- natural light
- a model carrying a powerful dive-light
- film that has a strong blue response.

Kodak's Underwater film is very useful in natural light if the wreck is deeper than 10m (33ft): the green water turns blue and the model's light gains red. Although this is perhaps unnatural, it does make for dramatic pictures.

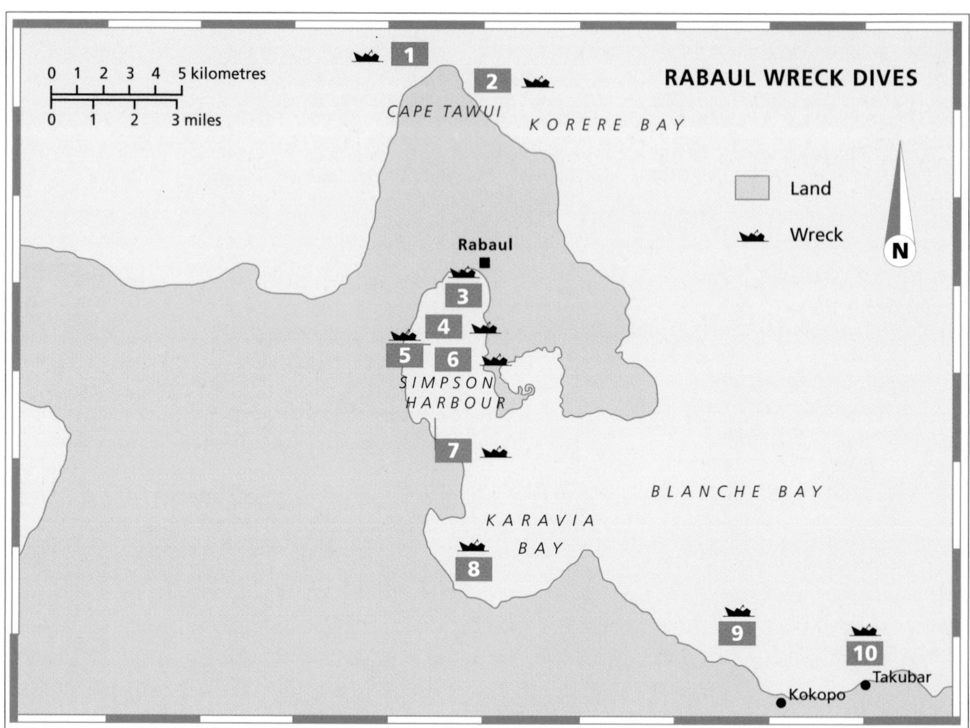

1 'PETE' BIPLANE

★★★★★★★

Location: About 1km (1100yd) west of Cape Tawui, off beach.
Access: By road or boat. Local knowledge necessary to find exact site of wreck. Arrange with villagers if diving from shore.
Conditions: Best in southeast wind conditions, when site completely sheltered and water very clear. Slight current runs over site.
Typical visibility: 40m (130ft)
Minimum depth: 3m (10ft)
Maximum depth: 27m (90ft)

You descend an attractive slope to find the aircraft upright in rubble at 27m (90ft). The craft is intact, and its splendid growths of soft corals and sponges make it very attractive and photogenic. This Mitsubishi Biplane, used as an observation plane during World War II, was code-named 'Pete' by the Allies. Fitted out as a seaplane, it was apparently sunk at its mooring – hence its good condition. Even to those not interested in wrecks this is a fascinating dive because of the marine life. You complete the dive by ascending the reef-slope, admiring the excellent corals and fish-life. Golden Cowries have been seen here.

The edge of the reef offers interesting snorkelling. The aircraft itself is too deep to snorkel, though competent skin divers can dive close enough to see it.

2 GEORGE'S WRECK

★★★★★★★

Location: Close to shore between Korere Bay and Cape Tawui.
Access: Can be dived from shore, but access difficult – boat far more convenient. Mooring on site for small craft only.
Conditions: Exposed to Southeast Trades, but usually calm.
Typical visibility: 40m (130ft)
Minimum depth: 15m (50ft)
Maximum depth: 55m (180ft)

A really unusual dive, since the wreck – an armed freighter – lies bow-up, very close to shore, on a steep underwater slope, and seems ready to slide down at the slightest shove. The clear water necessitates a warning: it is all too easy to swim down the deck without realizing how deep you're going, and find yourself at 55m (180ft). The starboard anchor, still in place, is the first thing you notice when descending. Just forward of midships are the remains of the bridge and crew-quarters; below them, the engine-room is accessible via a hole blown in the side by salvagers. The fallen funnel is behind the crew-quarters. The rudder and propeller are usually buried in the sand. Soft corals and colourful sponges decorate the wreck, and plenty of fish swim around. There is an attractive coral reef in shallow water for an enjoyable safety stop.

Snorkellers can easily see the bow of the wreck.

3 MITSU MARU AND SUGAR CHARLIE

★★

Location: Simpson Harbour.
Access: By boat.
Conditions: Usually calm.
Typical visibility: 20m (65ft) – but often (unpredictably) as low as 6m (20ft)
Minimum depth: 12m (40ft)
Maximum depth: 18m (60ft)

This relatively shallow dive makes a relaxing change from the many deep wrecks in Rabaul Harbour. Although small, *Mitsu Maru* is intact and has an exceptional fish-life, particularly anemonefish and lionfish. The engine-room is accessible but cannot be considered stable, and there is always danger from falling debris. A very interesting and puzzling feature is the tail-section of an 'Emily' flying boat, Sugar Charlie, up against the port bow; no other parts of the aircraft have been found. The wreck makes an interesting night-dive so long as you do not attempt penetration.

4 MANKO MARU

★★★

Location: Simpson Harbour.
Access: By boat.
Conditions: Usually calm.
Typical visibility: 20m (65ft) – usually less
Minimum depth: 20m (65ft)
Maximum depth: 35m (115ft)

A 1502-ton refrigeration vessel now resting upright on the bottom at 35m (115ft). The stern has been broken by the anchor of a modern ship – this wreck has suffered from lying close to the main Rabaul wharves. Nevertheless, it is well worth a dive, and, with bow and stern both at 25m (80ft), is shallower than many wrecks in the harbour, allowing you more time to fossick for artefacts. It is often shrouded with layers of misty water, giving a ghostly and enchanted feeling. Lionfish, Emperor and Moray Eels, black corals and sponges can be found, but the marine life is not as prolific as on wrecks outside the harbour.

5 YAMAYURI MARU

★★★

Location: Simpson Harbour.
Access: 12min by boat from Rabaul Yacht Club.
Conditions: Usually calm. This deep dive is for the experienced only.
Typical visibility: 25m (80ft) – often less
Minimum depth: 40m (130ft)
Maximum depth: 57m (190ft)

A 5028-ton freighter, upright and intact, with her bow at 43m (140ft) and stern at 40m (130ft). This wreck has yielded some interesting artefacts, including a mah-jongg set now displayed in the war museum ashore. Two big anchors rest on the foredeck near a gun; a second gun sits on the stern deck. The holds are very silty, so take great care not to reduce the visibility even further than it often is. Alongside the starboard side of the ship is a landing barge, complete with engine and propeller.

6 ITALY MARU

★★★

Location: Simpson Harbour.
Access: By boat.
Conditions: Usually calm.
Typical visibility: 25m (80ft) – sometimes less
Minimum depth: 30m (100ft)
Maximum depth: 45m (150ft)

This 5859-ton freighter now lies twisted and battered on its starboard side with both bow and stern distinguishable at 30m (100ft). A school of batfish lives on it, and it also has good stands of black coral and other marine life. Because the wreck is on its side, first-time divers may feel disorientated; however, after a few dives you can penetrate the engine-room through a large bomb-hole in the top (port) side – a favourite dive on the wreck.

7 HAKKAI MARU

★★★★

Location: Simpson Harbour.
Access: By boat.
Conditions: Usually calm.
Typical visibility: 25m (80ft), can be less
Minimum depth: 33m (110ft)
Maximum depth: 44m (145ft)

The *Hakkai Maru* was a 5114-ton Japanese naval engineering vessel sunk by dive bombers on 17 January 1944. The wreck is intact, upright, not excessively deep, and penetrations can be made inside the wreck to see machinery in the engineering workshop, bathrooms, cabins and the engine room. Many loose cables hang around inside the wreck ready to snare an unskilled diver, and silt can obliterate visibility so that only experienced divers should venture inside. Guns are still mounted on both the bow and stern, and a surprising amount of fish-life surrounds the wreck.

8 IWATE MARU

★★

Location: In Karavia Bay, offshore from old slipway.
Access: Usually from beach (small fee payable to landowners), 20min drive from town. Guide necessary to find wreck.
Conditions: Usually sheltered. Sometimes murky near surface, particularly after rain, but gets clearer deeper.
Typical visibility: 20m (65ft) – sometimes reduced
Minimum depth: as shallow as you like
Maximum depth: 22m (70ft)

The ship was originally 2928 tons but, as a shipping hazard, was blown up and now lies scattered around the bottom. Only the presence of an anchor reveals that one end was the bow. Nevertheless, many interesting artefacts can be found in the surrounding silty sand – broken china and ammunition, including 75mm (3in) shells, are common. The wreck has a thriving community of fish, and turtles often visit.

9 ZERO FIGHTER

★★★★

Location: 26km (15 miles) along the Kokopo road.
Access: Usually from beach rather than boat. Guide essential to find wreck.
Conditions: Usually calm.
Typical visibility: 30m (100ft)
Minimum depth: 27m (90ft)
Maximum depth: 30m (100ft)

After a short wade from the beach into waist-deep water, you descend the sloping sand bottom, past scattered coral bommies. You soon reach the aircraft, which is intact and upright. The wings sit flush with the sand bottom, and two of the three propeller blades stick out, with a small barrel sponge beside them. Two cannon are still attached forward of the cockpit, which is usually full of tiny baitfish. Fire Coral grows over much of the wreck, so don't touch it with your bare hands. A very fine example of this type of aircraft, offering photographers great opportunities.

10 TAKUBAR WRECK

★★★★

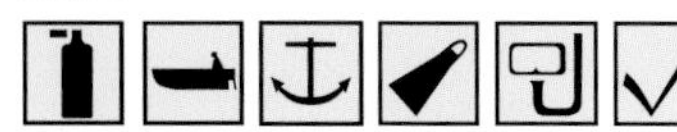

Location: Takubar, near Kokopo.
Access: 30min drive from Rabaul. Although possible to use boat to this site, usual access is from beach.
Conditions: Usually calm.
Typical visibility: 25m (80ft) – sometimes less
Minimum depth: 4m (13ft)
Maximum depth: 22m (70ft)

This wreck is believed to be of the 4981-ton freighter *Kinkasan Maru*, but identification has never been confirmed. The wreck, partly buried in the sand and resting on her port side, is broken and somewhat collapsed, but much is recognizable. You reach it after a short swim from the shore down a dark sand slope. There is good hard- and soft-coral growth, particularly near the stern, and a thriving fish community.

In good visibility this can be an interesting snorkel, since part of the wreck rises to 4m (13ft).

The common Lionfish, Pterois volitans, is probably one of the most photographed of PNG's fishes.

Diving Rabaul's Reefs

There is excellent reef diving in the area. The Submarine Base (Site 7), a current-swept vertical dropoff, and Midway Reef (Site 1), which has a brilliant mix of hard and soft corals, are two well known dives close to Rabaul, but even better diving can be found at Duke of York (Sites 11 and 13), Watom (Sites 4–6) and Pigeon (Credner) islands (Sites 9 and 10) – or near Cape Lambert (Site 15), a few hours' cruising northwest of Rabaul.

A short drive from town, some rare and exquisite marine creatures live on sand and rubble slopes that are easily accessible day and night. These include strange fish and invertebrates of many different types – but particularly molluscs. Rabaul was the centre years ago for a thriving shell-exporting business. Commercial activity has now ended, but keen photographers can find the rarest of molluscs on the deep slopes near Rabaul. Golden Cowries (*Cypraea aurantium*) and Gloriamaris cones are regularly discovered, and rarer species are not impossible to find. One species of cowrie is named *Cypraea rabaulensis.* Under no circumstances may you take live shells.

For more information on diving in this area, particularly on the wrecks, refer to *Rabaul's Forgotten Fleet* (1994) by Monica Forster with Peter Stone. Published before the eruption, the book describes, in fascinating detail, dives Monica and her husband Syd made on the wrecks during the many years they lived in Rabaul.

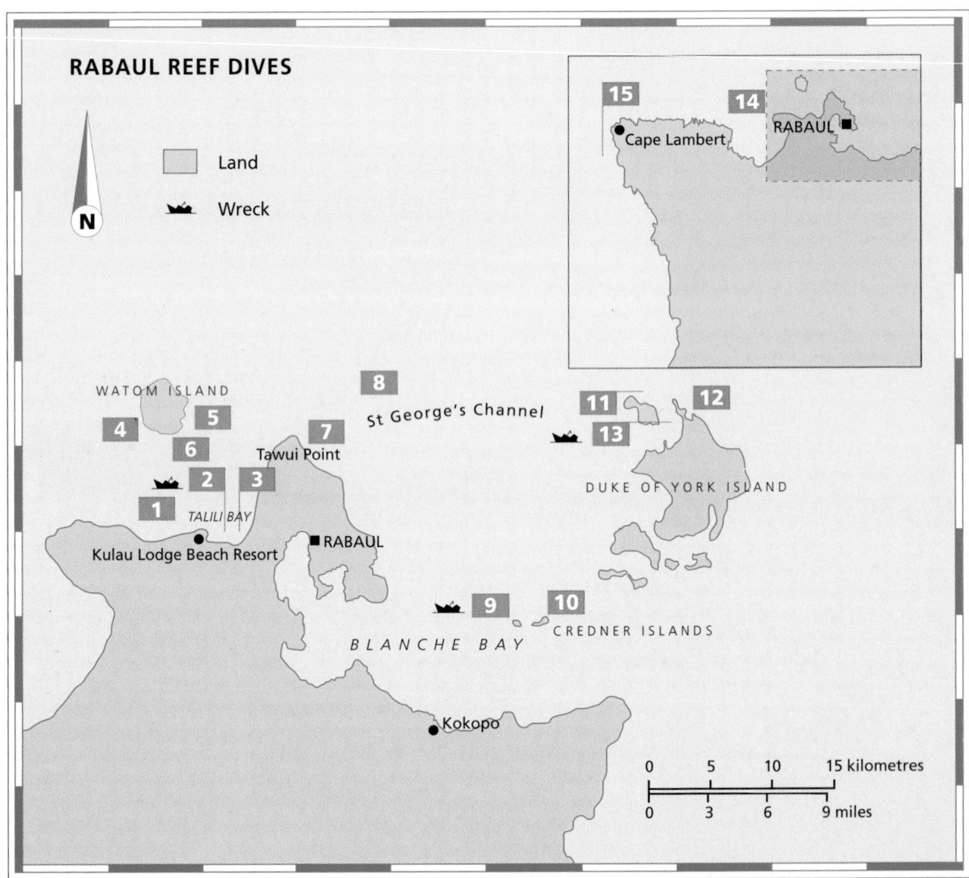

1 MIDWAY REEF

★★★★★★★★

Location: 3 n. miles (5.6km) west of Kulau Lodge Beach Resort.
Access: 10min by boat from Kulau Lodge Beach Resort.
Conditions: Usually calm. Slight currents.
Typical visibility: 35m (115ft)
Minimum depth: 3m (10ft)
Maximum depth: 38m (125ft)

Among the best reef dives in the Rabaul area. Several possible dive sites all have excellent hard and soft corals. From the southern tip, swim along the dropoff on the western side of the reef or descend to the sunken coral reef further south. At the northern end of this sausage-shaped reef you can explore both sides of the reef, although the western side is probably the more spectacular, being the steeper wall. The reef is cut with crevices and has a great variety of marine life, including soft corals and sea fans. Nudibranchs, clownfish and their anemones, turtles, reef sharks, pelagics and even dugong have been seen.

This is first-class snorkelling in usually ideal conditions; you can explore a large area where a great variety of reef creatures thrive.

2 KULAU LODGE BEACH WRECKS

★★★

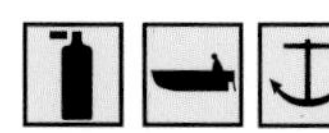

Location: 80m (88yd) offshore immediately in front of Kulau Lodge Beach Resort.
Access: By boat from beach.
Conditions: Usually calm.
Typical visibility: 25m (80ft) – sometimes reduced
Minimum depth: 8m (26ft)
Maximum depth: 35m (115ft)

A series of interesting wrecks sunk by Peter Leggett, the owner of the Kulau Lodge Beach Resort. They are connected by a guide-line, so can be easily found – even at night. The diveboat ties up to a mooring placed in 8m (26ft) near a garden of Giant Clams. The first wreck is a small coastal freighter, below which are the remains of a Japanese Zero aircraft. Further down is a small fuel tanker, and below that a small coastal freighter and a large Japanese fishing vessel. Scattered around are World War II bombs and ammunition. In and around the wrecks are some fascinating creatures. Stingrays are common, Shovelnose Sharks and dugong have been seen, and turtles come to the wrecks every night to rest. Frogfish and crocodilefish are harder to find but always there; juvenile Red Emperors are common. Going right to the deepest wreck is quite a long, deep swim, and it is surprisingly easy to run into decompression time, but the shallow grass beds near the mooring – harbouring cowfish, garden eels, live sea shells, colourful sea urchins and nudibranchs – make a safety stop a pleasure. The bottom is silty and easily stirred up, so control your diving.

3 BP WHARF

★★★

Location: Close to shore in Talili Bay.
Access: 5min by boat from Kulau Lodge Beach Resort. Swimming from shore not recommended. Take care wharf is clear for diving, and no large ships docked or likely to arrive.
Conditions: Usually calm.
Typical visibility: 10m (33ft)
Minimum depth: as shallow as you like
Maximum depth: 17m (55ft)

This fuelling wharf has been here for decades, and now has a magnificent display of marine creatures living on and around it. This is one of the few places where genuine stonefish are regularly found alongside commoner scorpionfish, lionfish, frogfish and batfish. Large soft corals decorate the wharf piles and shelter nudibranchs and pipefish. Octopus and squid are around. In the sand by the bottom of the wharf are flounders and pufferfish. This easy dive offers a trove of great macro photographic subjects. The wharf can also be dived at night, and is even more productive then.

4 WEST POINT

★★★★★★★★

Location: West coast of Watom Island.
Access: 20min by boat from Kulau Lodge Beach Resort. Only small boats can anchor on very shallow reeftop. Arrange with villagers before diving; they need to be assured nothing will be removed from reef.
Conditions: Usually calm; difficult if large northwesterly swells.
Typical visibility: 35m (115ft)
Minimum depth: 2m (6½ft)
Maximum depth: 50m (165ft) plus

The three possible dives here all start at the northwestern tip of the reef, which extends offshore in front of a village. The wall starts immediately, and you can either dive along it towards the village or go south along its outside. Both are good wall dives and offer a variety of marine life, including turtles, Eagle Rays, giant Dogtooth Tuna, batfish, anemonefish and plenty of other fish and invertebrates.

A deep dive, for experienced divers only, descends directly from the point of the reef to a sandy ledge at 53m (170ft). As on the other two dives, but more so, you can expect to see pelagics and sharks; Hammerhead Sharks and Tawny Sharks have been encountered.

There is first-class snorkelling along the edge of the dropoff.

5 THE GROTTO

★★★★★★★★

Location: East coast of Watom Island.
Access: 20min by boat from Kulau Lodge Beach Resort.
Conditions: Usually calm; best in late morning, with sun overhead. Exposed in Southeast Trades.
Typical visibility: 30m (100ft)
Minimum depth:10m (33ft)
Maximum depth: 50m (165ft) plus

A magnificent wall dive, with many grottoes cut into the wall. From the anchorage, where two World War II Japanese barges are sunk, the dive extends southerly to depths of 33m (110ft). A cave and a lava tube are on the side of a dropoff that descends to at least 75m (250ft). The crevices are full of colourful corals, and the scenery is excellent for wide-angle photography.

There is great snorkelling in shallow water along the dropoff's edge.

Dinah diving the spectacular 'Pete' Biplane Wreck.

DYNAMIC REEFS

Every diver deplores careless actions that result in damaged coral. A foolishly placed anchor or a clumsy overweighted diver – both can contribute to the degradation of a once beautiful reef. The good news is that coral reefs can heal physical damage if given time to do so. The problem is not so much the physical damage – such damage is anyway regularly inflicted by natural agents – but overuse of the reefs, with not enough time being allowed for recovery. There is no way a reef can survive hundreds of divers on it every day – or even perhaps just every week. We are fortunate in PNG that we have very many dive sites, and very few divers to dive on them. That is one reason why our reefs are so great.

6 GARDEN OF FANS

★★★★

Location: South side of Watom Island.
Access: 18min by boat from Kulau Lodge Beach Resort. Arrange with villagers.
Conditions: Mostly calm; exposed to Southeast Trades. Can be strong currents, so more suitable for experienced divers.
Typical visibility: 40m (130ft)
Minimum depth: 6m (20ft)
Maximum depth: 26m (85ft)

This series of sunken reefs off Watom Island is exposed to currents, so giant sea fans – some of them 2.5m (8ft) high – grow in a magnificent coral-garden setting. You're also likely to see large schools of fish, pelagics, turtles and reef sharks, and smaller creatures like nudibranchs and shells are common. Killer Whales have been seen.

7 SUBMARINE BASE

★★★★★★★

Location: Eastern side of Tawui Point.
Access: Accessible by sea, but no anchorage possible, so dive usually made from shore (fee payable to landowner for use of property and security of vehicles).
Conditions: Usually calm; sometimes current along wall.
Typical visibility: 40m (130ft) plus
Minimum depth: 3m (10ft)
Maximum depth: 50m (165ft) plus

After gearing up on the beach and wading into the water, just a few fin-kicks bring you to a wall plunging vertically into very deep water. Large pelagics, sharks, turtles and rays often patrol this, but you can discover many smaller creatures if you search the many cracks and crevices. The wall is particularly interesting at night. Many rare shells have been found here. If current is running, stay near the exit point.

There is good exhilarating snorkelling along the edge of the wall, and you can explore tunnels dug by the Japanese just off the beach; the Japanese used these to hold supplies for submarines – which, because of the vertical wall, could tie up directly to the beach.

8 ST GEORGE'S CHANNEL SEAMOUNT

★★★★

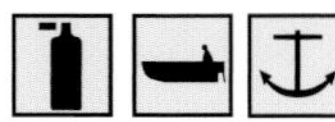

Location: In St George's Channel, 5 n. miles (9.3km) northeast of Cape Tawui.
Access: You must anchor in 27m (90ft).
Conditions: Calm weather and mild currents required. Recommended for experienced divers only.
Typical visibility: 40m (130ft) plus
Minimum depth: 27m (90ft)
Maximum depth: 40m (130ft) plus

A large seamount whose sides gradually slope to deep water; no dropoff has been found. The seamount's shallowest part is at 27m (90ft) and a current often flows, so a quick descent down the anchor-line is recommended and the dive should take place up-current of the anchor. Since the bottom has no distinct landmarks it is easy to get lost, so it is essential that a lookout with a pick-up boat remains on the surface, and that all divers carry Safety Sausages.

The reeftop is covered with giant barrel sponges, sea fans and whips, black coral and other hard and soft corals. Schools of fish roam over the reef, although with no point or dropoff they lack somewhere to congregate. Large Silvertip and other Sharks have been seen, and there is always the possibility of meeting other large fish, including Sailfish.

9 LITTLE PIGEON AND MALIS

★★★★★★★★

Location: Western of the two Credner Islands.
Access: By boat.
Conditions: Light winds required. Current assists divers.
Typical visibility: 45m (150ft)
Minimum depth: 1m (40in)
Maximum depth: 35m (115ft)

You enter the water on the northwestern side of the fringing reef around the island; the reef here is only 1m (40in) deep, but it drops vertically to about 35m (115ft). A current usually runs along the wall to the west and south, so you can drift with it along the wall, passing schools of small fish and the occasional shark. As you round the reef's western tip the wall ends and a sand slope starts. Swimming along this slope, which flattens out at about 15m (50ft), you meet a sunken steel freighter about 30m (100ft) long, the MV *Malis*, scuttled in 1985. The wreck is upright with a slight starboard list; in the usually clear water it makes an attractive prop for photographers. Beware the growths of stinging hydroids over much of the wreck. Dolphins are sometimes seen, and a Whale Shark has turned up at least once.

Snorkellers can drift around the reef-edge and see the wreck clearly.

10 REBECCA'S CORNER

★★★★★★★★

Location: Eastern of the two Credner Islands.
Access: May be too shallow to anchor. Boat should drop divers just east of rocks on northwestern side of island.
Conditions: Sheltered in southeast winds. Usually little current.
Typical visibility: 45m (150ft)
Minimum depth: 1m (40in)
Maximum depth: 35m (115ft)

An easy and very attractive dive in usually calm conditions. You descend the wall to about 25m (80ft) and swim east along it. It is covered with rich growths of sea fans and soft corals. Batfish and sharks are frequent, and you can find nudibranchs if you search the reef's many crevices. If it has been possible to anchor the boat, return along the wall in about 5–9m (16–30ft).

Snorkellers can enjoy swimming slowly along the edge of the dropoff.

11 RAINBOW REEF

★★★★★★★

Location: Off northwest end of Mait Island, Duke of York Islands.
Access: Anchor in one of two sand channels on reef in 12m (40ft).
Conditions: Partly sheltered in Southeast season. Some current over reef.
Typical visibility: 45m (150ft)
Minimum depth: 6m (20ft)
Maximum depth: 35m (115ft)

The name comes from the great array of colourful corals growing on the reef. Two sand gutters, sloping from 12m to 26m (40–85ft), divide this reef into three sections, all worth exploring. The reef is too large to dive on one tank, so you may profitably dive several times here. The staghorn and plate corals are unusually colourful, and sponges, sea whips and sea fans add further hues. When current flows there are many schools at the front of the reef, where spurs of coral point to the depths, and sharks mingle with them. Dugong have been seen on occasion, and a resident school of barracuda often greets you as you enter the water.

This is a little deep for comfortable snorkelling, but can be good in clear, still conditions.

12 HEAVEN'S GATE

★★★★

Location: Between northern tip of Duke of York Island and Mait Iri Island.
Access: Anchor in 8m (26ft) in channel close to dropoff.
Conditions: Partly sheltered in Southeast season. Current can be fierce.
Typical visibility: 45m (150ft)
Minimum depth: 8m (26ft)
Maximum depth: 25m (80ft) plus

On entering the water you descend into the channel, which bottoms at about 10m (33ft). Its floor changes to a sudden, very deep dropoff. Small bommies in the channel are festooned with colourful sea fans, staghorn corals, sea whips and juvenile Palette Surgeonfish (*Paracanthurus hepatus*). At the channel's mouth sharks, Dogtooth Tuna, barracuda, Eagle Rays and Bigeye Trevally mill around on the incoming tide. Many specimens of an unknown and unusual hard coral (it looks like purple tennis balls) litter the channel's bottom. On the wall, which drops steeply to about 25m (80ft), are magnificent stands of black coral, some with bases over 100mm (4in) thick.

13 JAPANESE WORLD WAR II TANKS

★★★★★★

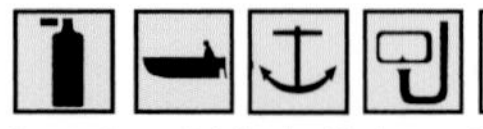

Location: Makada Harbour, Duke of York Islands, 20 n. miles (37km) from Rabaul.
Access: By boat.
Conditions: Very calm.
Typical visibility: 30m (100ft) plus
Minimum depth: 4m (13ft)
Maximum depth: 4m (13ft)

Usually a snorkel rather than a scuba dive, though underwater photographers seeking the very unusual wide-angle subjects here may wish to use scuba. The two tanks, a little apart, are upright and in good condition, although neither has guns. The remains of a landing-barge and other debris are nearby – possibly the barge capsized while carrying the tanks.

14 REIMER'S GARDEN

★★★★★★★★

Location: 10 n. miles (18.5km) west of Kulau Lodge Beach Resort.
Access: Anchor on southeast corner of reef for coral gardens.
Conditions: Usually sheltered and calm in morning; can get choppy in afternoon.
Typical visibility: 40m (130ft)
Minimum depth: 2m (6½ft)
Maximum depth: 40m (130ft) plus

The southeast corner of Reimer's Reef has a gently undulating coral garden, sloping away at the sides. The coral is mainly staghorn, though other corals and the occasional barrel sponge and sea fan are present. Crown-of-Thorns Starfish were common a few years back, but the reef has recovered to better than new.

For a more exciting dive on the same reef, move to the northern side, Reimer's Wall, which has a sheer dropoff. The site is terrific for a drift-dive, especially as there is sometimes a current along the wall. Sharks are seen, as are pelagics, turtles and a multitude of reef fish.

This large, shallow reef is excellent for snorkelling.

15 BANGKOK PASS

★★★★★

Location: Cape Lambert, 40 n. miles (75km) west of Rabaul.
Access: Anchor as close as possible to northern entrance to pass on the outer barrier reef southwest of Cape Lambert.
Conditions: Sheltered in Southeast Trades but exposed to northwesterly winds and swells. The current, which can be fierce, must be flowing into lagoon from west. For experienced divers only.
Typical visibility: 40m (130ft)
Minimum depth: 6m (20ft)
Maximum depth: 50m (165ft) plus

The current runs along the reef-face, then into the pass, so you have to get into position against it. (If there is no current there are few fish and the visibility drops dramatically.) Descend the steeply sloping reef, then plant yourself at about 25m (80ft) on the corner of the pass. In ideal conditions sharks and fish-life are fantastic. Big pelagics like Dogtooth Tuna and Spanish Mackerel continually patrol the reef, Eagle Rays and Silvertip and Grey Reef Sharks come to inspect you – but the jackpot occurs when schooling Hammerhead Sharks appear. This usually shy shark seems more confident here, and close encounters are possible.

Several nearby passes are good dives, but Bangkok Pass is the best.

Rabaul

How to Get There

The old Rabaul airstrip was buried in the 1994 eruption, and so services were diverted to Tokua Airstrip at nearby Kokopo, which was built with exactly this eventuality in mind. Air Niugini runs 3–4 flights daily from Port Moresby to Tokua (flight-time 1½hr for a direct flight – some are via Lae or other centres).

Air Niugini
PO Box 120, Rabaul
tel 675 92 8457

Where to Stay

Kulau Lodge Beach Resort
PO Box 65, Rabaul
tel 675 927 222
fax 675 927 226
Beautifully situated in Talili Bay on the north shore of New Britain, about a 12min drive east of Rabaul, the resort overlooks Rabaul's volcanoes; the eruption in 1994 gave it a light dusting of ash, but otherwise did not affect it. The owner, Peter Leggett, a very keen and able diver and a longtime Rabaul resident, knows the area very well. The resort has a mixture of beach cottages and deluxe apartments, totalling 22 rooms. It provides airport transfers, a 24-hour service and has a fully licensed restaurant.

Hamamas Hotel
PO Box 214, Rabaul
tel (not available at time of publication)
fax 675 92 8423
The Hamamas Hotel is the first to be opened in Rabaul Town since the '94 eruption. It has 28 rooms available with more planned, a bar lounge, post office, swimming pool, conference and function rooms. The restaurant specializes in Cantonese cuisine. Harbour tours are available.

Kaivuna Hotel
PO Box 395, Rabaul
tel 675 928 611
fax 675 928 514
The Kaivuna Hotel has been rebuilt since the eruption and now has 20 rooms back in service, with 12 more to be ready in 1996. The restaurant, featuring the hotel's famous pies and Kavieng lobsters, has also reopened, as have the bars. This was one of the best-known hotels for divers in Rabaul, well situated near the now-defunct Rabaul Yacht Club Jetty. Visiting this hotel gives an incredible insight into the destructive power of volcanoes – the hotel is an oasis in a mess of volcanic ash. Diving and other tours can be arranged, with prior booking advised.

Dive Facilities

Kulau Lodge Beach Resort
(address above)
Water sports from the palm-fringed private beach are the resort's speciality, and diving the main interest – although harbour cruises, game- and bottom-fishing, snorkelling, windsurfing and water bikes are also available. 15 complete sets of dive gear are available for hire and the resort has its own compressor and four fast diveboats. Instruction can be arranged with either NAUI or PADI certification.

Live-Aboards

The *Manta*/Frank Butler
c/o Walindi Plantation Resort
PO Box 4, Kimbe
tel 675 93 5441
fax 675 93 5638
Frank, the owner of the Rabaul Dive Centre (largely demolished during the eruption), was able to save his live-aboard boat, the *Manta*, and much of his equipment. Though it will be a long time before Rabaul town gets on its feet again, Frank will continue to provide a diving service to the area. Work is now underway to refurbish the *Manta*, lengthening it and replacing the engines; by the time you read this, the boat will be operating cruises from Walindi to Rabaul and return. Visiting divers will be able to book on the *Manta* and contact Frank through the offices of Walindi Diving. Not only will you still be able to dive the best of the Rabaul shipwrecks, you will be able to explore some of the excellent reef dives between Rabaul and Walindi including the Duke of York Islands (see page 132), the famous big-action dives at Cape Lambert – such as Bangkok Pass (see page 132) – and other reefs in this little-dived region.

The lengthened *Manta* has dormitory-style accommodation for 6/8 divers, two showers and a toilet, a spacious deck for diving and camera gear, 240V power, stereo and all the necessary navigational and diving equipment.

Local Highlights

The many local highlights are gradually being restored for visitors but the main feature of Rabaul, for several years to come, will be the new landscape created by the volcanic eruption.

Sadly, it will take a few years before Rabaul harbour looks like this again.

When we established an unofficial marine park at Horseshoe Reef near Port Moresby, we started to carry baits with us to the reef to feed the fish. We were able to buy frozen 'rubbish' fish from the supermarkets very cheaply, and every time we went to the reef we took some along. Fish in the wild respond very quickly to this kind of feeding, and within a few weeks we had a large Malabar Grouper and a huge Moray Eel feeding directly from our hands, along with a mass of other smaller fish. The grouper learned to recognize the sound of the boat so that, even if we anchored a couple of kilometres or so away from the feeding station, he would appear in the hope of an easy meal. He was a greedy beast, so we called him Gobbler.

The eel became Nessie, and was far better-mannered. She would emerge from her home on one of the small ships we had sunk near the reef and swim out to meet us, all excited and friendly – just like an affectionate pet. In fact, she once mistakenly swam out like this to a stranger on the reef; he thought he was being attacked and gave her a swipe across the head with his dive-knife. She recovered, although she was shy for a while, but ever after she bore the scar given to her by this ignoramus.

The dive was a favourite with many divers, as they were able to get very close to these animals. Our students were particularly impressed, and we were able to teach them that wild animals in the sea, particularly Moray Eels, are not necessarily dangerous at all. We played some games with the animals – particularly with Nessie, who would gently lift a bait from my mouth or, often, take my bare forearm in her mouth and hang on, without once inflicting so much as a prick from her dagger-like teeth, until I started to stroke her under her chin, which she seemed to really enjoy.

Problem Grouper

But, while Nessie became more and more a friend, Gobbler became more and more a problem. He learned to sneak around and grab unexpectedly at anything he thought could be food. This included divers' hands, especially if they picked up any marine life to study, though his favourite was blonde ponytails. He became a menace, and more and more frequently divers were surfacing with bleeding scratches through having been bitten by Gobbler. Worse still, for a time he was joined by a mate; once, while I was trying to feed them individually, they both charged me and bit me all over. I was wearing only a short wetsuit, and emerged bleeding from both knees and both elbows as well as my hands. Fortunately grouper teeth cannot do much more than give you a scratch, but even so I was a mess.

One diver on whom Gobbler had drawn blood after he had picked up a crinoid returned to the boat in shock and vomited. What had happened was that, after having been bitten on the hand, he had come face to face with a huge shark and assumed that, with his blood in the water, he was going to be eaten. The shark turned out to be in fact a harmless Whale Shark, but who could blame our diver for thinking, in the murky water, that he had met his maker?

Sometimes, though, Gobbler's greed gave us a few laughs. One of our trainee assistant instructors was running some students through their basic skills. The procedure was that he lined up four students in front of him, demonstrated the skill he wanted them to perform, and then pointed to each in turn for them to do it.

The next skill on the agenda was regulator recovery, so our assistant removed his regulator and tossed it away over his shoulder. To recover it again he leaned over, swept his arm back to catch the regulator hose, and tried to pull it round in order to put the mouthpiece back in his mouth. This time, for some reason, the regulator was stuck. Turning around to find out what was wrong, he discovered himself face-to-face with Gobbler, who had snuck up behind, curious about all the activity, and swallowed the regulator. After a few moments' tug-o'-war the grouper spat out the regulator and the assistant could breathe again. He then pointed to each of the students in turn, but all replied with vigorous negative shakes of the head . . .

Gobbler could also be used as an educational aid – for example, when we were trying to teach our students not to wave their hands around when swimming, but to get control using the fins only. Since flapping hands were a favourite Gobbler target, few of the students had too much trouble remembering to keep their hands neatly tucked away.

Hazards of Fish-Feeding

Now, except for shark feeds, we no longer take baits down to the reef. Although the practice can attract many large fish to come close, there are definite hazards, and divers regularly get injured. Moreover, fish will eat whatever is offered to them, even if it makes them get sick and pathetic. We never gave our fish anything but dead fish, but in other parts of the world fish have been fed things like eggs and chicken, and have ended up in a terrible state.

Paradoxically, sharks are very fussy about what they eat, and will not come to baits that are the wrong fish or are not completely fresh. Sharks seem to rely on smell rather than vision – which is probably why they never bite divers during shark feeds unless the divers are actually handling the baits.

We have found that, if we regularly dive a site and do not behave aggressively towards the fish, they learn to accept us as part of their natural environment and will allow us to get close without our having to use bait and risk getting bitten – a healthier situation all round.

Dinah feeding 'Gobbler'.

NEW IRELAND

The provincial capital of New Ireland Province, Kavieng, is situated on a beautiful harbour at the northern tip of the island of New Ireland. Between here and New Hanover, to the west, a maze of islands and passages makes for some of the most exciting diving in PNG. Inside the lagoons, which make perfect overnight anchorages, mangroves and calm waters are nurseries for a bounty of marine creatures which, since tidal currents regularly swing back and forth through the passes, are then swept to the outer reefs.

On the southwest side the reefs drop precipitously, forming dramatic dropoffs; where these are at the entrances to the passes, they are (literally!) breathtaking. But beware: the currents can be strong and good timing is necessary to catch the start or end of the incoming tide, when all the fish will be feeding and soft corals on display. With too much current the diving becomes difficult or hazardous for less experienced divers. I have found that the maximum incoming current coincides approximately with high tide at Port Moresby, and this can be used as a guide to choose the best time to dive.

Rainfall in the Kavieng area is fairly constant all year, with Dec/Jan being marginally the wettest period. The pattern tends to be that a few days of perfect conditions build up to a heavy afternoon downpour, which clears the air for a couple of days. The Northwest season, Jan/Mar, is probably the least desirable, with sudden rain-squalls and thunderstorms possible. The water is always warm, rarely dropping below 28°C (82°F) and in the shallows sometimes exceeding 30°C (86°F). I have never had the least desire to wear a wetsuit when diving out of Kavieng.

Kavieng has achieved a reputation as the pelagic capital of PNG diving. Its oceanic reefs abound with big fishes and the largest schools of barracuda and trevally in the country. Eagle Rays and giant Queensland Groupers abound. Many species of sharks are commonly encountered and the Silvertip Sharks at Valerie's Reef are now world famous. If Africa has its lions then PNG has its sharks and Kavieng is the place to go to see them. Reefs with big fish action are usually not the easiest of places to dive, so the diving in this area is more suitable for experienced divers.

Opposite: *The 'Kate' diver bomber wreck at Kavieng, site 12, page 142.*

Above: *Flashlightfish, Photoblepharon palpebratus, are best seen on moonless nights.*

1 KAPLAMAN REEF

★★★

Location: East of North Cape, New Ireland, off Kaplaman village.
Access: 15min by boat from Kavieng. Anchor on rubble patches on reeftop.
Conditions: Sheltered except from north and east. Currents on reef usually manageable.
Typical visibility: 40m (130ft)
Minimum depth: 15m (50ft)
Maximum depth: 40m (130ft)

Several reef ridges and pinnacles rise from deep water. Although there are some rubble patches, most of the reef is covered with healthy coral growth, with some sea fans and sea whips. The reef is best when a slight current runs; at the side receiving the current are many large fish and pelagics – Giant Grouper along with Grey Reef and Silvertip Sharks, Eagle Rays and schools of Spanish Mackerel, Bigeye Trevally, barracuda, Oceanic Triggerfish and Sea Perch.

2 ECHUCA PATCH

★★★★★

Location: 1 n. mile (1.85km) northwest of northern entrance to Kavieng Harbour.
Access: A few minutes by boat from Kavieng. Anchor on wreck at reef's northern end.
Conditions: Partly sheltered. Can have swells and current.
Typical visibility: 40m (130ft) plus
Minimum depth: 15m (50ft)
Maximum depth: 45m (150ft)

A large ridge reef rises to 15m (50ft) at its southern end, then gradually slopes away northwards. Near the northern end is the wreck of the *Der Yang*, a steel fishing boat sunk deliberately as an artificial reef. Two or three Queensland Groupers (*Epinephelus lanceolatus*), live in or near the wreck, and a school of barracuda swirl above it. Eagle Rays, tuna and other pelagics are regular visitors. Sea fans and sea whips decorate the ridge around the wreck, and schools of the rare Two-Spot Snapper (*Lutjanus biguttatus*) live around the plate corals. The wreck, lying on its starboard side, has a significant cover of soft and hard corals. The propeller makes a good subject for silhouette photos, especially when the barracuda circle directly above it.

Since the reeftop is quite deep and swells are often present, it is important a decompression-line is rigged for ascending divers. The reef is too big comfortably to circumnavigate in one dive.

FRESH SEAFOOD

The New Hanover region and other islands in the northern part of PNG have a bountiful supply of lobsters and mud crabs. Since many of the villagers in the area belong to the Seventh-Day Adventist faith they do not eat shelled seafood themselves, although they have no problem about catching the seafood and selling it to anyone who wishes to buy it – such as the occupants of passing diveboats; indeed, diveboats make a considerable contribution to the local economies. Since there is no refrigeration in the villages, lobsters and crabs are always sold live. This has caused chaos on board *Telita* before now, with mud crabs breaking their bonds and clambering around the boat!

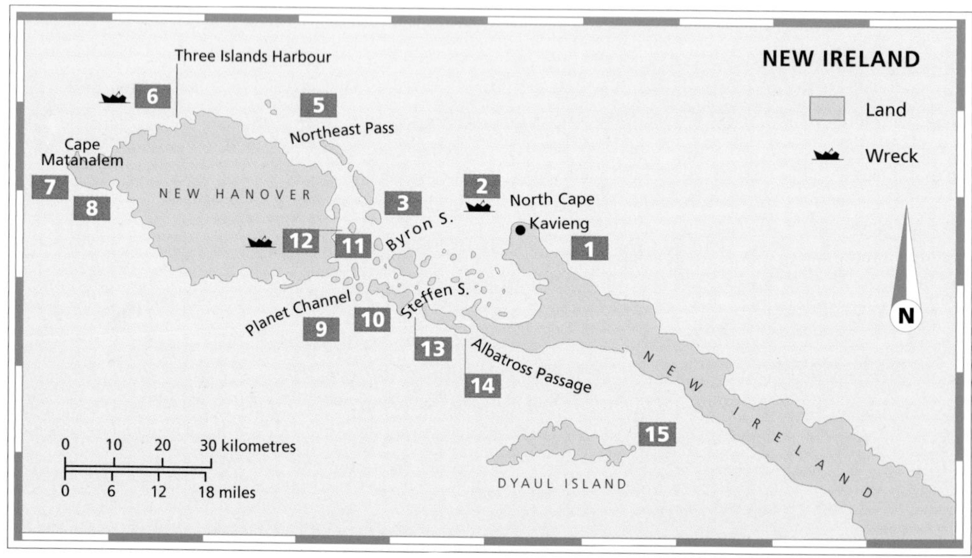

3 TURTLE REEF

★★★★★★★

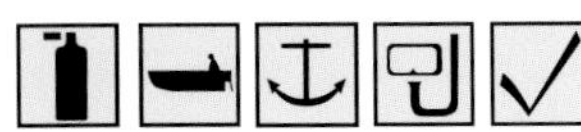

Location: 4 n. miles (7.4km) north of Bangatang Island.
Access: Anchor on northern side of reef.
Conditions: Usually divable. May be currents or swells.
Typical visibility: 45m (150ft)
Minimum depth: 8m (26ft)
Maximum depth: 40m (130ft)

A large and confusing reef, rising from deep water but without a well defined dropoff. The reef slopes and undulates, but has excellent growths of various hard corals in usually very clear water. There are some soft corals and fans, particularly deeper and around large coral bommies. Fish-life is scattered and sharks are not usually seen, but the resident Hawksbill Turtles (*Eretmochelys imbricata*) on the reef will approach and be gently handled. The turtles like to feed on sponges that grow under coral rocks.

The reef is easily snorkelled in calm conditions – you can meet turtles surfacing to breathe.

4 VALERIE'S REEF

★★★★★

Location: New Hanover, exact position withheld because of shark-finners.
Access: Refer to Telita Cruises.
Conditions: Best with slight current from southeast plus light winds. Often swells on site. Do not snorkel.
Typical visibility: 45m (150ft)
Minimum depth: 12m (40ft)
Maximum depth: 40m (130ft)

This has for many years been a feeding station for Silvertip Sharks; the initial dives were made from *Telita* with Valerie Taylor – hence the reef's name. The *Tiata* now regularly leads dives to this site: she is anchored on top of a sloping hard-coral reef, and at once sharks can be seen swimming below. As soon as the divers are in place on the reef, baits are lowered and the sharks take turns to come and feed. These sharks do not frenzy, and pass very close to the divers without being aggressive. No Grey Reefs have ever been seen, but a Great Hammerhead came to the baits once – the Silvertips immediately disappeared!

5 BIG FISH REEF

★★★★★

Location: 2 n. miles (3.7km) north of middle of Northeast Pass, New Hanover.
Access: Anchor on reeftop in rubble patches.
Conditions: Exposed to the north and east and can have strong currents, but usually divable.
Typical visibility: 45m (150ft)
Minimum depth: 12m (40ft)
Maximum depth: 40m (130ft) plus

This rectangular reef has fingers sloping away to deep water. Its edges are covered with excellent coral growth and, deeper, sea fans and orange Elephant-ear Sponges. Go to the side of the reef receiving the current (usually the southeast) to find giant schools of barracuda, trevally and batfish. Eagle Rays are common and the reef is thick with fusiliers. A Whale Shark made this its home one year, and other sharks are frequent; a large Bull Shark (*Carcharhinus leucas*) has been seen in the area.

6 JAPANESE MINI-SUBMARINE AND SHIPWRECK

★★★★★★★★★

Location: Three Islands Harbour, New Hanover; off Dunung Island.
Access: Anchor on sand next to shipwreck.
Conditions: Always sheltered; slight currents only.
Typical visibility: 15m (50ft) – sometimes reduced
Minimum depth: 4m (13ft)
Maximum depth: 22m (70ft)

Covered with lush growths of sea fans and soft corals, an armed freighter on its starboard side. The wreck has been salvaged and partly broken up, but has an incredible amount of marine growth on it. You can swim into great open sections – but take great care: much of the wreck is unstable, so avoid areas with loose plates and fittings. The crack where the wreck split in two is easily located; aft from it are a pair of masts.

If you swim out from the wreck in the direction of the masts you find, about 50m (55yd) across the sand, the mini-submarine. Discovered by Kevin Baldwin on *Telita* in 1987, this is now regularly dived from the *Tiata*:

Shark Callers

On the southwest coast of New Ireland, about 125km (80 miles) from Kavieng, is a village called Kontu. Here and at nearby villages is found the ancient tradition of Shark Calling. This involves much magic, and ends in the capture of deep-water sharks.

A solitary man paddles in a small canoe out to sea, where he calls the sharks by means of a coconut-shell rattle thrashed at the surface to imitate a school of nervous fish. When a shark is attracted it is lured close to the canoe and tricked into swimming into a noose, which is suddenly tightened around its head. The noose is attached to a large wooden propeller; this prevents the shark from swimming properly. Soon the exhausted animal is heaved aboard the canoe and beaten to death. The shark is shared among the villagers.

it is completely intact and, apart from the marine growth and corrosion, in perfect condition. It offers an excellent night-dive, but stay outside.

Snorkellers can see much of the shipwreck from the surface, but need to be able to skin dive to 18m (60ft) to see the submarine.

7 CHAPMAN'S REEF

★★★★★

Location: 350m (385yd) south of Ao Island, near Cape Matanalem.
Access: Anchor on southeastern end of reef in 10m (33ft).
Conditions: Often strong current, usually from southeast, but manageable by experienced divers. However, can experience swells and is partly exposed, so anchoring impossible in windy conditions.
Typical visibility: 50m (165ft)
Minimum depth: 10m (33ft)
Maximum depth: 50m (165ft) plus

A ridge reef parallel to the shore slopes deeply at the sides and has a massive dropoff at its eastern end. The trick of this fantastic dive is to get over the dropoff when there is a current flowing over it. This done, you're largely sheltered from current and can just pick a depth and watch the world go by. Sharks and Giant Grouper cruise through huge schools of fish. Pelagics hunt in the evenings. The reef is carpeted in soft corals, and there are sea fans down the drop. A deep crack across the ridge's eastern end is filled with fish.

The current is largely unpredictable, but we have observed that, oddly, it appears stronger on neap tides rather than springs. There is usually a period during the day when the current slackens, and then you can dive with the huge school of barracuda on top of the ridge and get them to circle around you.

8 TAUN REEF

★★★★★★★★★

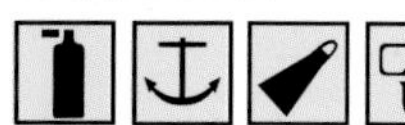

Location: In front of Taun village, New Hanover.
Access: Anchor on reeftop at western end in 5m (16ft).
Conditions: Inaccessible in strong southeast winds.
Typical visibility: 40m (130ft) plus
Minimum depth: 3m (10ft)
Maximum depth: 50m (165ft) plus

An oval reef which you can easily swim round on a single dive. The southern and eastern sides have a deep dropoff, and the northern side a passage between the main reef and the fringing reef off the village. There are sea fans and scenic areas with excellent fish-life. Sharks are frequent, and there is a resident barracuda school.

Snorkellers can enjoy both main and fringing reefs.

9 EAGLE RAY PASS

★★★★★

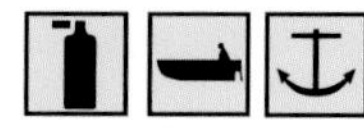

Location: Planet Channel, between Enang and Nusualana islands.
Access: By boat. Several different dives possible.
Conditions: Strong currents can flow through channel. Visibility and diving best when slight current flows into channel from south. Channel entrance exposed to southerly winds.
Typical visibility: 40m (130ft)
Minimum depth: 3m (10ft)
Maximum depth: 50m (165ft) plus

A ridge reef, defining a deep dropoff, runs directly across the channel's southern-side entrance. Between the fringing reef of Enang Island and the ridge is a pass, with 30m (100ft) depths inside. You can anchor on the ridge's western end in 5m (16ft) and dive the pass. Eagle Rays are often seen hanging in the current and feeding on the sandy floor.

The ridge deepens eastward, reaching about 18m (60ft) at the channel's midpoint. You can anchor here instead for a fantastic dive with huge schools of barracuda and trevally swimming over a reef prolific with sea fans and soft corals. Sharks and Giant Groupers are frequent. This is the most difficult dive in the area, being exposed to the full force of any current.

If the current is too strong to dive the ridge, an excellent drift-dive is possible along the channel's western side: you see many soft corals, giant sponges and sea fans as the drift takes you into the safe area of the lagoon.

Do not attempt the drift when the current is flowing out of the lagoon. In this case the only possible dive is on the western tip of the ridge, at the pass, which is largely unaffected by the outgoing current.

You can snorkel only at slack tide or along the edge of the channel, which is very shallow and always calm.

10 BYRON STRAIT

★★★★

Location: Southern entrance to Byron Strait.
Access: Anchor on reeftop in 6m (20ft) on western side of channel, furthest south possible.
Conditions: Requires an incoming current (from south). Exposed to southerly winds and swell.
Typical visibility: 40m (130ft)
Minimum depth: 6m (20ft)
Maximum depth: 50m (165ft) plus

You can dive in the passage or over the front face of the

dropoff. Eagle Rays, sharks and large schools of barracuda and trevally are frequent at the passage mouth. Down the outer drop, at 30m (100ft) and deeper, you can find exquisite fairy basslets (anthias) of various species including *Pseudanthias bicolor, P. randalli* and *P. cooperi*. The wall is alive with black corals, sea whips and sponges. Timing the current is important, as the water becomes dirty on the outgoing tide and fish-life is hard to find. However, a couple of small coral towers rising from deep water just 1/2 n. mile (930m) northwest of the entrance to Byron Strait can be dived on an outgoing current. The main one, Judy's Reef, has a dramatic ledge on its northwestern end at 30m (100ft).

On the eastern side of the passage is a similar, excellent, site.

11 MALACANTHUS PATCH

★★★

Location: Patch reef in the lagoon just southwest of Patio Island.
Access: Anchor on edge of patch. This is typically a good overnight anchorage.
Conditions: Always sheltered, sometimes a medium current running.
Typical visibility: 15m (50ft) often less.
Minimum depth: 8m (26ft)
Maximum depth: 20m (65ft)

A coral mound rises from a sand bottom at 20m (65ft). Its top has a scruffy coral reef with some soft corals and fans. Although this does not look very splendid, it is full of interesting creatures. Sand tilefish (*Malacanthus latovittatus*) are common – hence the patch's name. The best time to dive is at night, when Spanish Dancers, large and colourful Pleurobranchs and other molluscs will be found wandering about. Stonefish (*Synanceia verrucosa*) leave their lairs at night to lie in the open sand around the coral patches. Take care with the current, which can be uncomfortable; a current-line should be used to help divers to the bottom.

SHARKS IN DANGER

Sharks reproduce very slowly, so the deliberate fishing for them has a devastating effect on their population. They take 7–10 years, or even longer, to reach sexual maturity, and then are capable of reproduction only once every 2–3 years, giving birth to relatively small numbers of live young. Any local shark fishery is likely to fail, as the sharks get fished out very quickly. Since sharks play a vital role in keeping reefs healthy, the damage to the PNG reefs and village fisheries could be catastrophic. PNG sharks will produce far more revenue for the country alive, through tourism, than dead, through shark-finning. Sharks might not be as lovable as whales, but they need protection too!

One of a family of Silvertip Sharks, Carcharhinus albimarginatus, Valerie's Reef.

12 'KATE' DIVE-BOMBER

★★★★★★★

    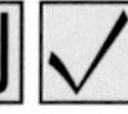

Location: Southwestern side of Anelaua Island, New Hanover.
Access: Anchor in narrow passage between island and reef approaching stone jetty.
Conditions: Calm in all weather. No current.
Typical visibility: 15m (50ft) – very variable
Minimum depth: 9m (30ft)
Maximum depth: 12m (40ft)

The aircraft is largely intact and upright in 10m (33ft), with its propeller against a reef-slope. The reef rises to 2m (6½ft), and the usual way to reach the aircraft is to swim along the slope (left shoulder to it) on the northwestern side of the narrow passage at 10m (33ft). We have experienced over 20m (65ft) visibility on the wreck, and it was then possible to take excellent photographs of the whole plane.

The area is suitable for snorkelling, and in clear conditions you can see the aircraft. There are interesting corals in the shallow water nearby.

13 STEFFEN STRAIT

★★★★

Location: Southern entrance to Steffen Strait.
Access: Anchoring possible on several patch reefs at entrance; alternatively (on incoming current only), drift-dive along edge of strait.
Conditions: Best with incoming current (can be very strong) from south. Exposed to southerly winds.
Typical visibility: 40m (130ft) plus – less on outgoing current
Minimum depth: 5m (16ft)
Maximum depth: 50m (165ft) plus

Several sites are close together. My favourite is a ridge reef, Peter's Patch, about 1km (1100yd) due south of the strait's eastern entrance. With a slight incoming current, you swim east along the top of a gradually descending narrow ridge. Both sides of the ridge have steep drops, and schools of Bigeye Trevally and batfish move from one side to the other; Grey Reef Sharks are common, and a marlin has been seen. The ridge's top is covered with plate and other corals, and there are many sponges, sea fans and whips. Golden Cowries have been seen. A deep dive is possible but most of the action takes place near the reeftop.

You can snorkel along the edge of the strait in shallow water.

14 ALBATROSS PASS

★★★★★

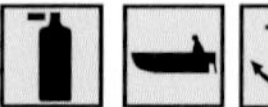

Location: Southern entrance to Albatross Channel, between New Ireland and Binnegem Island.
Access: Anchor in 8m (26ft) along dropoff in middle, or slightly to east of middle, of channel entrance.
Conditions: Current must be flowing into channel from south.
Typical visibility: 40m (130ft)
Minimum depth: 8m (26ft)
Maximum depth: 40m (130ft) plus

The reeftop has sand patches (with garden eels) and barren areas. It can be hard to get over the front edge against the current; in a strong current it is better to make the attempt at a point of the reef, rather than at a cut in it. Once over, the current becomes negligible and the near-vertical wall, dropping to 25–30m (80–100ft), is covered with large bushes of black coral of various species, plus gorgonians and soft corals; there are overhangs and even a swimthrough. At the wall's base a sand slope gradually falls to a second very deep dropoff. The best diving is on this slope: you can look back up at the wall and see all the fish patrolling along it. Many Grey Reef Sharks are always present, as are Giant Grouper, batfish, barracuda and trevally. Large Manta Rays and schools of Mobula are sometimes seen.

The shallow fringing reef on the channel's eastern side offers very attractive snorkelling, though crocodiles have been reported.

15 DYAUL POINT

★★★★★★★★★

Location: North side of east tip of Dyaul Island.
Access: Anchor on top of eastern coral tower.
Conditions: Sheltered and current-free in all but easterly winds.
Typical visibility: 60m (200ft) plus
Minimum depth: 5m (16ft)
Maximum depth: 50m (165ft) plus

A beautiful reef, with interesting formations and easy diving. Three coral towers rise at the edge of a steep dropoff. A small lagoon, 18m (60ft) deep, separates the towers from the shallow reef along the shore. The water is usually very clear and the coral excellent, with a mixture of staghorn and cabbage corals, plus patches of soft corals. The towers have ledges with soft corals, sea fans and many fish. Sharks are sometimes seen down the dropoff, but the best diving is in the shallows around the towers and in the lagoon.

There is excellent snorkelling over beautiful live reef in clear calm water.

Killer Whales

Many people do not realize that the Killer Whale (Orca) is found in the tropics, but every year divers around Papua New Guinea report encounters with this most awesome of creatures.

Contrary to early fears, it would appear that diving with Killer Whales is not a dangerous activity. We have snorkelled and scuba dived (sometimes unknowingly) with Orcas on many occasions without experiencing any aggressive actions.

The first experience I had in the water with a Killer Whale was at East Cape in Milne Bay – a site where they have been seen regularly over the years. A single large male, with an enormous dorsal fin, had killed and was eating an Ocean Sunfish (*Mola mola*). We decided to snorkel with him and, rather nervously, approached him on the calm, clear water. The whale was curious; he brought the dead sunfish towards us at the surface then let it drop. As it was falling through the water the whale backed off and watched. We made no move towards his meal and, when the sunfish had almost sunk from sight, he dived for it, brought it back to the surface and dropped it again. He did this several times before swimming away. I often wonder what might have happened had we got close to his meal.

Divers have swum with Orcas out of Port Moresby, Rabaul, Kimbe and, on one amazing dive, at Wuvulu Island. Here Jean-Michel Cousteau filmed Orcas diving and surfacing with sharks caught in their mouths. The whales could have surfaced anywhere with their prey, but chose to return to exactly the spot where the divers were waiting.

In 1994 divers at Walindi were in the water with Orcas when the whales suddenly dived. A few minutes later one surfaced with a large Hammerhead Shark in its mouth. A second Orca joined it and they proceeded to tear the shark apart and eat it in clear view of the divers. The practice of Orcas displaying their meals to divers may have some special significance – I don't think it necessarily means 'You're next'!

Other whales that divers have managed to swim with in Papua New Guinea are Sperm Whales, Pilot Whales, False Killer Whales, Humpback Whales and Minke Whales. Dolphins are common but difficult to swim with, although Walindi Diving has developed a technique whereby snorkellers hang on to lines attached to the bow of a slowly moving boat. Spinner Dolphins are attracted to the boat, and the divers can see them underwater.

The impressive killer whale – Orca.

Cape St George and the Northeast Islands

Cape St George at New Ireland's southern tip has a fascinating history. In 1879 an attempt to colonize the area (as Nouvelle-France) was made by the Marquis de Rays: without going to the inconvenience of actually inspecting the proposed site beforehand, he sold parcels of land here and shipped off 800 would-be colonists to one of the most rugged and inhospitable places imaginable. They mostly died of fever or starvation; he ended up in a lunatic asylum.

There is still virtually no development in the area, but as a dramatic example of nature's untamable beauty it is hard to better.

To the northeast of New Ireland and Bougainville are seven small island groups. Three are classic flat coral atolls – the Carteret, Green and Nuguria groups – and the other four are high volcanic islands with fringing reefs: the Feni, Tanga, Lihir and Tabar groups. Jump at any opportunity to visit these islands. Large pods of whales have been reported near the volcanic islands during December.

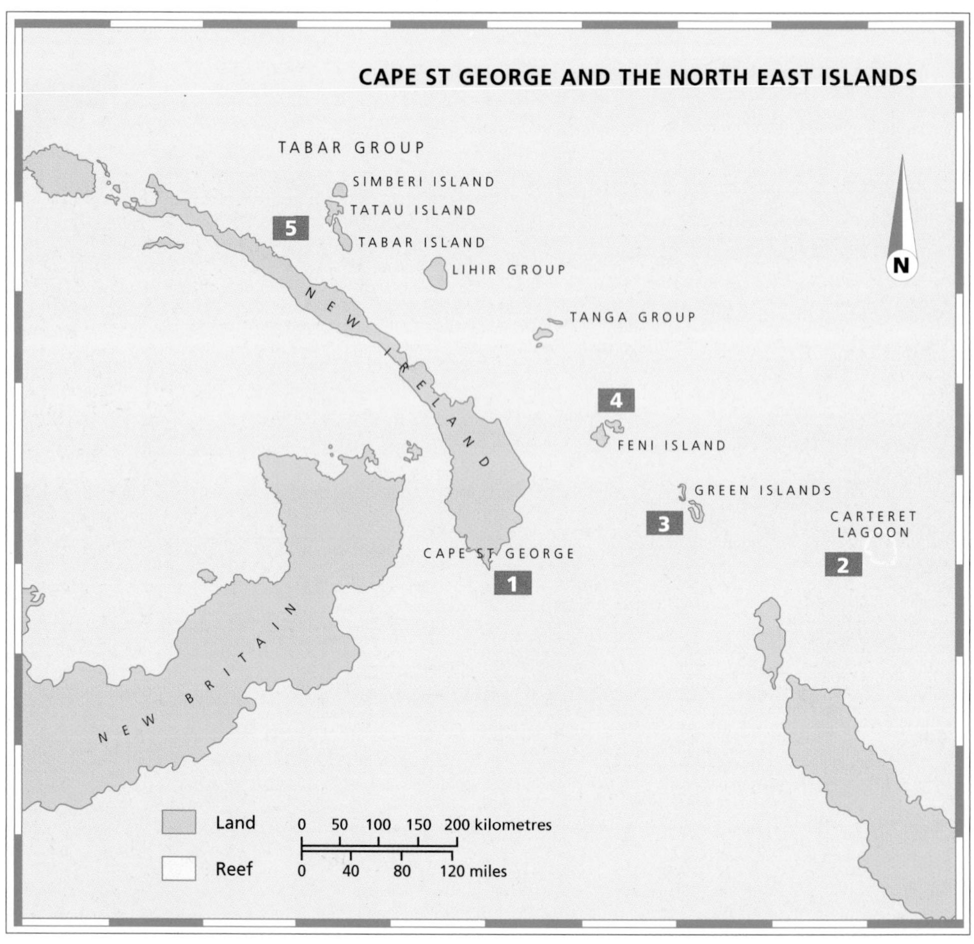

1 BALDWIN'S BRIDGE

★★★★★

Location: At small rocky island offshore immediately northeast of Cape St George.
Access: Anchor on sloping reef around base of rock – eastern side preferable.
Conditions: Impossible in southeast swells or wind: attempt only during Northwest season on days of complete calm. Can be fierce currents.
Typical visibility: 50m (165ft)
Minimum depth: 5m (16ft)
Maximum depth: 50m (165ft) plus

A huge natural underwater archway discovered by Kevin Baldwin and Dinah Halstead in 1986 – an incredible and unique site, superb for wide-angle photography. The rock, too steep to land on, is surrounded by a sloping reef that gradually becomes a wall. Swimming past the rock's southeast corner at 27m (90ft), you see the arch bridging the reef, with a second reef 50m (55yd) or so away. The arch is covered with pink soft corals and stinging hydroids, while giant sea fans and whip corals line the nearby reef-walls. Schools mill around the arch, and you can swim through it at a minimum of about 27m (90ft); sharks and Giant Grouper likewise swim through – all in all, an amazing sight. You can clearly see the seafloor about 60m (200ft) below.

The rock itself has vertical cracks and is full of lobsters.

2 WEST PASS, CARTERET ISLANDS

★★★★★★★

Location: Western entrance to Carteret Lagoon.
Access: Anchor on shelf on southern side of pass.
Conditions: Partly sheltered; can be current. Best when current flowing into lagoon.
Typical visibility: 40m (130ft) on incoming tide
Minimum depth: 6m (20ft)
Maximum depth: 40m (130ft) plus

The reef slopes to deep water, with a wonderful display of plate corals in layers down it. Sharks and pelagics are common and will approach closely. The water is very clear, so in low current there is a lot for snorkellers to see in the shallows.

An underwater marvel – Baldwin's Bridge near Cape St George.

3 ENTRANCE TO GREEN ISLAND LAGOON

★★★★★

Location: Southwest side of entrance to Green Island lagoon.
Access: Anchor as close to dropoff as possible.
Conditions: Partly sheltered; incoming current essential.
Typical visibility: 40m (130ft)
Minimum depth: 8m (26ft)
Maximum depth: 50m (165ft) plus

One of those great, unforgettable dives. Use a current-line or inflatable drop to get up-current at the wall, which plunges vertically at the lagoon's entrance; once you're over the wall the current's effects become negligible. Huge schools of Bigeye Trevally, surgeonfish, Sea Perch and fusiliers surge up and down and around you, and Grey Reef Sharks and Eagle Rays parade the edge – sometimes it seems a neverending stream of fish are pouring over the edge down onto you. The wall has soft corals and sponges, but the fish-life is what you'll always remember.

4 SALAT STRAIT, FENI ISLANDS

★★★★★★

Location: Northern end of pass between Feni Islands.
Access: Anchor in sand patches in pass.
Conditions: Sheltered; some current in pass.
Typical visibility: 40m (130ft)
Minimum depth: 5m (16ft)
Maximum depth: 20m (65ft)

Reef ridges scattered in the pass have sand patches between them. Schools of reef fish are common, but the main feature are the many large Black-blotched Stingrays (*Taeniura melanospila*) feeding in the sand patches. We found these rays very approachable. The coral ridges are healthy, but colourful soft corals and fans are rare.

The shallows at the edge of the strait offer easy snorkelling.

5 CHANNEL REEF, TABAR ISLANDS

★★★★

Location: Eastern side of entrance to channel between Tabar and Tatau islands.
Access: Anchor in channel near reef.
Conditions: Sheltered, but strong tidal currents flow over reef.
Typical visibility: 20m (65ft) – variable
Minimum depth: 2m (6½ft)
Maximum depth: 25m (80ft)

Pick a time when current is slight, then dive that side of the reef receiving current. The reef is covered with sponges, sea fans and whips and, even though relatively shallow, good stands of black coral. Bigeye Trevally and barracuda swarm around, along with a myriad other reef fish; you may meet active Grey Reef Sharks. The water is surprisingly clear for the circumstances. You can use the site as an anchorage, and in slack current enjoy a colourful night-dive.

Hawksbill Turtles at turtle reef have learned not to fear divers.

New Ireland

How to Get There

Air Niugini runs eight flights weekly into Kavieng from Port Moresby via Rabaul; some flights come via other centres.

Air Niugini
PO Box 63, Kavieng
tel 675 94 2135

Where to Stay

Malagan Lodge
PO Box 238, Kavieng
tel 675 94 2344
fax 675 94 1452
Perfectly situated on the beach at the northern entrance to Kavieng Harbour, this has its own white-sand beach leading to a shallow coral reef and sea-grass flats – ideal for snorkelling and learning scuba. A splendid way to end a day's diving is to lounge at the lodge admiring the spectacular sunsets over the palms on Nusa Island, on the far side of the harbour entrance. Owned by Melanesian Tourist Services, the lodge has 16 rooms, 12 single and 4 family/double, some air-conditioned, all with private bathrooms, TV, telephone and tea/coffee facilities. There are also conference facilities, a volleyball court, and private bar and restaurant. Snorkelling gear is available for hire. Land tours and harbour cruises are offered for K25 per person. Diving services are provided by Rob Padfield's Archipelago Divers and by the *Tiata* (addresses below).

Kavieng Hotel
PO Box 4, Kavieng
tel 675 94 2199
fax 675 942283
The well known Kavieng Hotel, situated in the town just a couple of minutes' walk from the beach, has recently been completely refurbished and now has 20 deluxe *en suite* rooms with satellite TV, air conditioning and telephone, and 14 backpacker rooms with fans, communal showers and toilets. Swimming pool. It offers land and sea tours, hire cars and boats, and diving and fishing tours. The diving services are provided by Rob Padfield's Archipelago Divers and by the *Tiata* (addresses below). A special feature is the opportunity to stay on one of the beautiful Islands near Kavieng. Paradise Island, in particular, acts as a scenic and convenient base for divers, with comfortable accommodation in several 'villas' and catering by an island manager.

Dive Facilities

Archipelago Divers
PADI instructor Rob Padfield and his wife Theresa have established a small land-based dive-tour business servicing the Kavieng hotels. Catering to individuals and small groups (up to 10), Rob and Theresa offer a personalized service and quick access to the best sites close to Kavieng. Archipelago Divers operates an 8m (26ft) fast diveboat and can supply hire gear (Scubapro), tanks and air-fills. Instruction is offered from Beginning Diver through to Divemaster certification. A new venture takes groups of four divers on a 6–8 day adventure around the New Ireland western archipelago, overnighting in village guesthouses and diving new sites each day.

Archipelago Divers
PO Box 479, Kavieng
tel 675 94 2531
fax 675 94 2531

Live-Aboards

Tiata
Telita Cruises
PO Box 141, Earlville
Cairns, Australia 4870
tel 61 (0)70 545401
fax 61 (0)70 547436
Based in Kavieng, the *Tiata* is a state-of-the-art purpose-built 20m (66ft) live-aboard diveboat commissioned in 1993. She is operated by Kevin Baldwin, one of the most experienced divers and diving instructors in PNG. She is completely air-conditioned and has five cabins for a maximum of 10 guests. The wheelhouse is equipped with an array of marine electronics including dual GPS navigation systems and plotters.

The *Tiata* runs cruises circumnavigating New Hanover and occasionally between New Ireland and New Britain. In the Northwest season she makes special expeditions or relocates to Alotau where she joins her sister ship, the *Telita* (see Milne Bay directory, page 71).

Taleo Tambu
c/o PO Box 37, Kavieng
tel/fax 675 94 2218
Now based in Kavieng, this 15m (50ft) sailing catamaran with accommodation for eight guests provides day trips and live-aboard cruises. For fanatical divers expecting five dives a day this is not the way to go, but if you wish to mix some diving and snorkelling with fishing, island and village visits – or just to enjoy sailing through the beautiful islands out of Kavieng – this could be a top choice. The owner/skipper, Alun Beck, is a longtime resident of PNG who fell in love with its natural beauty, chucked up his career in the TV business, and went cruising, sharing his enthusiasm with like-minded guests.

Local Highlights

Kavieng's historical artefacts – including a Japanese gun and relics dating from the time of the pre-World War I German Administrator, Baron Buluminski, famous for the excellent highway he built along the length of New Ireland – are scattered around the town. You can get help in finding them from the active and enthusiastic Tourist Bureau.

New Ireland Tourist Bureau
PO Box 103, Kavieng
tel 675 94 1449
fax 675 94 2346

The Tiata (see above)

MANUS ISLAND, THE WESTERN ISLES AND WUVULU

Manus Island itself does not have very many convenient dive sites. The whole of the north coast has a lagoon with typically murky water and poor reefs; outside it, instead of PNG's usual steep dropoffs, the reef gradually slopes from the barrier. These reefs have not been helped by the practice of blast-fishing. However, on the island's southeast side steep walls and clear water make for fine diving when the sea is calm.

Ndrova Island (Site 11), just 1 n. mile (1.85km) off Manus's southeast coast, has some particularly fine diving and provides shelter. The islands further southeast have been little explored, although good (if unexceptional) diving has been found. The water is usually clear, but strong currents are sometimes encountered. Reef-slopes are commoner than dropoffs. The best diving in the area is to the west. Kaniet (Site 1) and Sae (Site 2) islands are steep-sided with excellent walls and plenty of fish-life; their problem is that the reeftops are so shallow it is impossible to anchor.

The Hermit Islands Atoll (Sites 3–7) is a fascinating and perfect example of a remote coral atoll. The hilly central islands are surrounded by a ring of reefs and small islets, with two major passages enabling easy access to the sheltered anchorages by large vessels. The Ninigo Group (Sites 8–10) consists of three classic atolls and some offshore islands and reefs. Shelter is available in the large lagoon and also, for vessels with modest draft, in Heina Lagoon (Site 8) by means of a passage on the southwest side.

In 1995, during the windy season at its usual cruising grounds at Eastern Fields, the *Golden Dawn* (see Port Moresby directory, page 86) made an exploratory cruise around the coast to the town of Wewak on the north coast of the mainland and from there out to the Hermit and Ninigo Islands. This voyage was such a success that this is now planned as an annual event and the *Golden Dawn* will spend 3–4 months every year from about May to August running dive cruises to these remote atolls. So close to the equator (1–2°S), the water is always wonderfully warm – around 28°C (82°F). The best time for diving is during the Southeast season, May/Nov, when calm seas are the norm. The Northwest season, late-Dec/Mar, is wet and squally and should be avoided.

Opposite: *The remote Ninigo Islands where visitors are warmly welcomed and the diving is superb.*
Above: *A brilliantly coloured Fire Urchins, Astropyga radiata.*

Wuvulu Island

With such a magical name, Wuvulu just has to be special – and indeed it's the sort of place romantics dream of: a tiny tropical island inhabited by beautiful and friendly people and surrounded by blue, blue sea. Jean-Michel Cousteau realized its pristine nature and used it as a base for a series of educational tours called Project Ocean Search. A divers' lodge was built on the beach at Wuvulu, but the constant logistical problems of getting to and from the island have caused it to have limited success and the lodge is often closed.

Right in front of the lodge is a shallow reef-flat, dry at low tide, then an immediate and deep vertical dropoff with ledges, undercuts and swimthroughs. To the east of the lodge is a silty cave that enters straight into the dropoff at about 16m (52ft), wiggles a bit then ends in a chamber filled with stalactites. This dive requires lights and should not be attempted except by qualified cave-divers.

Around most of the rest of the island you have to cross a reef-flat several hundred metres wide before reaching the edge of the reef, and then there is a sloping dropoff rather than a vertical one. The reef is interesting, but not generally exciting. The best dive I had was off the southwest point (Site 12).

The water is always warm – 28–29°C (82–84°F) – and very clear, although sometimes milky in patches after low tide when water has run off the reef-flats. When there is enough water on them, the reef-flats are superb for snorkelling; otherwise reef walks are possible, with many creatures, including a unique volute shell, to see in the tide pools.

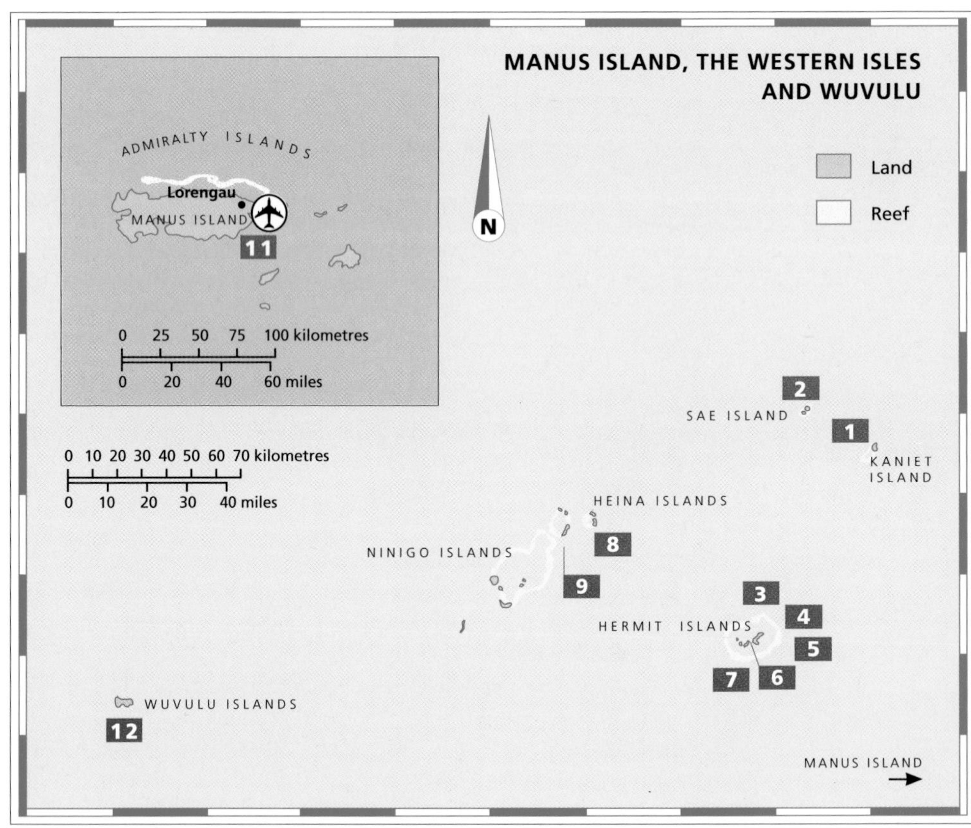

1 KANIET ISLAND

★★★★★★★★

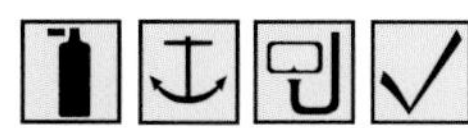

Location: Kaniet Island's northern tip.
Access: 'Live' boat diving necessary since anchoring impossible.
Conditions: Exposed in Northwest season.
Typical visibility: 40m (130ft) plus
Minimum depth: as shallow as you like
Maximum depth: 50m (165ft) plus

Divers are dropped in the water at the point and can drift or swim along the reef-wall, which has excellent hard-coral growths and some soft corals and sea fans. The plenteous fish-life includes resident Grey Reef Sharks and pelagics. Some abandoned long-line fishing gear litters the reef. The island's southern tip has less good visibility. There is superb snorkelling along the reef-edge.

2 SAE ISLAND

★★★★★★★★

Location: Sae Island, northwest side.
Access: 'Live' boat diving necessary since anchoring impossible.
Conditions: Little shelter – calm conditions necessary.
Typical visibility: 40m (130ft) plus
Minimum depth: as shallow as you like
Maximum depth: 50m (165ft) plus

Divers descend the wall and then drift or swim along it in any direction determined by current or interest. There are good hard- and soft-coral growths, plus many sharks. Turtles are frequent; they probably nest on the islands, which are also breeding-grounds for seabirds.

There is excellent snorkelling in shallow water.

3 HERMIT ISLANDS, NORTHWEST ENTRANCE

★★★★★★★

Location: Northwest entrance to Hermit Lagoon.
Access: Anchor on southwest or northeast side of

Eagle rays, Aetobatus narinari, are shy but common in northern PNG where they sometimes form large schools.

entrance, depending on current and wind.
Conditions: Can be dived in all conditions through selection of anchorage, as above.
Typical visibility: 15–40m (50–130ft), depending on current direction – incoming current always clearer
Minimum depth: 5m (16ft)
Maximum depth: 40m (130ft)
The southwest side of the entrance has good growths of soft corals and sea fans, and on an outgoing tide many fish. Being inside the lagoon, it is always sheltered from ocean swells, though visibility is not always perfect. This rich area has many interesting marine creatures in addition to the fish. The outer anchorage has less good coral but larger fish, including pelagics, Manta Rays and sometimes sharks; Hammerheads have been seen, and turtles are common. The outer reef slopes to a sandy plateau at about 40m (130ft).

At times of slack current you can snorkel around the shallow reef either side of the passage.

4 HERMIT ISLANDS, ALACRITY HARBOUR

★★★★

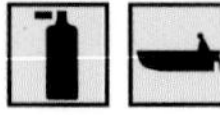

Location: Northeastern side of Hermit Lagoon.
Access: By boat from outside lagoon (only small boats can reach harbour from inside lagoon); anchor on south tip of northern finger reef which forms the harbour.
Conditions: Calm conditions required in Southeast season.
Typical visibility: 40m (130ft) plus
Minimum depth: 5m (16ft)
Maximum depth: 50m (165ft) plus
Decorated with large sea fans and whips, the reef slopes away steeply. There is good fish-life, with pelagics and sharks (including Silvertip). The coral on the reeftop is sparse, but the water is usually clear and there is the chance to see big fish.

5 HERMIT ISLANDS, SOUTHEAST ENTRANCE

★★★★★★★

Location: Southeast entrance to Hermit Lagoon.
Access: You can reach this entrance either by large boat outside lagoon or by small boat through boat passage inside lagoon. Site not accessible in strong Southeast Trades, when large swells form in passage.
Conditions: Calm or westerly winds required.
Typical visibility: 40m (130ft) plus
Minimum depth: as shallow as you like
Maximum depth: 50m (165ft) plus
Two passages, about 1km (1100yd) apart and separated by an isolated reef, form the southeast entrance. Either may be dived, as may the small lagoon behind the isolated reef. There is average coral, but plenty of fish. A school of dolphins lives nearby. Sharks and pelagics are frequent along the outer dropoff.

The small lagoon formed by the isolated reef between the passes reaches 20m (65ft) deep, but the coral gardens around the reef-edges are a perfect depth for snorkelling.

NAUTILUS

Deep down the PNG dropoffs, at 250m (800ft) and deeper, live two species of nautilus. *Nautilus pompilius* is the most common, being found throughout the country. *N. scrobicularis* is much rarer, having been caught live only from Manus, New Ireland and New Britain.

Telita Cruises were the first to enable sport divers to dive regularly with live nautilus. Overnight, we set a specially designed trap in 250–300m (800–1000ft) of water, baited with a fish carcase, then haul the trap up again first thing in the morning. Inevitably there are Nautilus in it. Divers quickly release them down a nearby dropoff, and are then able to observe and photograph these fascinating animals as they jet-propel themselves back down to their deep homes. As long as they are not held in the warmer waters for more than a few minutes, the Nautilus suffer no harm from this excursion to the shallows.

6 HERMIT ISLANDS, MANTA PASS

★★★★★★

Location: Hyane Passage, between Akib and Luff Islands.
Access: Anchor at edge of passage on down-current side.
Conditions: The passage is sheltered; current, usually manageable, runs through pass.
Typical visibility: 15m (50ft) – can be very variable
Minimum depth: as shallow as you like
Maximum depth: 22m (70ft)
Divers can be dropped off up-current by dinghy to drift slowly back through the pass to the anchored boat. Several bommies in the pass attract Manta Rays, which are apparently cleaned by Cleaner Wrasse (*Labroides dimidiatus*). To see this, remain still and as quiet as possible (controlling exhalation) beside one of the bommies – under no circumstances try to touch the mantas or they'll disappear. Other fish and coral may be seen in the pass, but the mantas are the attraction.

7 HERMIT ISLANDS, LEABON ISLAND

★★★★

Location: On outer barrier reef, south of Maron Island.
Access: Anchor near island inside barrier reef.
Conditions: Sheltered by reef from ocean swells; no current.
Typical visibility: 30m (100ft)
Minimum depth: as shallow as you like
Maximum depth: 6m (20ft)

This small island, a bird-breeding ground, can be reached by snorkelling, although it may not be desirable to land. The live surrounding reef, with the usual shallow-water fish species, offers easy snorkelling.

8 NINIGO ISLANDS, HEINA ISLAND

★★★★★★★

Location Heina Island.
Access: Vessels up to 25m (80ft) length can navigate the entrance to the Heina Lagoon, which provides very good anchorage.
Conditions: On lee side of island diving is possible in any wind direction.
Typical visibility: 50m (165ft)
Minimum depth: as shallow as you like
Maximum depth: 50m (165ft) plus

The steep dropoff all round Heina Island starts from very shallow water. The corals (hard and soft) are excellent. Although without any particular feature, anywhere around this island is worth diving. In places the reef-wall can be reached by swimming from the beach.

The reef-edge affords exciting snorkelling: you can see the deep- water dropoff from very close to shore.

9 NINIGO ISLANDS, PELLELUHU PASSAGE

★★★★★★★

Location: The passage between Pelleluhu and the main Ninigo Lagoon.
Access: You can anchor at edges of passage.
Conditions: Good shelter in most conditions. Currents through channel apparently modest and easily managed.
Typical visibility: 40m (130ft) plus
Minimum depth: 5m (16ft)
Maximum depth: 50m (165ft)

This channel is unusual in that both ends have deep oceanic water. The water is thus typically very clear, no

The Spine Cheeked Anemonefish, Premnas biaculeatus, gets darker in colour as it grows older.

matter what the tide, and big animals habitually swim through. You can dive from an anchored boat at whichever end is receiving current, or can drift from one end to the other (though you're unlikely to last the distance – the channel is about 4km [2½ miles] long). The channel's sides slope, rather than form vertical walls, and have very good hard corals but not many soft corals except on a spur of reef at the southwest end. There is plenty of variety among the small fishes. Keep scanning the channel's open water for larger sharks and rays.

The shallow edges of the channels offer good snorkelling.

10 NINIGO ISLANDS, TIATA REEF

★★★★★

Location: Uncharted reef south of Heina Island.
Access: Refer to Telita Cruises.
Conditions: Calm conditions essential as reef exposed. Often current on reef.
Typical visibility: 60m (200ft)
Minimum depth: 8m (26ft)
Maximum depth: 50m (165ft) plus

This newly discovered reef rises from very deep water and is surrounded by open sea. The reef ridge curves in an arc eastward and then southward, where there is a sudden dropoff. When current flows from the southeast, this end of the reef has huge numbers of pelagics, sharks and schooling fish – Rainbow Runners and Spanish Mackerel in particular. A Great Hammerhead has been seen. Hard corals dominate the shallower parts, with soft corals deeper. An exciting and exceptional dive.

11 NDROVA ISLAND

★★★★★★★★

Location: 1 n. mile (1.85km) offshore on southeast Manus Island.
Access: Small fast boats can reach site from Seeadler Harbour through shallow lagoon passages in under 1hr. Reeftop has coral reef cut with sand gutters, so you can anchor a larger boat here. South side drops away steeply from very shallow water: anchoring impossible.
Conditions: North side protected year-round.
Typical visibility: 45m (150ft)
Minimum depth: 3m (10ft)
Maximum depth: 50m (165ft) plus

The dropoff all around the island is steep and the water usually very clear. Coral growths are healthy, if not spectacular, and the reef has a good population of Grey Reef Sharks and the usual tropical fish. Here the rare *Nautilus scrobicularis*, known only from PNG, was first captured alive. (All nautilus captured during dive tours are released immediately after capture and return to their deep-water homes.) You can take nautilus portraits using a housed camera and 60mm lens, or Nikonos with 28mm lens and a close-up kit; beware of overexposure.

There is very pleasant snorkelling in sheltered water on the reeftop and at the edge of the dropoff.

COCONUT CRABS

Coconut Crabs are large land crabs that can climb coconut trees and husk and eat coconuts. These impressive beasts – growing to 60cm (2ft) or more across – are found on Wuvulu Island and some others, including Budi Budi in Milne Bay Province. The flesh, particularly of the body, is very oily, and generally only the claws are eaten: these contain great slabs of meat that are delicious if well cooked. Villagers at Budi Budi Island like to cook them on the coals of an open fire, but they can also be boiled.

12 SOUTHWEST POINT, WUVULU

★★★★★★★★

Location: Point west of Wuvulu Lodge.
Access: By boat from the lodge.
Conditions: Difficult if southerly winds blowing.
Typical visibility: 50m (165ft)
Minimum depth: as shallow as you like
Maximum depth: 50m (165ft) plus

Following the wall along to the west in the boat you eventually reach a spot where there is a sloping reef and sand patches before the dropoff. Sometimes there is a slight current here, and many fish gather to feed. There is no need to swim any great distance once down the slope. Hard corals predominate, although other parts of the reef have black corals and gorgonians. Snorkellers in the shallows will be rewarded with turtle sightings, and see harmless Blacktip Reef Sharks and many other fish.

Opposite: *This cave dive at Wuvulu Island should not be attempted without special training.*

Manus

How to Get There

Air Niugini runs a daily flight to Manus from Port Moresby, with a flight-time of 3–4hr, depending on the centre via which the flight comes.

Air Niugini
PO Box 170, Lorengau
tel 675 40 9092
The airstrip is a long 1hr drive from the town, which has poor facilities for visiting diveboats. *Tiata* found it convenient to anchor in Hyane Harbour, at the eastern end of the island, near the airstrip, in order to transfer divers to and from the diveboat.

Where to Stay

Lorengau Harbourside Hotel
PO Box 89, Lorengau, Manus
tel 675 40 9093/9262
fax 675 40 9392
This hotel was developed with tourism in mind, but probably caters more to business and to Government officials. It has a swimming pool and the usual amenities. Do try the mud crabs, if available; I once was lucky enough to feast on a dinner of these, and it was one of the most memorable meals I have ever had in PNG.

Wuvulu Lodge
Lus Development Corporation
PO Box 494, Wewak
tel 675 86 2788
A timber bungalow built on the beach, the lodge has accommodation for 12 guests (in fan-cooled rooms), with a small dining-room and a bar. The setting is very attractive, but sand gets everywhere; another nuisance is the long trek to the dive-room behind the lodge. The only surviving traditional Wuvulu canoe, with its distinctive and very beautiful spearlike prow and stern, rests on a stand in front of the lodge. The lodge has its own generator (turned off at night), and at one time had a good supply of tanks and a compressor. It is not known whether these are still in serviceable condition, and the lodge has not been used for diving tours for some time. However, the Wuvulu Lodge has a habit of being revived. For details of current status, contact the owners, Lus Development Corporation.

Dive Facilities

Ronnie Knight
PO Box 108, Lorengau
tel 675 40 9159
There are no established full-time dive operators in Manus, but Ronnie Knight has a diving compressor, boats and dive gear. He was very helpful to *Telita* when we visited in 1987, but has other interests now, and so you cannot rely on his services being available.

Live-Aboards

MV Tiata (see New Ireland directory – page 147) makes cruises to the Manus area by special arrangement.
MV Golden Dawn (see Port Moresby directory, p. 86) makes seasonal cruises (May to August) to the Hermit and Ninigo Islands from a temporary base at Wewak in the East Sepik Province.

Local Highlights

Manus is a fairly quiet place so far as activities go, its main tourist attraction being the nearby diving. There are some good beaches for swimming, and if you ask around you should be able to find some river canoeing on offer. The area is known for its shells – there's an exhibition at the Kohai Lodge, just out of town – and for its carvings, although these latter are rarely produced now; there's a carving exhibition at the Lorengau Council Office.

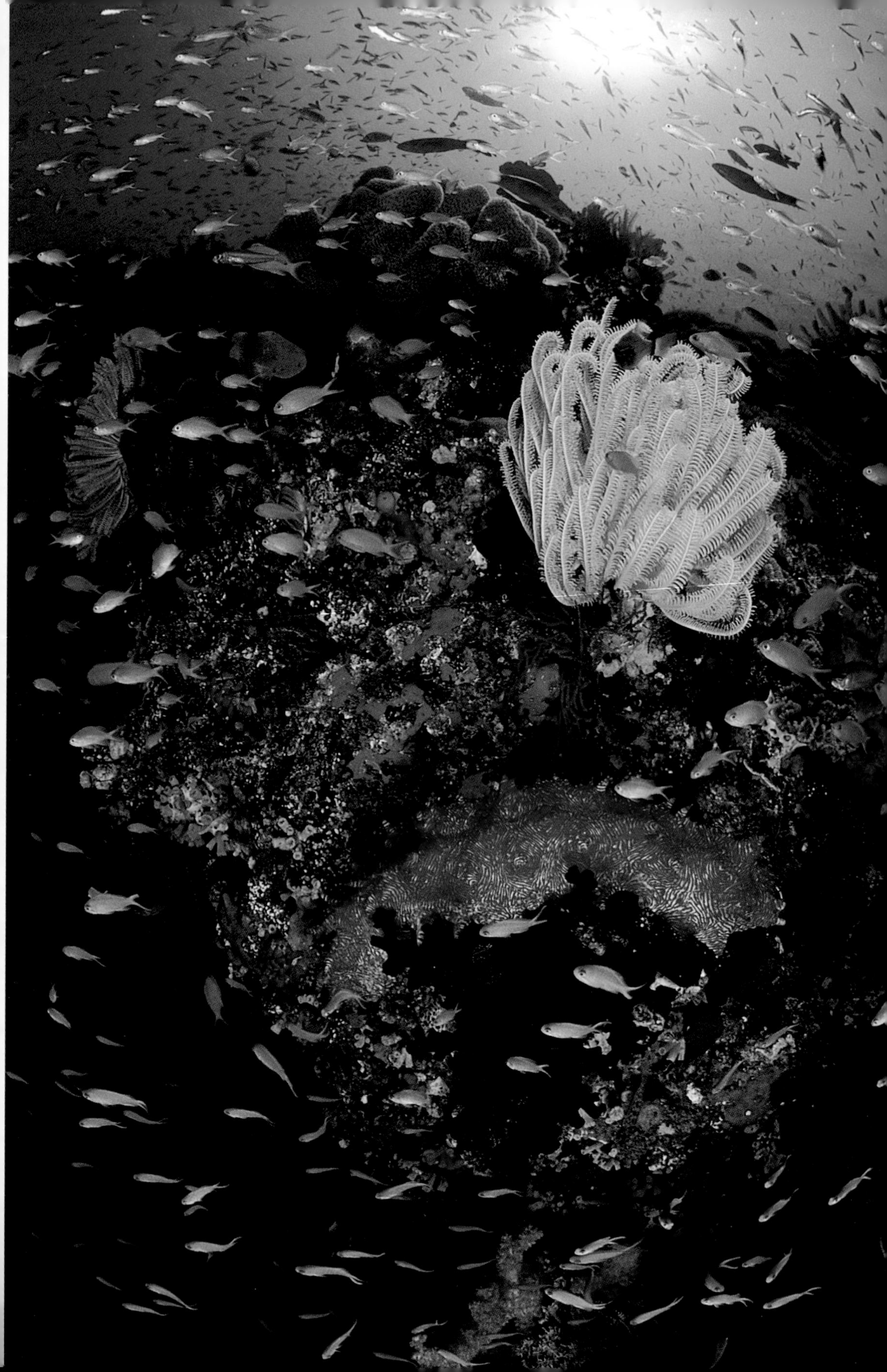

The Marine Environment

THE REEFS OF PAPUA NEW GUINEA

In terms of their biology and ecology, the reefs of Papua New Guinea are very similar to those of the Philippines, Indonesia and Eastern Australia (Great Barrier Reef). The geographical area in which they lie is recognised as the centre of marine biodiversity within the entire Indo-Pacific region.

THE NATURE OF CORALS AND REEFS

Tropical reefs are built mainly from corals, primitive animals closely related to sea anemones. Most of the coral types that contribute to reef construction are colonial; that is, numerous individuals – polyps – come together to create what is essentially a single compound organism. The polyps produce calcareous skeletons; when thousands of millions of them are present in a single colony they form large, stony (in fact, limestone) structures which build up as reefs.

What happens is that, when corals die, some of the skeleton remains intact, thus adding to the reef. Cracks and holes then fill with sand and the calcareous remains of other reef plants and animals, and gradually the whole becomes consolidated, with new corals growing on the surface of the mass. Thus only the outermost layer of the growing reef is alive.

There are about 450 species of reef-building coral in the seas around Papua New Guinea. Corals grow slowly, adding about 1–10cm (0.4–4in) growth in a year. Once over a certain age they start being able to reproduce, releasing tiny forms that float freely among the plankton for a few weeks until settling to continue the growth of the reef. The forms corals create as they grow vary enormously according to the species and to the place on the reef where it is growing. Colonies range in size from a few centimetres in diameter to giants several metres across and many hundreds of years old. Some are branched or bushy, others tree-like, others in the form of plates, tables or delicate leafy fronds, and yet others are encrusting, lobed, rounded or massive.

Microscopic plants called zooxanthellae are of great importance to the growth and health of corals. These are packed in their millions into the living tissues of most reef-building corals (and of various other reef animals, such as Giant Clams). Although reef corals capture planktonic organisms from the water, a significant amount of their food comes directly from the zooxanthellae. It is for this reason that the most prolific coral growths are in the shallow, well lit waters that the zooxanthellae prefer.

The presence of coral communities does not, in fact, necessarily lead to the development of thick deposits of reef limestone; for example, the Krakatoa Islands off the southern tip of Sumatra consist mainly of slabs of volcanic rock with a patchy veneer of corals.

Types of Reef

In most regions with plentiful coral communities, the calcareous skeletons have built up to form a variety of different types of reef:

- fringing reefs
- patch reefs, banks and shoals
- barrier reefs
- atolls

Fringing Reefs

Fringing reefs occur in shallow water near to land. Typically they extend to depths of 15m–45m (50–150ft), depending on factors such as the profile and depth of the seabed and the clarity of the water. Some of the mainland coastlines in Papua New Guinea are too close to river estuaries for reefs to develop, and instead support stands of mangroves – another marine ecosystem of enormous importance in the region. However, there are extensive fringing reefs, particularly along the northeast-facing coastline. Offshore islands, away from the influence of freshwater run-off, are mostly surrounded by reefs, some of which are precipitous and descend hundreds of metres.

Patch Reefs, Banks and Shoals

In theory, reefs can develop anywhere that the underlying rock has at some time been close enough to the surface for corals to become established and grow. Sea levels may have risen considerably since then, or other geological changes may have occurred to lower the depth of the bed beneath the surface; either way, there are many places where reefs exist as isolated mounds or hillocks on the seabed. Such patch reefs are widespread throughout the area region in relatively shallow waters surrounding the islands and on the continental shelf. They vary in size from tens to thousands of metres in diameter, usually with their tops coming to within a few metres of the surface – indeed, some emerge above the surface and are topped by sand cays. Patch reefs further offshore, lying in waters hundreds of metres deep and with even their tops 20m (66ft) or more below the surface, are usually referred to as banks or shoals.

Opposite: *Only recently described, the Red Line Sea Cucumber, Thelenota rubralineata, lives deeper than 18m where its red colour is not evident.*

Barrier Reefs

Barrier reefs occur along the edges of island or continental shelves, and are substantial structures. The major difference, apart from size, between them and fringing reefs is that they are separated from the shore by a wide, deep lagoon.

The outer edge of the barrier drops away steeply to the ocean floor beyond. Initially these reefs formed in shallow waters; then, as sea levels rose, they built progressively upwards so that their living topmost parts were still near the surface of the water.

There are several barrier reefs in Papua New Guinea. The best-developed is the 180km (110-mile) barrier running along the outside of the Louisiade Archipelago off the southern tip of the mainland.

Atolls

These are formations of ancient origin – millions of years old – and take the form of ring-shaped reefs enclosing a shallow lagoon and dropping away to deep water on their outsides. Atolls began life as fringing reefs around volcanic islands and kept growing as the underlying base gradually subsided beneath the water level.

Most of the world's atolls are in the Indian and Pacific oceans, but there are a number around Papua New Guinea. Egum Atoll in Milne Bay, PNG, is a good example, and there are others further afield waiting to be explored.

REEF LIFE

The reefs of Southeast Asia – and those off northern Australia – harbour a greater range of species than anywhere else in the Indo-Pacific: they are packed with all manner of bizarre and beautiful plants and exotic animals.

It is likely the region became established as a centre of evolutionary diversification millions of years ago; it has remained so, despite changes in sea levels and in the fortunes of individual reefs, right up until the present day.

On most reefs your attention is likely to be held initially by the fish life: in a single dive's casual observation you might see well over 50 species, while a more concentrated effort would reveal hundreds. Even that is only part of the story.

The reefs and associated marine habitats of Papua New Guinea support well over 1000 species of fish, but many are hidden from view within the complex framework of the reef – gobies, for example, usually in fact the most numerous of all the fish species on a reef, are seldom noticed.

Reef Zones and Habitats

Reefs can be divided into a number of zones reflecting differences in such features as depth, profile, distance from the shore, amount of wave action, and type of seabed. Associated with each zone are characteristic types of marine life.

The Back Reef and Lagoon

The back reef and lagoon fill the area between the shore and the seaward reef. Here the seabed is usually a mixture of sand, coral rubble, limestone slabs and living coral colonies. The water depth varies from a few metres to 50m (165ft) or more, and the size of the lagoon can be anywhere from a few hundred to thousands of square metres. The largest and deepest lagoons are those associated with barrier reefs and atolls, and may be dotted with islands and smaller reefs.

Sites within lagoons are obviously more sheltered than those on the seaward reef, and are also more affected by sedimentation. Here you will find many attractive seaweeds; most of the corals are delicate, branching types. Large sand-dwelling anemones are often found, and in places soft corals and 'false corals' are likely to form mats over the seabed. Especially where there is a current you may encounter extensive beds of seagrasses, the only flowering plants to occur in the sea. Among the many species of animals that make these pastures their home are the longest Sea Cucumbers you will find anywhere around the reef.

Although some typical reef fishes are absent from this environment, there is no shortage of interesting species. On the one hand there are roving predators – snappers, wrasse, triggerfish, emperors and others – on the lookout for worms, crustaceans, gastropods, sea urchins and small fish. Then there are the bottom-dwelling fishes that burrow into the sand until completely hidden, emerging only when they need to feed.

Most entertaining to watch – if you spot them – are the small gobies that live in association with Pistol Shrimps. In this partnership the shrimp is the digger and the goby, stationed at the entrance to the burrow, is the sentry. The small fish remains ever on the alert, ready to retreat hurriedly into the burrow at the first sign of disturbance. The shrimp has very poor eyesight; it keeps its antennae in close touch with the goby so that it can pick up the danger signal and, likewise, retire swiftly to the safety of the burrow.

The Reef Flat

Reef flats are formed as their associated reefs push steadily seaward, leaving behind limestone areas that are eroded and planed almost flat by the action of the sea. The reef flat is essentially an intertidal area, but at high tide it can provide interesting snorkelling.

The inner part of the reef flat is the area most sheltered from the waves, and here you may find beautiful pools full of corals and small fish. Among the common sights are `micro-atolls' of the coral genus *Porites*; their distinctive doughnut (toroidal) shape, with a ring of coral surrounding a small, sandy-bottomed pool, occurs as a result of low water level and hot sun inhibiting the upward growth of the coral. In deeper water, as on the reef rim, the same coral forms huge rounded colonies.

Towards the outer edge of the reef flat, where wave

action is much more significant, surfaces are often encrusted with calcareous red algae, and elsewhere you will usually find a fine mat of filamentous algae that serves as grazing pasture for fish, sea urchins, gastropods, molluscs and other animals. Some fish are permanent inhabitants of the reef-flat area, retreating to pools if necessary at low tide; but others, like parrotfish and surgeonfish, spend much of their time in deeper water, and then crowding over onto the reef flat with the rising tide.

The Seaward Reef Front

Most divers ignore the shoreward zones of the reef and head straight for sites on the reef front, on the basis that here they are most likely to see spectacular features and impressive displays of marine life. Brightly lit, clean, plankton-rich water provides ideal growing conditions for corals, and the colonies they form help create habitats of considerable complexity. There is infinite variety, from shallow gardens of delicate branching corals to walls festooned with soft corals and sea fans.

The top 20m (66ft) or so of the seaward reef is especially full of life. Here small, brilliantly coloured damselfish and anthias swarm around the coral, darting into open water to feed on plankton. Butterflyfish show their dazzling arrays of spots, stripes and intricate patterns as they probe into crevices or pick at coral polyps – many have elongated snouts especially adapted for this delicate task. By contrast, you can see parrotfish biting and scraping at the coral, over time leaving characteristic white scars.

Open-water species like fusiliers, snappers and sharks cover quite large areas when feeding, and wrasse often forage far and wide over the reef. But many species are more localized and can be highly territorial, on occasion even being prepared to take on a trespassing diver. Clownfishes (*Amphiprion spp*) and *Premnas biaculeatus* are among the boldest, dashing out from the safety of anemone tentacles to give chase.

Fish-watching can give you endless pleasure, but there is much else to see. Any bare spaces created on the reef are soon colonized, and in some places the surface is covered with large organisms that may be tens or even hundreds of years old. These sedentary reef-dwellers primarily rely on, aside from the omnipresent algae , waterborne food. Corals and their close relatives – anemones, sea fans and black corals – capture planktonic organisms using their tiny stinging cells. Sea squirts and sponges strain the plankton as seawater passes through special canals in their body-walls. Other organisms have rather different techniques: the Christmas-tree Worm, for example, filters out food with the aid of its beautiful feathery 'crown' of tentacles.

Apart from the fish and the sedentary organisms there is a huge array of other lifeforms for you to observe on the reef. Tiny crabs live among the coral branches and larger ones wedge themselves into appropriate nooks and crannies, often emerging to feed at night. Spiny lobsters hide in caverns, coming out to hunt under cover of darkness. Gastropod molluscs are another type of marine creature seldom seen during the day, but they are in fact present in very large numbers, especially on the shallower parts of the reef; many of them are small, but on occasion you might come across one of the larger species, like the Giant Triton (*Charonia tritonis*).

Some of the most easily spotted of the mobile invertebrates are the echinoderms, well represented on Papua New Guinean reefs. Most primitive of these are the feather stars, sporting long delicate arms in all colours from bright yellow to green, red and black. The best-known of their relatives, the sea urchins, is the black, spiny variety that lives in shallow reef areas and is a potential hazard to anyone walking onto the reef.

Many of the small, brightly coloured starfish that wander over the reef face feed on the surface film of detritus and micro-organisms. Others are carnivorous, browsing on sponges and sea mats, and a few feed on living coral polyps. The damage they cause depends on their size, their appetite and, collectively, their population density. Potentially the most damaging of all is the large predator *Acanthaster planci*, the Crown-of-Thorns Starfish; fortunately populations of this creature have so far reached plague proportions on relatively few of the Southeast Asian reefs, and so extensive damage caused by it is not yet commonplace.

Whether brilliantly attractive or frankly plain, whether swiftly darting or sessile, all the life forms you find on the reef are part of the reef's finely balanced ecosystem. You are not: you are an intruder, albeit a friendly one. It is your obligation to cause as little disturbance and destruction among these creatures as possible.

MARINE CONSERVATION

Reefs in Papua New Guinea are among the most biologically diverse in the world; they are also valuable to the local people as fishing grounds and as sources of other important natural products including shells. Unfortunately, in the past few decades they have come under increasing pressure from human activities, and as a result they are, in places, showing signs of wear and tear.

Corals are slow-growing: if damaged or removed they may require years to recover or be replaced. In the natural course of events, storm-driven waves from time to time create havoc on coral reefs, especially in the typhoon belt. But some human activities are similarly destructive, especially blast fishing and the indiscriminate collection of corals to sell as marine curios.

Overfishing is a further deadly hazard to reef environments, and has already led to perilously declining populations of target species in some areas. Another way overfishing can cause grave damage is through altering the balance of local ecosystems; for example, decreasing the populations of herbivorous fish can lead to an explosive increase in the algae on which those species feed, so the corals of the reef may be overgrown and suffer.

Some areas are being damaged by pollution, especially where reefs occur close to large centres of human population. Corals and other reef creatures are sensitive to dirty, sediment-laden water, and are at risk of being smothered when silt settles on the bottom. Sewage, nutrients from agricultural fertilizers and other organic materials washed into the sea encourage the growth of algae, sometimes to the extent that – again – corals become overgrown.

One final point affects us divers directly. Although, like other visitors to the reef, we wish simply to enjoy ourselves, and although most of us are conscious of conservation issues and take steps to reduce any deleterious effects of our presence, tourism and development in general have created many problems for the reefs. Harbours, jetties and sea walls are on occasion built so close to reefs – sometimes even on top of them! – that the environment is drastically altered and populations of reef organisms plummet. Visiting boats often damage the corals through inadvertent grounding or careless or insouciant anchoring. And divers themselves, once they get in the water, may, unintentionally cause damage as they move about on the reef.

Growing awareness of environmental issues has given rise to what is now known as 'ecotourism'. The main underlying principle is often summarized as 'take nothing but photographs, leave nothing but footprints', but even footprints – indeed, any form of touching – can be a problem in fragile environments, particularly among corals.

A better way to think of ecotourism is in terms of managing tourism and the tourists themselves in such a way as to make the industry ecologically sustainable. The necessary capital investment is minimal, and thereafter much-needed employment becomes available for the local population. In the long term the profits would exceed those from logging or overfishing.

Although divers, as well as many dive operators and resorts, have been at the forefront in protecting reefs and marine ecosystems, we all need somewhere to eat and sleep. If a small resort is built without a waste-treatment system, the nearby reefs may not be irreparably damaged; but if those same reefs start to attract increasing numbers of divers and spawn further resorts, strict controls become necessary.

In such discussions of ecotourism we are looking at the larger scale. It is too easy to forget that 'tourists' and 'divers' are not amorphous groups but collections of individuals, with individual responsibilities and capable of making individual decisions.

Keeping reefs ecologically sustainable depends as much on each of us as it does on the dive and resort operators. Here are just some of the ways in which you, as a diver, can help preserve the reefs that have given you so much:

- Try not to touch living marine organisms with either your body or your diving equipment. Be particularly careful to control your fins, since their size and the force of kicking can damage large areas of coral. Don't use deep fin-strokes next to the reef, since the surge of water can disturb delicate organisms.
- Learn the skills of good buoyancy control – too much damage is caused by divers descending too rapidly or crashing into corals while trying to adjust their buoyancy. Make sure you are properly weighted and learn to achieve neutral buoyancy. If you haven't dived for a while, practise your skills somewhere you won't cause any damage.
- Avoid kicking up sand. Clouds of sand settling on the reef can smother corals. Snorkellers should be careful not to kick up sand when treading water in shallow reef areas.
- Never stand on corals, however robust they may seem. Living polyps are easily damaged by the slightest touch. Never pose for pictures or stand inside giant basket or barrel sponges.
- If you are out of control and about to collide with the reef, steady yourself with your fingertips on a part of the reef that is already dead or covered in algae. If you need to adjust your diving equipment or mask, try to do so in a sandy area well away from the reef.
- Don't collect or buy shells, corals, starfish or any other marine souvenirs. The exception to this in PNG is nautilus shells which after dying naturally, are collected by villagers and sold to tourists.
- On any excursion, whether with an operator or privately organized, make sure you take your garbage back for proper disposal on land.
- Take great care in underwater caverns and caves. Avoid lots of people crowding into the cave, and don't stay too long: your air bubbles collect in pockets on the roof of the cave, and delicate creatures living there can 'drown in air'.
- If booking a live-aboard dive trip, ask about the company's environmental policy – particularly on the discharge of sewage and anchoring. Avoid boats that cause unnecessary anchor damage, have bad oil leaks, or discharge untreated sewage near reefs.
- Don't participate in spearfishing for sport – it is anyway now banned in many countries. If you are living on a boat and relying on spearfishing for food, make sure you are familiar with all local fish and game regulations and obtain any necessary licensing.
- Don't feed reef fish. It may seem harmless but it can upset their normal feeding patterns and provoke aggressive behaviour – and be unhealthy for them if you give food that is not part of their normal diet.
- Don't move marine organisms around to photograph or play with them. In particular, don't hitch rides on turtles: it causes them considerable stress.

MARINE CONSERVATION IN PNG

Protected Animals

Animals in PNG are protected under two classifications, the Papua New Guinea Fauna Protection and Control Act (1966, with subsequent revisions) and CITES (the Convention on International Trade in Endangered Species), which PNG signed in 1976. Those marine animals protected are indicated in the table below.

Dugong	*Dugong dugon*	P	I
Sei Whale	*Balaenoptera borealis*	P	I
Blue Whale	*Balaenoptera musculus*	P	I
Fin Whale	*Balaenoptera physalus*	P	I
Humpback Whale	*Megaptera noveangliae*	P	I
Saltwater Crocodile	*Crocodylus porosus*	R	II
Loggerhead Turtle	*Caretta caretta*	R	I
Green Turtle	*Chelonia mydas*	R	I
Leathery Turtle	*Dermochelys coriacea*	R	I
Hawksbill Turtle	*Eretmochelys imbricata*	R	I
Pacific Ridley	*Lepodochelys olivacea*	R	I
Flatback Turtle	*Natator depressus*	R	I
Southern Giant Clam	*Tridacna derasa*	–	II
Giant Clam	*Tridacna gigas*	–	II
Black corals	*Order Antipatharia*	–	II
Stony corals	*Order Scleractinia*	–	II
Fire corals	*Order Milleporina*	–	II
Blue coral	*Heliopora coerulea*	–	II
Organ-pipe coral	*Tubipora musica*	–	II

Legend:

P Fauna Protection and Control Act: *protected*
R Fauna Protection and Control Act: *restricted for*
.... *trade, allowed for*
.... *traditional utilization*
I CITES: .... *trade prohibited*
II CITES: .... *trade authorised*
.... *only under permit*

CREATURES TO LOOK OUT FOR IN PNG

Hammerhead shark

Hammerhead sharks are most often seen swimming along the edge of deep drop-offs. In PNG they are rarely deep preferring the first 25m (80ft) and often very close to the surface. The males are more inquisitive than the females and will occasionally make a close pass though usually they are both shy of divers. The sharks can form large schools at certain times of the year.

Shrimpfish

Schools of Shrimpfish are found on shallow reefs and grass patches in sheltered bays. They swim with their heads down trying to disappear among blades of sea grass, urchin spines or coral fingers. They are extremely thin, which explains their other common name of "Razorfish". When approached they turn away from divers and virtually vanish. They are related to pipefish and sea horses.

Also protected are 35 other species of mammals, 148 species of birds, 20 other species of reptiles, 45 species of freshwater fishes and 22 species of butterflies.

Biodiversity

Recent research has confirmed that PNG's biodiversity – in the sense of number of different species – is very considerable. A few are endemic, but most have a wider distribution, being found also on the reefs of Eastern Australia, the Phillippines and Indonesia. This rich biodiversity is probably related to the extraordinary range of environments which exist in PNG. Families which are well represented in Papua New Guinea, and are of interest to divers include the following:

Sponges (*Porifera*); Corals (*Scleractinia*); Shells (*Mollusca*); Nudibranchs (*Mollusca*); Sharks (*Chondrichthyes*); Bony Fishes (*Osteichthyes*); Marine Mammals (*Mammalia*).

CITES

The Convention on International Trade in Endangered Species (CITES) invited nations to protect endangered species by refusing to trade in them or in products derived from them. PNG has been a signatory to this convention since 1976. This fact has protected many species in PNG – including turtles, Giant Clams and dugong – from large-scale commercial exploitation. However, small-scale commercial exploitation still occurs within the country. Villagers are allowed to continue the 'traditional' hunting of turtles and dugong. Although this is supposed to be only for traditional feasts, the animals regularly turn up for sale in markets. It is also very hard to accept hunting as 'traditional' when it is carried out with guns in outboard-powered dinghies. To its credit, the Government has acted to stop export of corals, and has programmes educating the public on the importance of the nation's wildlife.

Scalloped hammerhead shark, *Sphyrna lewini*, (up to 3.5m)

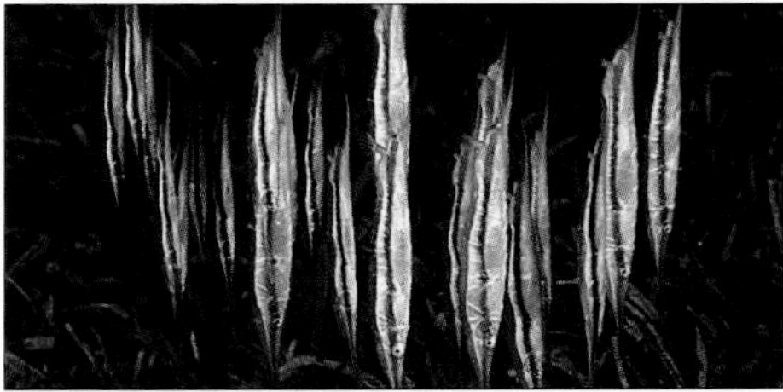

Shrimpfish, *Aeoliscus strigatus*, (up to 14cm)

Cuttlefish

Cuttlefish are relatives of the squid but have an internal shell or "bone". The bone floats after the cuttlefish has died and these are collected and sold to owners of pet birds. They have a remarkable ability to change their body colours, patterns and textures in order to blend in with their background or make threatening or other displays. They often use a pulsating colour to mesmerise prey. Cuttlefish are common in all habitats but often missed because of their superb camouflage.

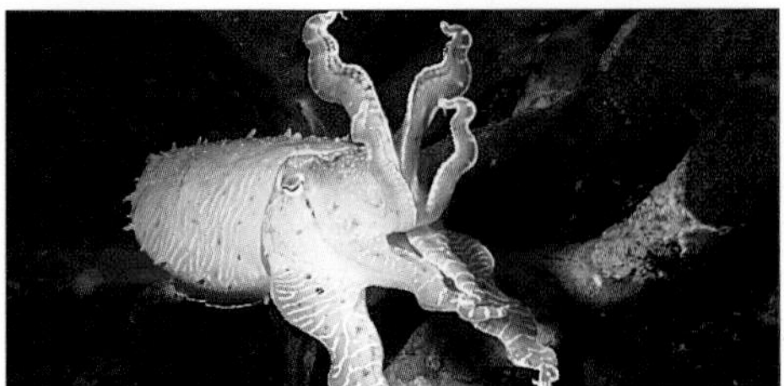

Cuttlefish, *Sepia sp.*, (up to 20cm)

Crocodilefish

Often confused with scorpionfish, these harmless fish are actually members of the flathead family. They lie motionless, usually in the open, on rubble and sand patches on top of reefs. They grow up to 50cm (20in) long and have fantastic frilly "eyebrows" – a popular subject for macro photographers, particularly as the Crocodilefish will obligingly stay still even with very close approach and gentle contact. A completely black variety is less frequently found typically on white sand patches where it mimics a black sponge.

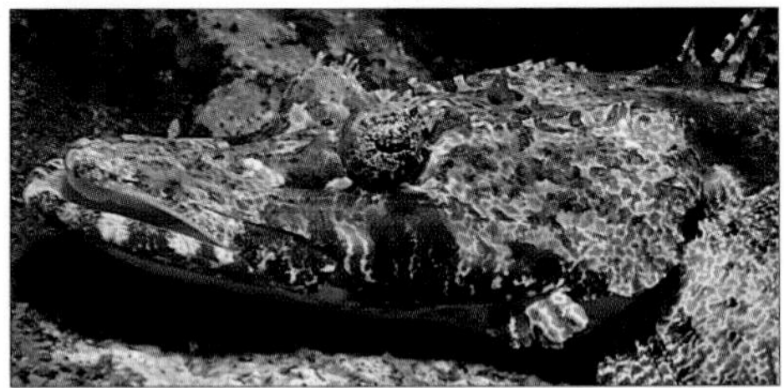

Crocodilefish, *Cymbacephalus beauforti*, (up to 20cm)

Two spot lionfish

Of the five species of Lionfish found in PNG this is the least often seen mainly because it hides inside coral heads during the day only emerging in the evening and night to hunt. It is very sensitive to light and will dart into cover if light is shone directly on it. Contact with its dorsal spines is to be avoided as they can, in common with all other Lionfishes and Scorpionfishes, inject a potent venom causing great pain. The fish is easily identified by the two (or sometimes three) spots on the soft dorsal fin .

Two spot lionfish, *Dendrochirus biocellatus*, (up to 20cm)

Barramundi cod

This fish is a prize catch for the dinner table in many parts of the world and is becoming rare. PNG still has plenty and they can be found, often in pairs, at medium depths on coral reefs that are not far offshore and have some current usually flowing over them. The exquisite juveniles have fewer black spots on a brilliant white background and prefer shallow sheltered water. They are an inquisitive fish and will often emerge from the shelter of a hole in the coral to watch divers.

Barramundi cod, *Cromileptes altivelis*, (up to 65cm)

Black and white sea perch

This photograph shows a juvenile. These are usually found swimming near crinoids, soft corals and black coral bushes. The juveniles are solitary. As they grow they lose their black and white stripes and spots and end up with blue squiggly lines on a yellow background. The adults form large schools and hang around in the current on the edge of a reef feeding on current-borne plankton. The very similar Black Snapper (*Malcolor niger*) also has a juvenile with black and white spots and stripes, but the adult is coloured a uniform scruffy black.

Black and white sea perch, *Malcolor macularis*, (up to 12cm)

Blue-girdled angelfish
This is one of the most fabulous of the many beautiful angelfishes that are common on PNG reefs. As with all angelfishes it can be distinguished from butterfly fishes by the spine on the gill cover. Although the adult is very common the juveniles, which are blue with white vertical lines, are very hard to find. Angelfish are territorial and, if a reef is dived often, individuals get used to divers and allow close approach.

Blue-girdled angelfish, *Pomacanthus navarchus*, (up to 25cm)

Banded sea snake
The silver and black Banded Sea Snake is actually a Krait and will leave the water occasionally, even boarding moored boats. They possess a potent venom, however they are docile and even if molested will not always inject venom if they bite. Since they breath air they can be seen swimming up to the surface where they rest for a few moments before swimming down to the reef again. They spend their day hunting for small fishes in holes in the reef. Divers sometimes find themselves with an inquisitive snake investigating them, but if the diver stays calm the snake will soon depart.

Banded sea snake, *Laticauda sp.*, (up to 97cm)

Decorated dartfish
These dartfish live in holes in the sand and rubble close to reefs. They are commonly in pairs and never venture very far from their holes into which they will dive at the slightest sign of danger. The Decorated Dartfish lives deep down the reef slopes, usually at 30m (100ft), but its close relative the Fire Dartfish, *N. magnifica*, can be found from 9m (30ft) down. They both feed on plankton which drifts near their holes.

Decorated dartfish, *Nemateleotris decora*, (up to 75mm)

Yellownose shrimp goby
There are very many species of Shrimp Gobies in PNG, but the Yellownose is one of the most distinctive. It lives in symbiosis with a blind shrimp which maintains the sand burrow that they both live in. When the shrimp is cleaning out the burrow using its claw as a bulldozer, the goby stands guard, ready to warn the shrimp of any danger approaching. The shrimp usually has at least one feeler in constant contact with the goby when it emerges from the burrow. They are found down sand slopes usually at 20m (66ft) or deeper.

Yellownose Shrimp Goby, *Stonogobiops xanthorhinica*, (up to 6cm

Twostripe goby
This fish is particularly fascinating because it builds rubble mounds next to its burrows. The Twostripe Goby lives in pairs and can be seen spending a lot of time during the day picking up pieces of broken coral or debris, carrying them to their mounds and dropping them on top. The mounds can grow to 80cm (32in) across and 40m (16in) high, requiring thousands of pieces of rubble to build. Some pairs have more than one burrow and associated mound. They are found in shallow and deep water on sandy patches near reefs.

Twostripe goby, *Valenciennea helsdingeni*, (up to 12cm)

Cabbage coral
This coral creates a living sculpture with the most wonderful undulating shapes. It is usually in isolated patches on reef flats or slopes in water no deeper than 18m (60ft). The patches can be up to 10m (33ft) across. Sweetlips often live with other fishes in the shelter of coral. It is very hardy and often ignored by Crown of Thorns Sea Star - a sea star that can devour coral. The large leafy plates can be snapped by careless divers or boat anchors. However, broken pieces will quickly mend if placed back together.

Cabbage coral, *Turbinaria sp.*

Porcelain crab
Anemonefishes are protected from predators by living among the tentacles of anemones - and so are Porcelain Crabs. They are most commonly found living with Panda Clownfish, *Amphriprion polymnus*, in the sand anemone *Stichodactyla haddoni* in shallow sea grass beds, but can be found on other anemones. The crabs feed on plankton drifting past and can be seen perched on the host anemone scooping the water with net-like feelers.

Porcelain crab, *Neopetrolisthes ohshimai*, (3-10cm)

Mantis Shrimp
The Mantis Shrimp is famous for its ability to smash aquarium glass with its modified forelegs, known as "jack-knife claws". The shrimp is able to strike prey, and potential predators (and divers!), with an incredibly fast and hard blow. They build vertical burrows in the rubble near reefs in shallow water and are commonly seen perched at the entrance to their burrows or scampering round the reef. They can often be teased from their burrows by dropping a piece of debris into the hole - the shrimp will carry the debris and dump it outside.

Mantis shrimp, *Odontodactylus scyllarus*, (5-8cm)

Imperator shrimp
This elegant shrimp is seen on sea stars but most often on the very long segmented cucumbers known as Synaptids which many novice divers mistake for sea snakes. They are mostly found in very shallow water on sand and rubble bottoms by very carefully examining every Synaptid seen. Most will have the shrimp, but they tend to hide underneath the cucumber when disturbed. The same species of shrimp, but with a different colour, lives among the gills of Spanish Dancers and other nudibranchs.

Imperator shrimp, *Periclimenes imperator*, (5-8cm)

Spanish dancer
The largest, and arguably the most beautiful, of all the nudibranchs, the Spanish Dancer can grow to 50cm (20in). The very large ones are found deep [40m (130ft)] down outer drop-offs when they are in the open even in daytime. More usually smaller specimens are found wandering over the reef during night dives in shallow water. If one is carried into open water and released it will swim with exaggerated undulating motion making it look like its namesake. Occasionally they will swim around an anchored boat at night apparently attracted by the light.

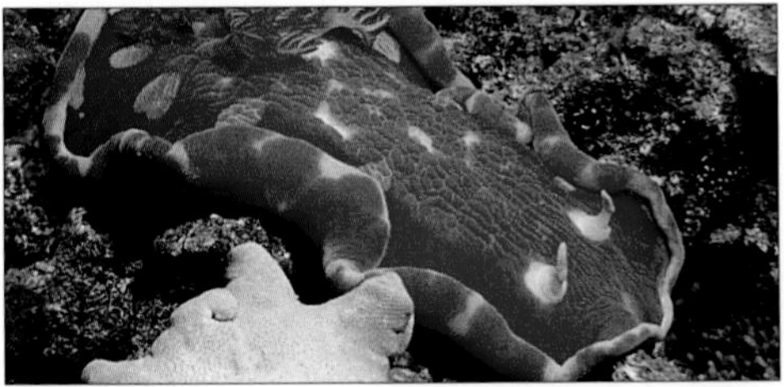

Spanish dancer, *Hexabranchus sanguineus*, (up to 40cm)

Underwater Photography

Photography has become one of the most popular underwater pastimes. Being able to capture on film some of the amazing creatures we see underwater is highly rewarding, but can also prove incredibly frustrating, as the real difficulties of underwater photography – backscatter, fish that refuse to stay still, flooded camera housings and so on – become apparent. You need a lot of perseverance – and luck – to get really good results, but if you're prepared to persist you'll find you've developed a passion that will last for a lifetime of diving.

Shallow-Water Cameras

There are several cameras on the market that are suitable for snorkelling. Kodak and Fuji both offer cheap, single-use cameras that are waterproof down to about 2m (6ft) and work well enough in clear, sunlit waters. If you object to disposables, Minolta and Canon make slightly more expensive cameras that can be used down to depths of about 5m (16ft).

Submersible Cameras and Housings

You have essentially two main options for serious underwater photography. The first is to lash out on a purpose-built waterproof camera; the second is to buy a waterproof housing for your normal SLR or land camera. Each system has its pros and cons. The submersible camera used by most professionals is the Nikonos, a 35mm non-reflex camera with TTL (through-the-lens) automatic exposure system and dedicated flashguns. (A popular alternative is the Sea & Sea Motor Marine II.) The specially designed Nikonos lenses give sharper results underwater than any housed lenses, but the lack of reflex focusing makes it difficult to compose pictures, and you can easily cut off part of a subject. They range from 15mm to 80mm in focal length, but must be changed in air. Underwater, the 35mm lens is of much use only with extension tubes or close-up outfits, though it can be used in air. The 28mm lens should be considered the standard. Other companies supply accessories for the Nikonos: lenses, lens converters, extension tubes and housings to accommodate fish-eye and superwide land-camera lenses. Lens converters are convenient: they can be changed underwater. The Motor Marine II makes good use of these, with converters for wide-angle and macro. The Nikonos close-up kit can also be changed underwater. Nikonos have recently introduced the RS-AF, a fully waterproof reflex camera with autofocus and dedicated lenses and flashgun, but it is extremely heavy and expensive. It is a poor buy by comparison with land cameras like Nikon's 801, F90 and F4 in housings; these are more versatile, weigh less, and can be used also on land.

Land cameras can be used underwater in specialist metal or plexiglass housings. Housings without controls, as used for fully automatic cameras, require fast films to obtain reasonable shutter speeds and lens apertures in the low ambient light underwater. Housings are available for all top-grade reflex cameras, but there are advantages and disadvantages to each system:

- Metal housings are strong, reliable, work well at depth and last a long time if properly maintained; they are heavier to carry, but are buoyant in water. Their higher cost is justified if your camera is expensive and deserves the extra protection.
- Plexiglass housings are fragile and need careful handling both in and out of the water; they are available for a wide range of cameras. They are lightweight, which is convenient on land, but in water are often too buoyant, so that you have to attach extra weights to them. Some models compress at depth, so the control rods miss the camera controls ... but, if you adjust the rods to work at depths they do not function properly near the surface! However, as most underwater photographs are taken near the surface, in practice this drawback is not usually serious.

Tips on Underwater Video

Stills photography is all very well in recording a marine subject held in one tiny moment in time, but when you are faced with a pack of sharks patrolling the lower regions of a cliff wall or watching the underwater ballet of the manta ray, then video is what you need. Nothing tells the story of our marine wonders better. The only drawback of taking underwater video is that the format is changing constantly and your modern state-of-the-art video and housing may soon be obsolete. These days equipment is so light that one of the greatest problems you encounter may be camera shake, which can even be caused by the rise and fall of your breathing when you are neutrally buoyant. To minimize this, use a camera tripod to keep the equipment steady when working in close-up situations. This will allow you to zoom in on the subject without the loss of image quality. Natural light shots are perhaps the easiest of all, but the lack of colour may make the subject matter appear dull. When using artificial light, get in close to the subject for better colour saturation. These lights can be attached to the video housing or hand-held by your diving buddy. (Make sure your buddy knows exactly what you are planning.) Remember to treat each shot of video footage as if it were a complete story in itself and do not linger too long on any one subject. If you do want to concentrate on one thing, then change the view, get in closer, or move underneath the subject. Take 'cut-away' shots or small portraits of divers' faces, or fish, which can then be inserted at a later date, during editing. A useful tip is to remember some famous film scene and try to recreate it.

Editing is where all your hard work can come together. Do not be tempted to bore your audience with too long a video. Be ruthless in your selection of video clips. Rather, keep it short and sweet and leave them wanting more! Include a soundtrack wherever possible to enhance the image that you are portraying.

'O' Rings

Underwater cameras, housings, flashguns and cables have 'O' ring seals. These and their mating surfaces or grooves must be kept scrupulously clean. 'O' rings should be lightly greased with silicone grease to prevent flooding; too much grease will attract grit and hairs. Silicone spray should not be used, as the cooling can crack the 'O' ring.

Removable 'O' rings should be stored off the unit to stop them becoming flat, and the unit itself should be sealed in a plastic bag to keep out moisture. User-removable 'O' rings on Nikonos cameras and flash-synchronization cables are best replaced every 12 months; non-removable 'O' rings should be serviced every 12–18 months. The 'O' rings on housings usually last the life of the housing.

Lighting

Sunlight can give spectacular effects underwater, especially in silhouette shots. When the sun is at a low angle, or in choppy seas, much of the light fails to penetrate surface. To get the best of it, photograph two hours either side of the sun's highest point. Generally you should have the sun behind you and on your subject.

Water acts as a cyan (blue–green) filter, cutting back red, so photographs taken with colour film have a blue–green cast. Different filters can correct this in either cold or tropical waters, but they reduce the already limited amount of light available. The answer is flash, which will put back the colour and increase apparent sharpness.

Modern flashguns have TTL automatic-exposure systems. Underwater, large flashguns give good wide-angle performance up to 1.5m (5ft). Smaller flashguns have a narrower angle and work up to only 1m (40in); diffusers widen the angle of cover, but you lose at least one f-stop in output. Some land flashguns can be housed for underwater use.

Flashguns used on or near the camera make suspended particles in the water light up like white stars in a black sky (backscatter); the closer these are to the camera, the larger they appear. The solution is to keep the flash as far as possible above and to one side of the camera. Two narrow-angle flashguns, one each side of the camera, often produce a better result than a single wide-angle flashgun. In a multiple-flash set-up the prime flashgun will meter by TTL (if available); any other flashgun connected will give its pre-programmed output, so should be set low to achieve modelling light.

When photographing divers, remember the eyes within the mask must be lit. Flashguns with a colour temperature of 4500K give more accurate skin tones and colour.

Fish scales reflect light in different ways depending on the angle of the fish to the camera. Silver fish reflect more light than coloured fish, and black fish almost none at all, so to make sure you get a good result you should bracket exposures. If using an automatic flashgun, do this by altering the film-speed setting. At distances under 1m (40in) most automatic flashguns tend to overexpose, so allow for this. The easiest way to balance flash with available light is to use TTL flash with a camera set on aperture-priority metering. Take a reading of the mid-water background that agrees with your chosen flash-synchronization speed, and set the aperture one number higher to give a deeper blue. Set your flash to TTL and it will correctly light your subject.

Once you have learnt the correct exposures for different situations you can begin experimenting aesthetically with manual exposure.

FILM AND CAMERA TIPS

- If you have to buy film locally, do so from a top photography outlet or a major hotel, where the turnover of stock will be reasonably swift and where the film will have spent most of its storage life in cool conditions.
- If you keep film refrigerated, give it at least two hours to defrost before putting it in a camera.
- Do not assemble underwater cameras in cool air-conditioned rooms or cabins. Condensation is likely to form inside them when you take them into the water.
- Normal cameras that have been in an air-conditioned environ ment will mist up when you take them out into the warm atmosphere. You need to wait at least 10 minutes for the con densation to dissipate before you can take clear photographs.

Film

For b/w photography, fast 400 ISO film is best. For beginners wishing to use colour, negative print film is best as it has plenty of exposure latitude. (Reversal film is better for reproduction, but requires very accurate exposure.) Kodachrome films are ideal for close work but can give mid-water shots a blue–green water background; although this is in fact accurate, people are conditioned to a 'blue' sea. Ektachrome and Fujichrome produce blue water backgrounds; 50–100 ISO films present the best compromise between exposure and grain, and pale yellow filters can be used to cut down the blue.

Subjects

What you photograph depends on your personal interests. Macro photography, with extension tubes and fixed frames, is easiest to get right: the lens-to-subject and flash-to-subject distances are fixed, and the effects of silting in the water are minimized. Expose a test film at a variety of exposures with a fixed set-up; the best result tells you the exposure to use in future for this particular setting and film. Some fish are strongly territorial. Surgeonfish, triggerfish and sharks may make mock attacks; you can get strong pictures if you are brave enough to stand your ground. Manta rays are curious and will keep coming back if you react quietly and do not chase them. Angelfish and Butterflyfish swim off when you first enter their territory, but if you remain quiet they will usually return and allow you to photograph them.

Diver and wreck photography are the most difficult. Even with apparently clear water and wide-angle lenses there will be backscatter, and you need to use flash if you are going to get a diver's mask to show.

Underwater night photography introduces you to another world. Many creatures appear only at night, and some fish are more approachable because half-asleep. However, focusing quickly in dim light is difficult, and many subjects disappear as soon as they are lit up, so you need to preset the controls.

On the Shoot – Tips

- Underwater photography starts before you enter the water. If you have a clear idea of what you wish to photograph, you are likely to get better results. And, remember, you can't change films or prime lenses underwater.
- Autofocus systems that work on contrast (not infrared) are good underwater but only for high-contrast subjects.
- When you are balancing flash with daylight, cameras with faster flash-synchronization speeds – 1/125sec or 1/250sec – give sharper results with fast-moving fish. The lens aperture will be bigger, so you must be accurate in your focusing.
- Masks keep your eyes distant from the viewfinder. Buy the smallest-volume mask you can wear.
- Cameras fitted with optical action finders or eye-piece magnifiers are useful in housings but not so important with autofocus systems.
- Coloured filters can give surrealistic results, as do starburst filters when photographing divers with shiny equipment, lit torches or flashguns set to slave.
- Wear a wetsuit for warmth.
- Refraction through your mask and the camera lens makes objects appear one-third closer and larger than in air. Reflex focusing and visual estimates of distances are unaffected but, if you measure a distance, compensate by reducing the resultant figure by one-third when setting the lens focus.
- When there is a flat port (window) in front of the lens, the focal length is increased and the image sharpness decreased due to differential refraction. Most pronounced with wide-angle lenses, this should be compensated using a convex dome port. Dome ports need lenses that can focus on a virtual image at about 30cm (40in), so you may have to fit supplementary +1 or +2 dioptre lenses.

A major problem for travelling photographers and videographers is battery charging. Most mainland towns have stockists for AA or D cell batteries, though they may be old or have been badly stored – if the weight does not preclude this, it is best to carry your own spares. Despite their memory problems, rechargeable nickel–cadmium batteries have advantages in cold weather, recharge flashguns much more quickly and, even if flooded, can usually be used again. Make sure you carry spares and that your chargers are of the appropriate voltage for your destination. Quick chargers are useful so long as the electric current available is strong enough. Most video cameras and many flashguns have dedicated battery packs, so carry at least one spare and keep it charged.

Health and Safety for Divers

The information in this section is intended as a guide only, it is no substitute for thorough training or professional medical advice. The information is based on currently accepted health and safety information but it is certainly not meant to be a substitute for a comprehensive manual on the subject. We strongly advise that the reader obtains a recognised manual on diving safety and medicine before embarking on a trip.

- Divers who have suffered any injury or symptom of an injury, no matter how minor, related to diving, should consult a doctor, preferably a specialist in diving medicine, as soon as possible after the symptom or injury occurs.
- No matter how confident you are in formulating your own diagnosis remember that you remain an amateur diver and an amateur doctor.
- If you yourself are the victim of a diving injury do not be shy to reveal your symptoms at the expense of ridicule. Mild symptoms can later develop into a major illness with life threatening consequences. It is better to be honest with yourself and live to dive another day.
- Always err on the conservative side when considering your ailment, if you discover you only have a minor illness both you and the doctor will be relieved.

GENERAL PRINCIPLES OF FIRST AID

The basic principles of first aid are:

- doing no harm
- sustaining life
- preventing deterioration
- promoting recovery

In the event of any illness or injury a simple sequence of patient assessment and management can be followed. The sequence first involves assessment and definition of any life threatening conditions followed by management of the problems found.

The first thing to do is to ensure both the patient's

and your own safety by removing yourselves from the threatening environment (the water). Make sure that whatever your actions, they in no way further endanger the patient or yourself.

Then the first things to check are:

- A: for AIRWAY (with care of the neck)
- B : for BREATHING
- C: for CIRCULATION
- D: for DECREASED level of consciousness
- E: for EXPOSURE (the patient must be adequately exposed in order to examine them properly)

- **Airway (with attention to the neck):** - is there a neck injury? Is the mouth and nose free of obstruction? Noisy breathing is a sign of airway obstruction.
- **Breathing:** Look at the chest to see if it is rising and falling. Listen for air movement at the nose and mouth. Feel for the movement of air against your cheek.
- **Circulation:** Feel for a pulse next to the wind pipe (carotid artery)
- **Decreased level of consciousness:** Does the patient respond in any of the following ways:
  A - Awake, Aware, Spontaneous speech
  V - Verbal Stimuli, does he answer to 'Wake up!'
  P - Painful Stimuli, does he respond to a pinch
  U - Unresponsive
- **Exposure:** Preserve the dignity of the patient as far as possible but remove clothes as necessary to adequately effect your treatment.

Now, send for help

If you think the condition of the patient is serious following your assessment, you need to send or call for help from the emergency services (ambulance, paramedics). Whoever you send for help must come back and tell you that help is on its way.

Recovery Position

If the patient is unconscious but breathing normally there is a risk of vomiting and subsequent choking on their own vomit. It is therefore critical that the patient be turned onto his side in the recovery position. If you suspect a spinal or neck injury, be sure to immobilize the patient in a straight line before you turn him on his side.

Cardiopulmonary Resuscitation (CPR)

Cardiopulmonary Resuscitation is required when the patient is found to have no pulse. It consists of techniques to:

- ventilate the patient's lungs - expired air resuscitation
- pump the patient's heart - external cardiac compression.

Once you have checked the ABC's you need to do the following:

Airway

Open the airway by gently extending the head (head tilt) and lifting the chin with two fingers (chin lift). This will lift the tongue away from the back of the throat and open the airway. If you suspect a foreign body in the airway sweep your finger across the back of the tongue from one side to the other. If one is found, remove it. Do not attempt this on a conscious or semi-conscious patient as they will either bite your finger off or vomit.

Breathing

- If the patient is not breathing you need to give expired air resuscitation, in other words you need to breath air into their lungs.
- Pinch the patient's nose closed
- Place your mouth, open, fully over the patient's mouth, making as good a seal as possible.
- Exhale into the patient's mouth hard enough to cause the patient's chest to rise and fall.
- If the patient's chest fails to rise you need to adjust the position of the airway.
- The 16% of oxygen in your expired air is adequate to sustain life.
- Initially you need to give two full slow breaths.
- If the patient is found to have a pulse, in the next step continue breathing for the patient once every five seconds, checking for a pulse after every ten breaths.
- If the patient begins breathing on his own you can turn him into the recovery position.

Circulation

After giving the two breaths as above you now need to give external cardiac compression.

- Kneel next to the patient's chest
- Measure two finger breadths above the notch at the point where the ribs meet the lower end of the breast bone.
- Place the heel of your left hand just above your two fingers in the centre of the breast bone
- Place the heel of your right hand on your left hand
- Straighten your elbows
- Place your shoulders perpendicularly above the patient's breast bone
- Compress the breast bone 4 to 5cm to a rhythm of 'one, two, three . . .'
- Give fifteen compressions

Continue giving cycles of two breaths and fifteen compressions checking for a pulse after every five cycles. The aim of CPR is to keep the patient alive until more sophisticated help arrives in the form of paramedics or a doctor with the necessary equipment. Make sure that you and your buddy are trained in CPR. It could mean the difference between life and death.

DIVING DISEASES AND ILLNESS

Acute Decompression Illness

Acute decompression illness means any illness arising out of the decompression of a diver, in other words, by the diver moving from an area of high ambient pressure to an area of low pressure. It is divided into two groups:

- Decompression Sickness
- Barotrauma with Arterial Gas Embolism

It is not important for the diver or first aider to differentiate between the two conditions because both are serious and both require the same emergency treatment. The important thing is to recognise Acute Decompression Illness and to initiate emergency treatment. For reasons of recognition and completeness a brief discussion on each condition follows:

> **TRAVELLING MEDICINE**
>
> Many doctors decline to issue drugs, particularly antibiotics, to people who want them 'just in case'; but a diving holiday can be ruined by an otherwise trivial ear or sinus infection, especially in a remote area or on a live-aboard boat where the nearest doctor or pharmacy is a long and difficult journey away.
>
> Many travelling divers therefore carry with them medical kits that could lead the uninitiated to think they were hypochondriacs! Nasal sprays, eardrops, antihistamine creams, anti-diarrhoea medicines, antibiotics, sea-sickness remedies ... Forearmed, such divers can take immediate action as soon as they realize something is wrong. At the very least, this may minimize their loss of diving time. Remember that most decongestants and sea-sickness remedies can make you drowsy and therefore should not be taken before diving.

Decompression Sickness

Decompression sickness or 'the bends' arises following inadequate decompression by the diver. Exposure to higher ambient pressure underwater causes nitrogen to dissolve in increasing amounts in the body tissues. If this pressure is released gradually during correct and adequate decompression procedures the nitrogen escapes naturally into the blood and is exhaled through the lungs. If this release of pressure is too rapid the nitrogen cannot escape quickly enough and physical nitrogen bubbles form in the tissues.

The symptoms and signs of the disease are related to the tissues in which these bubbles form and the disease is described by the tissues affected, e.g. joint bend.

Symptoms and signs include:

- Nausea and vomiting
- Dizziness
- Malaise
- Weakness
- Joint pains
- Paralysis
- Numbness
- Itching of skin
- Incontinence

Barotrauma with Arterial Gas Embolism

Barotrauma refers to the damage that occurs when the tissue surrounding a gaseous space is injured following a change in the volume or air in that space. An arterial gas embolism refers to a gas bubble that moves in a blood vessel usually leading to obstruction of that blood vessel or a vessel further downstream.

Barotrauma can therefore occur to any tissue that surrounds a gas filled space, most commonly the:

- Ears • middle ear squeeze • burst ear drum
- Sinuses • sinus squeeze • sinus pain, nose bleeds
- Lungs • lung squeeze • burst lung
- Face • mask squeeze • swollen, bloodshot eyes
- Teeth • tooth squeeze • toothache

Burst lung is the most serious of these and can result in arterial gas embolism. It occurs following a rapid ascent during which the diver does not exhale adequately. The rising pressure of expanding air in the lungs bursts the delicate alveoli of lung sacs and forces aïr into the blood vessels that carry blood back to the heart and ultimately the brain. In the brain these bubbles of air black blood vessels and obstruct the supply of blood and oxygen to the brain, resulting in brain damage.

The symptoms and signs of lung barotrauma and arterial gas embolism include:

Shortness of breath, chest pain and unconsciousness

Treatment of Acute Decompression Illness

- ABC's and CPR as necessary
- Position the patient in the recovery position with no tilt or raising of the legs
- Administer 100% Oxygen by mask (or demand valve)
- Keep the patient warm
- Remove to the nearest hospital as soon as possible
- The hospital or emergency services will arrange the recompression treatment required

Carbon Dioxide or Monoxide Poisoning Carbon dioxide poisoning can occur as a result of skip breathing (diver holds his breath on SCUBA); heavy exercise on SCUBA or malfunctioning rebreather systems.Carbon monoxide poisoning occurs as a result of: exhaust gases being pumped into cylinders; inferior systems; air intake too close to exhaust fumes. Symptoms and signs would be: Blue colour of the skin; shortness of breath; loss of consciousness.

Treatment: Safety, ABC's as necessary; CPR if required;100% oxygen through a mask or demand valve; remove to nearest hospital

Head Injury All head injuries should be regarded as potentially serious.

Treatment: The diver should come to the surface, the wound should be disinfected, and there should be no more diving until a doctor has been consulted. If the diver is unconscious, of course the emergency services

ROUGH AND READY NONSPECIALIST TESTS FOR DECOMPRESSION SICKNESS

A Does the diver know:
who he or she is?
where he or she is?
what the time is?

B Can the diver see and count the number of fingers you hold up?
Place your hand 50cm (20in) in front of the diver's face and ask him/her to follow your hand with his/her eyes as you move it from side to side and up and down. Be sure that both eyes follow in each direction, and look out for any rapid oscillation or jerky movements of the eyeballs.

C Ask the diver to smile, and check that both sides of the face bear the same expression. Run the back of a finger across each side of the diver's forehead, cheeks and chin, and confirm that the diver feels it.

D Check that the diver can hear you whisper when his/her eyes are closed.

E Ask the diver to shrug his/her shoulders. Both sides should move equally.

F Ask the diver to swallow. Check the Adam's apple moves up and down.

G Ask the diver to stick out the tongue at the centre of the mouth — deviation to either side indicates a problem.

H Check there is equal muscle strength on both sides of the body. You do this by pulling/pushing each of the diver's arms and legs away from and back towards the body, asking him/her to resist you.

I Run your finger lightly across the diver's shoulders, down the back, across the chest and abdomen, and along the arms and legs, both upper and lower and inside and out, and check the diver can feel this all the time.

J On firm ground (not on a boat) check the diver can walk in a straight line and, with eyes closed, stand upright with his/her feet together and arms outstretched.

If the results of any of these checks do not appear normal, the diver may be suffering from decompression sickness, so take appropriate action (see previous page).

should be contacted; if breathing and/or pulse has stopped, CPR (page 168) should be administered. If the diver is breathing and has a pulse, check for bleeding and other injuries and treat for shock; if wounds permit, put sufferer into recovery position and administer 100% oxygen (if possible). Keep him or her warm and comfortable, and monitor pulse and respiration constantly. **DO NOT** administer fluids to unconscious or semi-conscious divers.

Hyperthermia (increased body temperature) A rise in body temperature results from a combination of overheating, normally due to exercise, and inadequate fluid intake. The diver will progress through heat exhaustion to heat stroke with eventual collapse. Heat stroke is an emergency and if the diver is not cooled and rehydrated he will die.
Treatment: Remove the diver from the hot environment and remove all clothes. Sponge with a damp cloth and fan either manually or with an electric fan. Conscious divers can be given oral rehydration salts. If unconscious, place the patient in the recovery position and monitor the ABC's. Always seek advanced medical help.

Hypothermia Normal internal body temperature is just under 37°C (98.4°F). If for any reason it is pushed much below this – usually, in diving, through inadequate protective clothing – progressively more serious symptoms may occur, with death as the ultimate endpoint. A drop of 1C° (2F°) leads to shivering and discomfort. A 2C° (3°F) drop induces the body's self-heating mechanisms to react: blood flow to the peripheries is reduced and shivering becomes extreme. A 3C° (5°F) drop leads to amnesia, confusion, disorientation, heartbeat and breathing irregularities, and possibly rigor.
Treatment: Take the sufferer to sheltered warmth or otherwise prevent further heat-loss: use an exposure bag, surround the diver with buddies' bodies, and cover the diver's head and neck with a woolly hat, warm towels or anything else suitable. In sheltered warmth, re-dress the diver in warm, dry clothing and then put him/her in an exposure bag; in the open the diver is best left in existing garments. If the diver is conscious and coherent, a warm shower or bath and a warm, sweet drink should be enough; otherwise call the emergency services and meanwhile treat for shock, while deploying the other warming measures noted. Never give alchohol.

Near Drowning Near drowning refers to a situation where the diver has inhaled some water. He or she may be conscious or unconscious. Water in the lungs interferes with the normal transport of oxygen from the lungs into the blood.
Treatment: Remove the diver from the water and check the ABC's. Depending on your findings commence EAR or CPR where appropriate. If possible, administer oxygen by mask or demand valve. All near drowning victims may later develop secondary drowning, a condition where fluid oozes into the lungs causing the diver to drown in his own secretions, therefore all near drowning victims should be observed for 24 hours in a hospital.

Nitrogen Narcosis The air we breathe is about 80% nitrogen; breathing the standard mixture under compression, as divers do, can lead to symptoms very much like those of drunkenness - the condition is popularly called `rapture of the deep'. Some divers experience nitrogen narcosis at depths of 30-40m (100-130ft). Up to a depth of about 60m (200ft) - that is, beyond the legal maximum depth for sport diving in both the UK and USA - the symptoms need not (but may) be serious; beyond about 80m (260ft) the diver may become unconscious. The onset of symptoms can be sudden and unheralded. The condition itself is not actually harmful: dangers arise through secondary effects, notably the diver doing something foolish.
Treatment: The sole treatment required is to return immediately to a shallower depth.

Shock Shock refers not to the emotional trauma of a frightening experience but to a physiological state in the body resulting from poor blood and oxygen delivery to the tissues. As a result of oxygen and blood deprivation the tissues cannot perform their functions. There are many causes of shock, the most common being the loss of blood.

Treatment: Treatment is directed as restoring blood and oxygen delivery to the tissues, therefore maintain the ABC's and administer 100% oxygen. Control all external bleeding by direct pressure, pressure on pressure points and elevation of the affected limb. Tourniquet should only be used as a last resort and only then on the arms and legs. Conscious victims should be laid on their backs with their legs raised and head to one side. Unconscious, shocked victims should be placed on their left side in the recovery position.

GENERAL MARINE RELATED AILMENTS

Apart from the specific diving related illnesses, the commonest divers' ailments include sunburn, coral cuts, fire-coral stings, swimmers' ear, sea sickness and various biting insects.

Cuts and Abrasions

Divers should wear appropriate abrasive protection for the environment. Hands, knees, elbows and feet are the commonest areas affected. The danger with abrasions is that they become infected so all wounds should be thoroughly scrubed with fresh water and an antiseptic as soon as possible. Infection may progress to a stage where antibiotics are necessary. Spreading inflamed areas should prompt the diver to seek medical advice.

Swimmer's Ear

Swimmer's ear is an infection of the external ear canal resulting from constantly wet ears. The infection is often a combination of a fungal and bacterial one. To prevent this condition, always dry the ears thoroughly after diving and, if you are susceptible to the condition, insert

- 5% acetic acid in isopropyl alcohol *or*
- aluminium acetate/acetic acid solution

drops after diving. Once infected, the best possible treatment is to stop diving or swimming for a few days and apply anti-fungal or antibiotic ear drops.

Sea or Motion Sickness

Motion sickness can be an annoying complication on a diving holiday involving boat dives. If you are susceptible to motion sickness, get medical advice prior to boarding the boat. A cautionary note must be made that the antihistamine in some preventative drugs may make you drowsy and impair your ability to think while diving.

Biting Insects

Some areas are notorious for biting insects. Wear protective clothing, take a good insect repellent and some antihistamine cream to relieve the effects.

Sunburn

Take precautions against sunburn and use high protection factor creams.

Tropical diseases

Visit the doctor before your trip and make sure you have the appropriate vaccinations for the specific countries you are visiting.

Fish that Bite

- **Barracudas**

  Barracudas very rarely bite divers, although this has been known to happen in turbid or murky shallow water, where sunlight flashing on a knife blade, camera lens or jewellery has confused the fish into thinking they are attacking their normal prey, such as sardines.

  Treatment: Thoroughly clean the wounds and use antiseptic or antibiotic cream. Bad bites will also need antibiotic and anti-tetanus treatment.

- **Moray Eels**

  Probably more divers are bitten by morays than by all other sea creatures added together – usually through putting their hands into holes to collect shells or lobsters.

  Often a moray refuses to let go, so, unless you can persuade it to do so with your knife, you can make the wound worse by tearing your flesh as you pull the fish off.

  Treatment: Thorough cleaning and usually stitching. The bites always go septic, so have antibiotics and anti-tetanus available.

- **Sharks**

  Sharks rarely attack divers, but should always be treated with respect. Attacks are usually connected with speared or hooked fish, fish or meat set up as bait, lobsters rattling when picked up, or certain types of vibration such as that produced by helicopters. The main exception is the Great White Shark, whose normal prey is sea lion or seal and which may mistake a diver for one of these. You will not see a Great White when diving in Papua New Guinea waters, but you might encounter another dangerous species, the Tiger Shark, which sometimes comes into shallow water to feed at night. Grey Reef Sharks can be territorial; they often warn of an attack by arching their backs and pointing their pectoral fins downwards. Other sharks often give warning by bumping into you first. An important tip in defending against shark attack is to face the shark and make eye contact with it. If you are frightened, a shark will detect this from the vibrations given off by your body. Calmly back up to the reef or boat and get out of the water.

FIRST-AID KIT

Your first-aid kit should be waterproof, compartmentalized and sealable, and, as a minimum, should contain:

- a full first-aid manual – the information in this appendix is for general guidance only
- relevant contact numbers for the emergency services
- pencil and notebook
- tweezers
- scissors
- 6 large standard sterile dressings
- 1 large Elastoplast/Band-Aid fabric dressing strip
- 2 triangular bandages
- 3 medium-size safety pins
- 1 pack sterile cotton wool
- 2 50mm (2in) crepe bandages
- eyedrops
- antiseptic fluid/cream
- bottle of vinegar
- sachets of rehydration salts
- sea-sickness tablets
- decongestants
- painkillers
- anti-AIDS pack (syringes/needles/drip needle)

Treatment: Victims usually have severe injuries and shock. Where possible, stop the bleeding with tourniquets or pressure bandages and stabilize the sufferer with blood or plasma transfusions **before** transporting to hospital. Even minor wounds are likely to become infected, requiring antibiotic and antitetanus treatment.

- **Triggerfish** Large triggerfish – usually males guarding eggs in 'nests' – are particularly aggressive, and will attack divers who get too close. Their teeth are very strong, and can go through rubber fins and draw blood through a 4mm (1/6 in) wetsuit.
  Treatment: Clean the wound and treat it with antiseptic cream.

Venomous Sea Creatures

Many venomous sea creatures are bottom-dwellers, hiding among coral or resting on or burrowing into sand. If you need to move along the sea bottom, do so in a shuffle, so that you push such creatures out of the way and minimize your risk of stepping directly onto sharp venomous spines, many of which can pierce rubber fins. Antivenins require specialist medical supervision, do not work for all species and need refrigerated storage, so they are rarely available when required. Most of the venoms are high-molecular-weight proteins that break down under heat. Apply a broad ligature between the limb and the body — remember to release it every 15 minutes. Immerse the limb in hot water (e.g., the cooling water from an outboard motor, if no other supply is available) at 50°C (120°F) for 2 hours, until the pain stops. Several injections around the wound of local anaesthetic (e.g., procaine hydrochloride), if available, will ease the pain. Younger or weaker victims may need CPR (page 168). Remember that venoms may still be active in fish that have been dead for 48 hours.

- **Cone Shells** Live cone shells should never be handled without gloves: the animal has a mobile tube-like organ that shoots a poison dart. The resultis initial numbness followed by local muscular paralysis, which may extend to respiratory paralysis and heart failure. *You should not be collecting shells anyway!*
  Treatment: Apply a broad ligature between the wound and the body. CPR may be necessary.
- **Crown-of-Thorns Starfish** The Crown-of Thorns Starfish has spines that can pierce gloves and break off under the skin, causing pain and sometimes nausea lasting several days.
  Treatment: The hot-water treatment (30min) helps the pain. Septic wounds require antibiotics.
- **Fire Coral** Fire corals (*Millepora* spp) are not true corals but members of the class Hydrozoa – i.e., they are more closely related to the stinging hydroids. Many people react violently from the slightest brush with them, and the resulting blisters may be 15cm (6in) across.
  Treatment: As for stinging hydroids .
- **Jellyfish** Most jellyfish sting, but few are dangerous. As a general rule, those with the longest tentacles tend to have the most painful stings. The Box Jellyfish or Sea Wasp (*Chironex fleckeri*) of Northern Australia is the most venomous creature known, having caused twice as many fatalities in those waters as have sharks; it has yet to be found in Asian waters but its appearance one day cannot be precluded. Its occurrence is seasonal, and in calmer weather it invades shallow-water beaches; it is difficult to see in murky water. It sticks to the skin by its many tentacles, causing extreme pain and leaving lasting scars. The victim often stops breathing, and young children may even die.
  Treatment: Whenever the conditions are favourable for the Box Jellyfish, wear protection such as a wetsuit, lycra bodysuit, old clothes or a leotard and tights. In the event of a sting, there is an antivenin, but it needs to be injected within three minutes. The recommended treatment is to pour acetic acid (vinegar) over animal and wounds alike and then to remove the animal with forceps or gloves. CPR (page 168) may be required.
- **Lionfish/Turkeyfish** These are slow-moving except when swallowing prey. They hang around on reefs and wrecks and pack a heavy sting in their beautiful spines.
  Treatment: As for stonefish.
- **Rabbitfish** These have venomous spines in their

fins, and should on no account be handled.
Treatment: Use the hot-water treatment.

- **Scorpionfish** Other scorpionfish are less camouflaged and less dangerous than the stonefish, but are more common and dangerous enough.
Treatment: As for stonefish.
- **Sea Snakes** Sea snakes have venom 10 times more powerful than a cobra's, but luckily they are rarely aggressive. However their short fangs can pierce a lycra suit.
Treatment: Apply a broad ligature between the injury and the body and wash the wound. CPR may be necessary. Antivenins are available but need skilled medical supervision.
- **Sea Urchins** The spines of sea urchins can be poisonous. Even if not, they can puncture the skin – even through gloves – and break off, leaving painful wounds that often go septic.
Treatment: For bad cases give the hot-water treatment; this also softens the spines, helping the body reject them. Soothing creams or a magnesium-sulphate compress will help reduce the pain. Septic wounds require antibiotics.
- **Stinging Hydroids** Stinging hydroids often go unnoticed on wrecks, old anchor ropes and chains until you put your hand on them, when their nematocysts are fired into your skin. The wounds are not serious but are very painful, and large blisters can be raised on sensitive skin.
Treatment: Bathe the affected part in methylated spirit or vinegar (acetic acid). Local anaesthetic may be required to ease the pain, though antihistamine cream is usually enough.
- **Stinging Plankton** You cannot see stinging plankton, and so cannot take evasive measures. If there are reports of any in the area keep as much of your body covered as possible.
Treatment: As for stinging hydroids.
- **Sting Rays** Sting rays vary from a few centime tres to several metres across. The sting consists of one or more spines on top of the tail; though these point backwards they can sting in any direction. The rays thrash out and sting when trodden on or caught. Wounds may be large and severely lacerated.
Treatment: Clean the wound and remove any spines. Give the hot-water treatment and local anaesthetic if available; follow up with antibiotics and anti-tetanus.
- **Stonefish** Stonefish are the most feared, best camouflaged and most dangerous of the scorpionfish family. The venom is contained in the spines of the dorsal fin, which is raised when the fish is agitated.
Treatment: There is usually intense pain and swelling. Clean the wound, give the hot-water treatment and follow up with antibiotic and anti-tetanus.
- **Others** Venoms occur also in soft corals, the anemones associated with Clownfish and the nudibranchs that feed on stinging hydroids; if you have sensitive skin, do not touch any of them.

Cuts

Underwater cuts and scrapes – especially from coral, barnacles or sharp metal – will usually, if not cleaned out and treated quickly, go septic; absorption of the resulting poisons into the body can cause bigger problems. After every dive, clean and disinfect any wounds, no matter how small. Larger wounds will often refuse to heal unless you stay out of seawater for a couple of days. Surgeonfish have sharp fins on each side of the caudal peduncle; they use these against other fish, lashing out with a sweep of the tail, and occasionally may do likewise when defending territory against a trespassing diver. These `scalpels' are often covered in toxic mucus, so wounds should be cleaned and treated with antibiotic cream.As a preventative measure against cuts in general, the golden rule is do not touch! Learn good buoyancy control so that you can avoid touching anything unnecessarily.

Fish-feeding

You should never feed fish anything other than their natural foods. It is not always advisable to feed fish anyway since it can upset the natural balance of the reef community by leading to an increase in the population of species which accept food against those that don't. It can also create expectations which may have unpleasant consequences for divers who follow if they are unaware that the fish are normally fed at a particular site.

Allen, Gerald, and Swainston, Roger (1993) *Reef Fishes of New Guinea.* Christensen Research Institute, PO Box 305, Madang, PNG

Coleman, Neville (1989) *Nudibranchs of the South Pacific.* Sea Australia Resource Centre, PO Box 702, Springwood, Australia 4127

Coleman, Neville (1993) *Encyclopedia of Marine Animals.* Collins/Angus & Robertson, Sydney, Australia; Neville Coleman, PO Box 702, Springwood, Australia 4127

Cousteau, Jean-Michel, and Richards, Mose (1989) *Cousteau's Papua New Guinea Journey.* Abrams, New York

Deacon, Kevin (1989) *Australia and the South Pacific, Exploring the Islands and Underwater World.* Simon & Schuster, Brookvale, Australia

Doubilet, David (1989) *Light in the Sea.* Thomasson-Grant, Charlottesville, USA

Doubilet, David (1992) *Pacific.* Little Brown, Boston/Toronto/London

Fautin, Daphne, and Allen, Gerald (1992) *Field Guide to Anemonefishes and their Host Sea Anemones.* Western Australian Museum, Perth, Australia

Forster, Monica, and Stone, Peter (1994) *Rabaul's Forgotten Fleet.* Ocean's Enterprises 303 Commercial Rd., Yarram, Australia

Gert de Couet, Heinz, and Green, Andrew (1989) *The Manual of Underwater Photography.* Verlag Christa Hemmen, Wiesbaden, Germany

Kirkland, David (1991) *Impressions of Papua New Guinea.* Robert Brown, Buranda, Australia

Kuiter, Rudie (1992) *Tropical Reef-Fishes of the Western Pacific, Indonesia and Adjacent Waters.* Penerbit PT Gramedia Pustaka Utama, Jl. Palmerah Selatan 24-26, Jakarta, Indonesia

Lieske, Ewald, and Myers, Robert (1994) *Coral Reef Fishes.* Collins Pocket Guide, HarperCollins, London/New York

Randall, John, Allen, Gerald, and Steen, Roger (1990) *Fishes of the Great Barrier Reef and Coral Sea.* University of Hawaii Press, Honolulu; Crawford House Press, Bathurst, Australia

Stafford-Deitsch, Jeremy (1991) *Reef, a Safari through the Coral World.* Headline, London

Steen, Roger (1990) *Coral Reefs, Nature's Richest Realm.* Crawford House Press, Bathurst, Australia; Letts, London

Ward, Peter Douglas (1988) *In Search of Nautilus.* Simon & Schuster, New York

Wheeler, Tony, and Murray, Jon (1993) *Papua New Guinea: A Travel Survival Kit* (5th edn). Lonely Planet, Hawthorn, Australia

Whiting, Neil (1994) *Wrecks and Reefs, Port Moresby, Papua New Guinea.* Robert Brown & Ass., PO Box 1299, Cooparoo DC, Australia 4151; Neil Whiting, PO Box 7078, Boroko, PNG

Index